# A MAN CALLED YARRA

# A MAN CALLED YARRA

STAN YARRAMUNUA WITH ROBERT HILLMAN

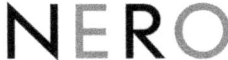

Published by Nero,
an imprint of Schwartz Publishing Pty Ltd
Level 1, 221 Drummond Street
Carlton VIC 3053, Australia
enquiries@blackincbooks.com
www.nerobooks.com

9781863959650 (paperback)
9781743820513 (ebook)

 A catalogue record for this
book is available from the
National Library of Australia

Cover design by Tristan Main
Cover image by Tobias Titz
Text design and typesetting by Tristan Main

# CONTENTS

*This book is dedicated to Frankie and Charlotte, my parents.*
*Even through the struggle, they always showed me hope.*

# CHAPTER 1

# MY OLD MAN

The dirty old heap called Staffer House up in Nicholson Street, Fitzroy, was an important place in my life when I was a kid. It's not there anymore. I know, because I went around to Nicholson Street a year ago to take a peep and found it had become something much fancier than the broken-down rooming house I once knew. Back then poor people stayed there, mostly whacked out on booze or smack. Staffer was the place my dad, Frankie, and I stayed whenever we reached Melbourne after knocking about the state together.

This was between 1974 and 1977, when I nine and ten and eleven. Of all the ages you can be, ten is one of the best. Maybe the best of all. Strength was coming into my skinny body, and lots of fresh ideas for making strife filled my mind. I'd wake up in the morning to the rackety trams rolling down Nicholson, eat God knows what for breakfast, then mosey out to see what mischief I could find.

I can picture myself down at the Champion, a pub in Gertrude Street just around the corner from Staffer House, a place I knew as well as other kids knew the school they attended. As a matter of fact, the Champ *was* my school; also the Rob Roy, down there in Fitzroy, and the Builders Arms. All three working men's pubs. My dad and my uncle Darryl used to hustle at the three pubs, particularly the Champ, lords of the pool table, me watching on, knowing the script my dad was following down to the pauses and gestures and nods and shakes of the head.

"So, what, you want to play for stakes? Two bucks a frame, three bucks a margin of twenty points? Something like that?"

And the ning-nong my old man was hustling would say: "Five bucks a frame, ten bucks a margin of twenty."

"Woo! A flash bloke like yerself, don't know if I can risk it."

And the ning-nong: "No guts?"

"Okay, then. Expect you'll take me shirt and hat, but what the hell."

I had a quiet little smile to myself as Dad let the punter win two frames by a margin of thirty. My quiet smile was still there as Dad got this bozo to up the stakes to fifty a frame, a hundred bucks for a margin of sixty. And cleared the table on the one break, pop, pop, pop. This might seem – what would you say? – an *unwholesome* environment for a kid. Well, yeah. But you learn a great deal about your fellow man by studying an expert hustler like my dad in a pub. He *played* them, my dad; he played the bozos. Never went too far with his 'I'm just a pitiful amateur' thing. He worked out what it was that the punter wanted to hear, and he gave it to him. Made lots of dough. My dad at the Champ, he was an artist of the con. Handy with his dukes, capable of knocking back a dozen glasses of the frothy stuff without losing his wits. But there was more to him than scamming. Never had employment of the skilled sort, but he could roll up his sleeves and take on a hundred different jobs that required muscle and stamina. People looked up to him; not just other whitefellas, but Aborigines too. I can say with a full heart that my dad was a role model for me; a role model of a fairly dodgy sort, yeah, but someone to look up to, someone to admire. He was always trying to educate me, in his way, to pass on his wisdom.

My dad and his brother Darryl were in the Champ this one time, and there was something going on between Darryl and Dad, some bone of contention. I wasn't at the pub at this point, but Dad told me the full story later. As it happened, Darryl did his block and smacked Dad in the face – whack. Darryl knew what a punch was and when he smacked my dad, he meant it to sting. Which it did. Now, my dad didn't respond immediately, just rubbed his jaw, had a bit of a think. And what he thought was that he could teach me something about the right way to reply when someone – your brother, your buddy, your worst enemy, anyone – gives you a smack on the kisser. So he headed off back to Staffer House to get me and took me to the Champ, where Darryl was still propping up the bar. He whispered in my ear: "Watch this, Stannie." He paid at the bar for a couple of pots, carried them over to where Darryl was yarning with a mate next to the juke-box. One of the pots was for Darryl – all is forgiven, that sort of thing. He said to Darryl – and I was watching closely – "Here, mate, hold these and I'll put a tune on for you." Meaning on the jukebox. He handed over the two pots, and while Darryl's hands were full, reached behind him, clamped a mitt on his neck and slammed his face into the jukebox. Not hard enough to kill him – of course not, this was his brother – but hard enough to let Darryl know who was boss. I was watching and thinking: "Woo!" Darryl recovered, washed away the blood, muttered a few words of admiration for my dad's ruse, sank another pot of beer. What I was meant to learn from this little scene was not that every problem can be solved by flattening a bloke's face on the surface of a jukebox, but instead that I shouldn't put up with rubbish from anyone; don't turn the other cheek.

As for me, if I'd been charged and found guilty of all the mischief my ten years had spanned I would've had a record as long as Ned Kelly's. Theft was against the law, sure, but not in my dad's scheme of things – he was what the law would call a 'petty criminal'. He might take possession of a few items in a clandestine way; might be seen driving around in a car that, technically speaking, belonged to someone else. For him, the unforgivable thing about theft was getting caught. Not that he sent me out to steal and scam; I wasn't Oliver Twist, and my dad wasn't Fagin. He just let me know that I should use my wits and my ingenuity. I'm in a shop, nobody's looking, I slip a block of Cadbury's down my jumper – that sort of thing. I wasn't above a bit of purse snatching, either; in fact, I was pretty good at it. The thing about purse snatching, you need some luck – a clear path of escape. You don't want to be snatching a handbag in an elevator, do you?

I was mooching down by the Champ one fine day when a woman appeared on the footpath with a big juicy handbag hanging loose on her shoulder. I thought: "Stan, my friend, you and that handbag have got to become better acquainted." I shuffled up behind the lady, made my move, dashed away without any witnesses. Well, except for two detectives who'd just stepped out of a car about ten feet away. They heard the lady scream, looked at me, gave chase. I ran in through the front door of the Champ intending to exit through the side door and almost barged into my uncle Darryl. It took him a split second to size up the situation, and when the detectives came through the door he clobbered one with his left fist, one with his right. I raced out the side door and up Gertrude Street.

I came to know damned near everything about street life. I could dodge and weave; I could run like the wind; I could get in one window and out of another so fast all you'd see was a blur. I knew what to do with my fists when I needed to, and I could give cheek like you wouldn't believe. But there was always a big problem with the sort of knowledge I picked up, and it was this: I couldn't build anything with it. I could survive, but that was it. A life that uses nothing but street savvy, sure, it's exciting in its way, even thrilling on certain days, but if I look at it in another way it's like I was shuffling down a path between huge heaps of mullock, the washed-out left-behinds of miners, like the ones up at Ballarat where I lived for a bit. Shuffling along, no idea of my destination.

I've had a better life than that. I've had a terrific life. I'm glad every day for the sun and the sky. But it took me time to get here. Ten years old – that was a great age, but you can't be ten years old at twenty and thirty. My old man was pretty much a kid until the day he died, and that was the life he passed on to me. He even said it sometimes: "Never grow up, Stannie, never." But I did, eventually, and I'm glad of it.

CHAPTER 2

# THE SOLES OF MY FEET

**B**efore I was ten I was nine, eight, seven, six, and so on. I was born in Swan Hill, up on the Murray in Victoria, and spent many of the 'so on' years in a shack outside of town. What's the difference between a shack and a house? Wear and tear? A fair bit of wear and tear on the Dryden family home: the corrugated iron roof crusty, rusty spouting in a sorry state, the weatherboards desperate for a coat of paint, dirt floor. Our place was on an orchard and vineyard – apples, oranges, table grapes – and may have been the original house on the spread. This is a common thing with farmers, graziers, orchardists. They have four or five good seasons in a row and they think about building a bigger house on the property. The old house is rented out, or it becomes a pickers' shack. So I'd have to say that our old place was a bit closer to a shack than a house, not by much.

Twelve of us lived in that shack, sometimes more: my dad, Frankie 'Duke' Dryden, rarely called by his legal first name of Percy; my mum, Charlotte; Davy, my younger brother; Lynette, who was the baby of the family; and Judy, my older sister, who wasn't actually my dad's daughter, although Mum and Dad let her think she was because her real dad had disappeared years before Charlotte took up with Frankie. And Nan Lily Charles, who was living with a German by the name of Karl. I don't know how Karl got to Swan Hill, but he was a good bloke and devoted to Nan Lily. Dad's brother Darryl was with us off and on. Uncle Ian on my mum's side of the family – the Aboriginal side – wandered in and out of our lives, and Uncle Ian's son, Derryk, my cousin, had his small corner in the shack and stayed there even if his dad disappeared for a month or two. Mum's sister Aunty Yvonne came for a visit and stayed; also Grandma Lette with her pure white hair. Grandma Lette was really my great-grandma on Mum's side, and had heaps of clout in the family because of her age.

Twelve people in a not-very-big shack makes a crowd, but I never felt cramped. Just the opposite. I felt comfortable with uncles and aunties and cousins and brothers and sisters around me most of the time. I didn't need more space when I was indoors, and when I was outdoors I had all the space in the world. I didn't care about the noise, either – a good thing because nobody ever spoke in a quiet voice, nobody whispered. Everything was shouted. Mum might be cooking at the stove and calling over her shoulder nonstop for Davy to stop annoying Lynnie, or to ask Aunty Yvonne to make a cup of tea for Nan Lily, or to tell Frankie to take some argument he was having with Uncle Darryl outside. Mum was the boss of the indoors. If anyone needed a dispute settled, Mum was the umpire, and there were always disputes to settle. Indoors at our place was a big, rowdy mess from dawn to dark and later.

When it came time to go to bed, Lynnie went off first, to a mattress in a corner, then Derryk and Davy and me were ordered to get ourselves asleep and we'd wedge ourselves together on the same mattress as Lynnie. The grown-ups would please themselves. Dad and Darryl and Uncle Ian would maybe stay up boozing and laughing and singing and fighting for hours. Strangers turned up from time to time, Aborigines like me, and suddenly I'd have an Uncle Tom I'd never seen before, an Aunty Mary, usually with some kids in tow. We squeezed up and made room.

Man, there were fabulous times with my mob – brothers, sisters, cousins, mates. Like paradise some days. An orchard on the Murray was not a bad place at all for a kid to grow up. I had the sunshine three hundred and sixty-five days of the year and an endless supply of oranges. And the river itself, for swimming. No school, so I stayed around the place all day or wandered about in the mulga inventing games, looking for strife, mischief, flirting with disaster. Might climb a tree, might investigate a wombat burrow by wriggling down it. A lot of cider gums up on the Murray, red gums, spinning gums, black wattle, blueskin wattle. Lots of wombat burrows, too.

Aborigines, we're made for the outdoors. The sun, the soil – that's the best thing. On riverbanks, out in the mulga, looking up at the clouds: that's where I felt freedom. Doing nothing, a lot of the time. Except listening. Except seeing. Except feeling the story of the earth through the soles of my feet. That was special, when my feet told me the story of everything that lives, everything that has ever lived, people, rocks, the blue sky itself, goannas, galahs.

I wasn't going to starve with oranges, grapes and apples all around me, but I wasn't likely to live like a prince either. Mum kept us on what she got from welfare and Dad chipped in whenever he was on the scene – money from picking grapes, from his off-and-on work with the council, pick and shovel stuff. So I can't say the Stan Dryden wardrobe was anything to brag about. Don't know that I even owned a pair of shoes, but that didn't bother me – going barefoot was best.

The only time we saw kids who enjoyed what might be called a posh life (wouldn't have been all that posh, just in comparison to the Drydens) was in Swan Hill, where we went now and again. I saw kids getting into the back seats of new cars as if it was just a normal thing and I thought: "That'd be good, big flash car." But I didn't feel any envy. My family had been poor for so long, it was just the way things were – rich and poor.

I didn't think of race all that much, either. My dad, when I came to know him better at the age of about seven, had no time for racism. He was white, his wife and kids were black, never saw him making any sort of big deal about it. He was a working-class white man, the class that had practically invented Australian racism, certainly upheld it – but Dad? None of it in him. Another way in which he could be considered a good role model, his general dodginess aside. Hell, I'm glad he told me to hold my head high. I've never had to suffer the sort of self-consciousness that can get into some Indigenous people. They've got this big, fat, powerful white-dominated culture all around them, and they think: "It's the white man who builds everything, the white man who invents things, the white man who can afford to buy things. Us blackfellas, we could never do that." Really, really bad for any Aboriginal soul, that kind of feeling of inferiority.

As a kid, I was aware that you could find white men who looked down on Aborigines, but I didn't get it. I thought it was wacky. I remember Frankie mentioning it back when I was on the road with him, a few years after Swan Hill. I heard him saying that such-and-such a bloke was 'racist' – didn't care for black people, for Aborigines. I thought: "Really?" Then about the same time, out on the road, this white bloke abused me and called me a useless black bastard. It shocked me. I thought: "This is that racism Dad was talking about." So I went hurrying off to find Dad. "Dad, Dad! This bloke down the road, he's doing that racism thing!" And Dad took off to find him and clobber him, which he did.

Some days on the orchard, paradise; but not every day. There were rotten arguments between Mum and Dad; Mum and Uncle Darryl, Uncle Ian; or between Ian and Darryl, Darryl and Dad, that gave me a pain in the guts. Lots and lots of kids experience this sort of pain. I loved Mum, I loved Dad, I loved my uncles, my aunties. I didn't want to hear the people I loved having a go at each other, shouting, slamming doors. I wanted to say: "Please, can't you just get on? How hard would that be?" But it wasn't a kid's place to speak up like that. Us kids, we put on blank looks as if it was all going over our heads. But it wasn't.

The arguments were hard on Mum, too, but not just the arguments. Frankie was too restless to be a husband or a normal sort of father. By the time I was five, I'd somehow accepted that he might be at the Swan Hill shack for breakfast, then gone by dinner time. When he took off into the mulga, Mum was lonely even with the noise going on and people around her from first light to bedtime. Sure, she had her differences with Dad, but she could probably remember back to the time when it was all fresh, when my dad had her on a pedestal. She said to me one time: "Met your dad at the pub, Stannie, and he was the best thing I'd ever seen. You were made with pure love." But Jesus, being a mother to four kids, never enough money coming in – how women do it is a mystery to me. Must be like serving a life sentence with hard labour. There's that song, 'Try a Little Tenderness'. Wouldn't have hurt if Mum had enjoyed a bit more tenderness at certain times. Dad was never physically abusive, never raised a hand to Mum. But there're more ways of breaking a woman's spirit than by biffing her.

One morning we'd been into town in the car with Mum, the four of us kids, and I could see by just glancing at her profile that she was suffering in a worse way than usual, her face drawn into a mask of sorrow. As we came up to the bridge over the Murray, she cried out: "I just feel like driving off the bridge into the water, that's what I want to do." And I'm like: "Hell, Mum, no, don't do that!" And my sister Judy in the front seat beside Mum let out a scream: "Mum, no, no!" and grabbed the steering wheel. Davy and Lynnie, they went hysterical. I mean, for the love of Jesus, I didn't want my mum to go driving the car into the bloody river. She was all we had when Dad was off the track and into the bush. But that's what despair is.

Mum wasn't the only one in the family who loved Dad, and missed him. Me, Davy, Judy and Lynette, we felt it like a kick in the guts. When Dad took off and stayed away for longer than the usual two or three days, mostly I was waiting for him to come back. It didn't seem that life was still going on without him; it was like I was just doing what they call 'marking time'. The things I loved were sort of faded. The blue sky, such a fabulous thing to stare at – it was like the blue sky was missing something. That good, hot, hot sun burning down was just the sun without Dad around. I loved my mum, of course. But Mum couldn't be a hero to me, even though she was more truly heroic than Dad. Mum was just there, and sure, I wanted her to be there, and I wanted her to be cooking and all that sort of thing, and I didn't mind her yelling at me, but she wasn't my hero.

I had only the one hero in my life, and that was Dad. And doesn't a kid need a hero! Dad had this easy way of walking, as loose as a goose, big grin, impressed everyone. He could knock you out just by sticking his hands in the pockets of his jeans and lifting his chin to smile at you. The time came when I saw John Wayne in the movies, and I thought: "That's my old man." I wanted my dad around not just because he was my dad but because he made me braver and happier, and I knew I had to make the most of him when he was there. Mooching about with Davy and Lynnie and Derryk and a few other stray cousins, I'd come across Frankie on his council gig with a road gang and I'd hang about just to watch him at work. He'd notice me and call out: "Stannie!" and I'd wave back. Then Davy and Lynnie would call out, and Frankie'd lift both thumbs and flash a big smile. He was always the leader of the road gang, made up of a dozen Aborigines from around Swan Hill putting in a couple of weeks' work for cash in hand. They'd do anything Frankie asked them to do, and do it well because it was Frankie asking them. They respected him.

One morning we found Frankie with his gang laying pipes along a road that skirted the Murray, and Frankie had each guy swinging his pick in unison. As I watched, one of the men jumped into the air and screamed out: "Snake! Snake! Big bugger!" Frankie held up a hand, signalling for everyone to stop work. The men on the gang formed a line behind Frankie. He hadn't asked them to do that, but somehow they thought they should. Frankie reached out with a long-handled shovel and prodded in the dry grass. Then he took a step to one side, and all the men took a step to one side. He prodded again, took another step to the side; the men shuffled to the side, keeping behind him. It made me laugh. Frankie was so accepted as the boss that the gang imitated everything he did. He was laughing as he prodded for the snake, and I knew why. He was the white guy, all the others were blackfellas, but he was the one with the bush savvy. This funny dance they were doing, it was the sort of entertainment that he could give again and again. I loved it.

Weeks later, the old man vanished. I had a sick feeling in the guts while I was looking for him out in the yard. It was early in the morning and I'd expected to find him finishing a longneck around the side of the shack near where the vines started. I went back inside and asked Mum where he'd gone. "Adelaide," she said. She didn't say why and I didn't ask. I spent the next few hours with my head on my chest, mooching about down by the river. I knew I'd get over it, but for a time I had to put up with brushing tears out of my eyes and keeping away from everyone. Mum knew to leave me be when-ever the old man took off. All she ever said was: "He'll come back, love, don't worry." It usually took a fortnight of Dad gone missing before I became my normal self again and was content to look for trouble and swing out on the rope over the river and give cheek and gorge myself on oranges. Frankie would turn up when he was good and ready.

Except this time he didn't turn up, not after a month, not after two months, three. I wasn't worried; he'd be back in time. Then Mum told me that she'd heard from a mate of Dad's, Kenny. "Yeah? What'd he say?"

And Mum said: "He's in jail, Stannie. In Adelaide."

"For what?"

"He biffed a bloke is what Kenny says. Pretty bad. Give him two years."

Well, two years was just the same as forever. I nodded and went outside and mooched. Mum found me and said: "Might get good behaviour, Stannie. Might only be a year." Good behaviour? Frankie? I kept mooching. I just had to cop it. One year was half of forever.

What was going on in the minds of my parents I didn't always know, as a kid. I woke up some mornings and I was told: "Get dressed, we're going to Brisbane, we're going to Perth, we're going to Timbuktu." Really? But why? "Don't worry about why. We're going to Timbuktu and that's that." This one morning I woke up and Mum told me we were going to the city, to Melbourne; more precisely, to Elsternwick, where one of our rellies had a place. Never heard of Elsternwick, but that's where we were headed, apparently. So off we went, in the car, old blue Zephyr, the whole tribe of us, and hours later the Drydens of Swan Hill were the Drydens of Elsternwick. A while later – months, I think – I woke up one morning and Mum said: "Get dressed, we're going to Ballarat." What? How come? "Don't be asking me how come. We're going and that's it." We got in the car, and a few hours later we were in a house my Uncle Ian had found – the Drydens of Ballarat.

# CHAPTER 3

# THE EUREKA STOCKADE BLOODY PRIMARY SCHOOL

T he house we shared with Uncle Ian and his mob was in South Ballarat, an old weatherboard monster, what would be called Victorian architecture. South Ballarat was full of old houses like that. It was said that most of the city was built in gold-rush days, when people from all over the world were wandering about with a pick and shovel and digging fat gold nuggets out of the ground. Something interesting I heard from my uncle Darryl about the gold rush: he said that blackfellas didn't smelt metal; didn't go about searching for iron and tin and copper. "Aborigines used stone," he told me. So all that gold was just left sitting there. The white men came along, the goldseekers, and they picked it up and put it in the bank. If my people had got it into their heads at any time in our sixty thousand years on the continent to take ore and melt it with flame – no gold rush, no Ballarat, no Bendigo, no Melbourne. "The whitefellas, they owe blackfellas," said Uncle Darryl.

Okay, no gold left in Ballarat, but what they did have was something new in my life: school. Bloody hell. The government wanted every kid in the state to attend school. Including the Drydens. Mum told me that us kids were going to school, and I said: "Huh?"

She said: "Yeah, school. They put all the kids from everywhere into rooms and teach 'em stuff. About numbers, and writing."

"For how long?" I said.

"Five days a week."

I thought: "You must be bloody joking." But Mum was fair dinkum about it. We were going to school. And we did. And I hated it. We had this galah in a suit saying: "What's two and two? You, Stan Dryden, what's two and two?"

And me: "What's two and two what?"

"Just two and two. What is it?"

"Two and two cockies? Two and two rocks? Two and two people? What?"

"Don't worry about what. Just tell me what's two and two."

I thought: "He's insane." David and Lynette and Judy, they thought the same as me, that the teacher was insane. So we gave up on him, and instead of sitting in the classrooms, we skived off down to the riverbank, under the black wattles and sheoaks. A few other kids came along, too – kids who couldn't see the beginning or middle of anything sensible in sitting inside for hours when the whole outdoors was waiting. Might take a bottle of Coke with us. Might take a packet of smokes. Needed money for Cokes and smokes, but we'd found what might be called a reliable stream of income.

There was an old lady, Stella, a lady of maybe seventy, maybe more, who lived down our street a little ways. When we first moved to Ballarat, she'd give Mum five dollars, ten dollars every now and again to get us kids some ice-creams, just out of the goodness of her heart. She'd say: "Here you go, Missus Dryden, I'd like to see those kids enjoying a Drumstick. You'll accept this note, will you?" It evolved over the months that Mum might send us to see Stella and ask her for a fiver or a tenner to see the family through to pay-day. I'd knock on Stella's door and when she answered, I'd say: "Me mum was wondering if you could spare five dollars for some bread and milk, we're a bit short, she asked me to tell you. Or ten." I made sure I looked pitiful on these occasions. As if I could barely hold myself up from being starved. Then it occurred to me that I could go and see Stella without any say-so from Mum. Just on my own initiative. I couldn't say: "I need a tenner for fags and lollies." Of course not. But I could say: "Missus Stella, things are crook, can you spare a tenner to save us?" And Stella, looking a little sceptical, would say: "Here you go. Don't come back too soon." The other kids would be hiding around the corner. We'd race down to the milk bar for lollies, ice creams, Coke, fags. In those days kids like me could buy fags if we said they were for our mum or dad: "Yeah, deadset, for me mum, she's a chain-smoker. Benson & Hedges." Ten minutes later, stretched out in the shade of the wattles, not a care in the world, me instructing Davy on the technique of blowing smoke rings. Man, that was heaven.

Until the teacher, the insane guy I mentioned, sent the big kids in Grade Six to fetch us back to school. "Okay, Dryden, teacher wants to see you." Might have had to put me in a stranglehold, but those big kids, sucks that they were, hauled us back to Eureka Stockade Primary. Imagine that. A place of imprisonment – the school – named after a site that was all about the struggle for freedom – the Eureka Stockade. A bloody injustice.

So, I couldn't get any joy out of school – and this is the way it is for lots of Indigenous kids. Bugger of a job for white teachers keeping them interested. In my heart, I know what the problem is for Indigenous kids when they're forced to go to whitefella schools.

Blackfellas, we find it real hard to believe that the most important things about the world are written down in words, scribbled in numbers. Okay, we know this is the twenty-first century; we know a kid has to read and write and add numbers together to make a go of it in the world. But in a funny way, we don't believe it's true.

Listen to this, which happens to be a fact from white culture, a famous fact: what goes up must come down. Gravity, and so on. First put into those words by Isaac Newton, English cove of the long ago and far away. In the way black Australians look at the world, going back long before old Isaac, things that go up don't necessarily come down. Some things have always been up; found their way up, and stay up, forever. 'Up' is where certain things live, and also certain spirits. I've never made it a hard and fast rule of physics that what goes up must come down. But I do have beliefs that can never be chucked away. The life force of various animals may be the life force in me. Me and the goanna, we might be one and the same. Doesn't stop me eating him. Me and the bush turkey, could be we enjoy the one spirit. I would never say that any of these things are 'facts'. In sixty thousand years, we blackfellas never made a big deal of what's a fact and what isn't. What we did have, and still have, are things that are true, and will always be true.

There I was, then, in the classroom, with the teacher standing in front of a big wall map, pointing at places with the long wooden ruler that he also used for whacking. "This here's Africa," he said. "Lots of countries in Africa. Look at this one. Country called Egypt. What's the capital of Egypt? Stan Dryden, the capital of Egypt, what is it?"

"Dunno, sir."

"Of course you don't, Dryden. You don't know anything. Foolish of me to have even asked you."

He wanted me to accept that I was stupid, ignorant. But here's the thing. I knew I wasn't stupid. When he said things like that, it didn't make me hang my head in shame. Because I happened to know I was clever. Ask me the capital of silly old Egypt, I couldn't give you an answer. A thousand other things, sure, you'd get a good answer from me. The thousand other things were important in my life; Egypt, no. And so as I was sitting at my desk, I wasn't there. I was up a big cider gum, with the bush spread out below. Bit of wind, not too much. A smile on my face. In thousands and thousands of other gums, north, south, east and west, from down south to the far north, heaps of other Aboriginal kids, wind in their hair, smiles on their faces. Before those big ships pulled into Sydney Harbour, no blackfella on the whole continent would've thought: "That's strange, kid sitting up in a cider gum with a big smile." And nobody would've stood at the bottom of the tree in suit and tie and leather shoes and socks asking the capital of Egypt.

One day I was doing something or other outdoors, before or after school maybe, then I came back to the house and my mum had this funny look on her face. She said: "See that blanket on the couch, Stannie? Go and pick it up. Something under that blanket I want you to see." I was thinking: "What the hell?" There was a shape under the blanket, long enough to be a log. I lifted the blanket, and found a bloke grinning at me, a bloke old enough to be my father, a bloke who *was* my father, in fact. Mum said: "Stannie, it's your dad." Huh? I'd forgotten what Dad looked like. I knew really well the *feeling* of Dad, but it was only when I saw him on the sofa that his looks came back to me. Dad said: "Yep, I'm back, Stannie. Gimme a hug."

Which I did – and such a rush of emotion. I let him take me in his arms and hug me tight. I never, never wanted to be without him again, and for a while, I wasn't.

There was a big meatworks on the outskirts of town, and that's where Dad went to work, cutting up animals into chops and T-bones. Kept his family, the whole mob of us, for a time. Seeing Dad each day, it was as if I'd had him close all my life. But then a day came, a bad day, when he got jack of the job at the meatworks and took off again, leaving me behind; just headed down that long street in Ballarat and didn't turn around.

Since he'd come back from Adelaide, Dad'd nicked off for a day or two or three, but this time I knew it was different. And it tore my heart out. The time away from me in jail I could accept. He'd had no choice about that. The bloke he'd almost biffed the life out of had deserved it, so Dad told me. But never again, he'd said. "You and me, cobber. Frankie and Stannie." This bond I had with Dad, it was a powerful thing, and I truly believed him when he said it was me and him for good.

My guess is that lots of kids in our day and age would feel as if they could never forgive a dad or a mum who abandoned them in the way my dad did. A grievance would get into their guts and twist them out of shape. But as heartsore as I was I never felt for a moment any grudge against Frankie. It was just the way he was, a restless sort of coot who had to keep moving. There's a great Patsy Cline song, 'The Wayward Wind'. She sings about this bloke who breaks her heart when he hears a train whistle blow and slips away to catch a boxcar. Has to wander. Frankie had to wander. This is what I think, at least, and my guess has to be given some weight because brother! I've seen many wanderers in my time. I think Frankie, without knowing it, was looking for a home. Somewhere he could look around and say: "Yeah, this'll do me." He never found that home, and neither do any of the other wanderers. But deep down I think it's what he wanted – to find the impossible place that didn't exist where he would want to put down roots. As a matter of fact, I'm Frankie's true heir in the wandering department. At the back of the Stan brain there's an idea of a home that I'll worship forever. I wander. I'm restless every day of my life. When I wander these days, I do it by jet liner – up to Sydney, to Brissy, further off to Bali, to Perth. Or it could be somewhere close enough for me to drive the Ferrari, the Merc. Man, that's the ultimate, powering down the highway with the wind in my hair, on my way to some place I'll want to leave behind after a day or two. For Frankie, it was something in his blood, very much like the wandering instinct of my people that runs in my veins. That's what gave him the genius he had for knowing what was going on in the head and heart and soul of an Aborigine. But with a difference – Frankie had this need to find a home, somewhere he could look around and say: "Yeah, this'll do me." For Indigenous people, nah, not so much. Country, yeah – we have that powerful connection with country. But we don't have to plonk a three-bedroom weatherboard house down somewhere and say: "This spot here is home." What can I say? We're a nomadic people. Whitefellas, at some point in their history, they made the switch from wandering about to the three-bedroom weatherboard house, or brick house it could be. Can't wait to sink the foundations somewhere, whack up a paling fence, stick a sign out by the front gate: 'No Trespassing'.

So, Dad was off on his travels and I was up in Ballarat in Uncle Ian's place with an expectation that I'd turn up each day at bloody Eureka Stockade Primary. If I nicked off, I had these Education Department people showing up on Uncle Ian's doorstep like the coppers and the squatter in 'Waltzing Matilda': "Where is that skinny kid? Why isn't he at the wonderful Eureka Stockade school? Everyone's happy at Eureka Stockade Primary. All of 'em learning stuff. Capital of Egypt. Two plus two. What goes up must come down. Good stuff for that skinny kid to know." I'd be hiding behind the door, thinking: "Dad, come and get me!"

And then he did. He turned up as he was always going to. After a few days, he had a big blue with Mum. "Okay," he said, "I'm off. But I'm taking Stan. Damned right. I'm taking Stan." And off we went, me and my old man, Frankie and Stan, on the road.

"Where we going, Dad?"

"Adelaide," said Dad.

I'm thinking: "Adelaide? Where the hell even is Adelaide?" But who cared. I was with Dad. That was the best thing, best ever.

# CHAPTER 4

# PRIDE

Travelling with Frankie was an adventure of a certain sort, also dangerous. My dad had a code that told him how he should behave in certain situations. The code was based on honour and justice and was usually enforced with violence. I think of him as a sort of knight from the olden days, wandering about the countryside and setting things to rights when it was called for. I was his apprentice, what was called a 'squire' back then.

An incident in Orange a couple of years down the track from Ballarat gives an example of what I'm talking about. Dad and I were in a park in the middle of town, Cook Park on Clinton Street. My sister Lynette with us; must have picked her up from wherever Mum was living at the time. Dad was sitting cross-legged on the grass guzzling down the chilled stuff with maybe even more dedication than usual, stubby after stubby up to his lips, little twirl of the wrist, gone. The style of drinking of a man who was in earnest about filling his system with grog. I could see how many beers Dad was putting away but it never worried me. I might have thought: "Bloody hell, my old man's an alcoholic, this is serious." No. Dad couldn't do any wrong in my eyes. Whenever I saw people giving him a concerned glance – other blokes in the park, could be, as if they were worried about a piss-pot left in charge of two or three kids – I'd always look at them and think: "What's the matter with you?" Dad always kept a little bit of his brain sober even deep into a session on the piss, enough to notice if anyone was showing disrespect towards him or his kids. He didn't go about looking for a blue, but if he saw the need to swing his fists, then, boy – get out of the way! Dad's code of honour, it might as well have been printed on a card and handed out wherever we stopped: "Frankie Dryden. Don't give me grief. No racist shit. Slap your missus, you're going down."

At Cook Park that day Lynette, with tears in her eyes, shuffled up to where Dad was sitting on the ground. Said the bloke further along had told her to "fuck off" and called her a "black bitch". Now, lots of Aboriginal kids, they're used to racist insults, they let it slide when some white rat abuses them. But the Dryden kids didn't let anything slide. The way we thought – and this was both Frankie's influence and Mum's, because Mum was a strong, strong woman herself, wouldn't abide being slagged off – was that nobody on earth had the right to throw shit at us. We thought we deserved the respect of every human being on the planet.

Anyway, Frankie looked up at Lynette, listening to what she'd said. "He said what?"

"Dad, he said 'black bitch'."

Dad shook his head, put down his stubby. He knew he wouldn't be able to get to his feet unaided, so he told Lyn and me to grab him under his arms and lift him to his knees. We hoisted him up, held him steady as he shuffled on his knees to within range of the bloke who'd been so unwise as to insult Frankie's daughter. Other blokes in the park turned around casually to see what Frankie was up to.

His target was guzzling away, not fearing any danger from a pisspot on his knees. How wrong he was. Frankie drew back his fist – and his fist was like a block of cement after all the punches it had landed over the years – and pow! It caught the bloke on the side of the face with such force that it dislodged the poor bugger's right eyeball from its socket; it was left dangling down his cheek. I was thinking: "Bloody hell, never seen that before." The bloke was unconscious, good and proper; could've been dead. Dad was looking pleased with himself in a dozy sort of way, still on his knees. But we had to get the hell out of town, avoid any awkward questions from the cops. Caught the bus to Sydney, left the one-eyed bloke to work things out for himself. You can be sure he'd have been thinking twice before he called a sweet little kid like Lynette a black bitch again.

Most of the time I was travelling with my old man, it was just Frankie and his squire, Stan. But every so often, our travels took us back to wherever Mum, David, Judy and Lynette were staying. When we hit the road again, it might be the whole tribe, or it might be that just Lynette came with us, or Davy. Dad's plans were usually spur-of-the-moment things. He might suddenly think: "You know what? The whole lot of us, we have to head off for Sydney." And he'd announce his decision and the time of our departure: "Tomorrow, five in the morning." Mum, she barely had a say in it. She was expected to adopt any plan that popped into Dad's head. Sometimes she jacked up, and if any of Dad's plans were too ridiculous, she'd put her foot down.

Mum never took a backward step in arguments with the old man. She stood up for herself, damned right. In fact, she was known as 'Sarge' among her family and friends, because she had such authority. Everyone respected her; everyone listened when she gave advice. Dad's respect for Mum, though, it went up and down. At times he seemed completely devoted to her; at other times, not so much. One of the themes of his complaints about Mum was that she 'wasn't loyal'. He had this idea that she was seeing other blokes when he wasn't around. I don't know about that – well, of course not. If Mum was messing around, she didn't flaunt it. But hell's bells – Frankie left Mum by herself so often that it wouldn't have been surprising if she found a little thrill somewhere else. What I do know, and it's a funny thing, is that Mum could still show Frankie true affection at times. Her love for him never faded away entirely. But, boy, her affection was put to the test when he swooped in from wherever he was and took us kids away from her. He sometimes took all of us in one go, except for Judy. Swoop! The three of us. He thought it was his right. One time when he swooped, Mum got onto the cops, and the cops called in the Feds, who put it down as kidnapping. From that time on – 1975 – the Feds were looking for Frankie. Well, they could look if they liked. My old man had a whole radar system in his brain that told him when cops were around. He could suss them out on the other side of a mountain.

That night when Frankie swooped and gathered me up for our trip to Adelaide, he barely had a zack to his name, so he was relying on hitching rides. He stuck out his thumb but couldn't get a car to stop, so he peeled off the highway to a stand of pines that ran along the road. Under the pines it was soft sleeping because of all the needles that had built up. And that's what we did, slept on the needles until dawn. I thought: "Too right!" I could see the moon through the boughs of the pines, hear an owl hooting away. Whenever I glanced over to my left, there was Dad stretched out and gazing up at the Milky Way. I'd have been happy to sleep under pine trees every night, if that was the plan. With Dad there, I was super secure, didn't need to worry about a damned thing. "Adelaide," I thought. "Yeah, right-o." I knew a bit about Dad's time in Adelaide from Mum, but I wanted to hear more from Dad. I called across to him: "You been to Adelaide before?"

"Yeah. I came here from Adelaide. More than two years over there."

"Doing what, Dad?"

"Doing what? Doing time." And he laughed. "Doing time in Port Lincoln clink."

"Yeah? What for, Dad?"

"Biffed a bloke. He was putting shit on this one-armed guy. Didn't like that. Biffed him. Might've done a bit of harm."

It was only later that I heard the full story of the one-armed man, who was being ridiculed by the foreman on a work site in Adelaide. Dad listened to the abuse this poor bloke was copping and thought: "That's it." I mean, the one-armed bloke had it hard enough finding work in his condition, and here was this foreman slagging him off for not working fast enough. Frankie had heard enough; he strode up to the foreman and clocked him. I've made the point about being punched by Frankie. Same as being done over with a sledgehammer. So the foreman's off to hospital with injuries of one sort and another, and Dad's off to court. Now, biffing the foreman, that shows a sense of justice, a sense of right and wrong. But in other situations – no, I'd have to say that Frankie was pretty much blind to right and wrong.

A friend of Dad's told me about this one time in Melbourne when Frankie needed a suit for a job interview (sounds weird, I know, but he was a man of many resources) and didn't have anything even resembling one. What to do? He waited in the Champ until he saw a bloke in a suit heading from the bar into the gents. "Your old man followed him in," said Dad's mate. "Five minutes later, Frankie comes out wearing the suit, the shirt and tie, the shoes. I didn't go and look at what sort of mess Frankie'd left behind. But yeah, that's your dad, not a bloke who lets not having a suit get in the way of his plans." So you'd have to say that Dad's sense of right and wrong deserted him on that day.

We woke up to the sound of kookas singing on the fence after sleeping under the pines that first night out of Ballarat. Breakfast would've been nice, but Dad said we'd have to wait. Brushed the pine needles off, stood on the roadside and had a ride within a few minutes that took us to Bordertown. A sandwich and an orange juice, then a second ride right into Adelaide, where we took up residence in the park at Whitmore Square while we waited for an empty house, Dad boozing his brains out, me looking about for mischief. That's what took the place of games in my childhood – mischief. But not mischief just for the sake of it, I'm proud to say; no, mischief for profit. Might be a few handbags that needed to find their way into my possession. Might be a few items on the supermarket shelves that would be better off down my shirt. And so on. If I scored, Dad would say: "What you got there? Look at that, a Cherry Ripe. Is that for your old dad?" The goldmine of the world that Dad hoed into every so often was becoming my goldmine, too. It would be true to say that I was in training for a life of theft and scamming, and doing really well at it, likely to graduate with honours. I didn't think in that way, didn't really occur to me that I was doing much wrong. The time would come – oh, years further along, years – when I would start to value my imagination, my creativity, over simple mischief, but there in Whitmore Square at the age of ten, I wouldn't have traded my life with Frankie for anything.

It was a recognised refuge for the homeless, Whitmore Square. And for boozers. The whole area around the square was half posh, half rubbish. Nice houses running down from Sturt Street and Morphett Street, but a bit further around, strip clubs, hookers, dealers. We slept on the ground at night while we waited for a house to turn up. Among the homeless, there was a sort of unofficial real estate service being run: someone would tell you about an empty down in Morphett Street, say, or further away, above North Terrace. Nearly all the places we heard about were old Victorian buildings. Most of these Victorian places were worth a fortune and were never empty, but here and there one would pop up, maybe a place that had been home to some old couple for decades until the two of them had died with no heirs, and the house would stand vacant sometimes for three, four, five years until all the legal business was worked out.

Never any running water in these empties, and of course no gas or electricity. Usually just a mattress or two on the floor. Homeless people might stay for a month before heading off to another city, letting somebody know that the place would be available on such-and-such a date. The number of people who could doss down in an empty depended on how many mattresses were lying about. Or sometimes people improvised, sleeping on newspapers, on scraps of fabric, maybe even using newspapers as blankets as well. Wasn't a problem that there was no gas or electricity because homeless people live on takeaway, no cooking. The organisation that the homeless most appreciate is Macca's. I could get myself a full belly for five bucks. All those ads on telly with happy white mums and dads and cheerful young couples stopping at Macca's for a feed? Nah. The people that Macca's counts on are the homeless.

Sometimes you might find a fireplace in an empty, hustle up some wood, get a blaze going. People who've never known what it is to be homeless might think that these empties were just dumps of misery and despair, boozers pissing their trousers, kids crawling around in rubbish. And yeah, you saw some of that; some slum dwelling. But they could also be places of comradeship, laughter, joking. Me and Frankie, we might meet up with someone we hadn't seen for a couple of years, hear about his travels, all that good gear. In the empties I knew there was never any wife bashing, girlfriend bashing, never anyone giving a backhander to his kids because it was known that Frankie Dryden wouldn't stand for it. Me, if I'd been told that I'd live in empties for my whole life, I would have said: "Sweet." At times, though, I must admit, I wouldn't have minded a telly and few more blankets. When we were able to live in rented places with gas and electricity, it was good having a telly. But I didn't suffer from feelings of being poor. Didn't experience envy for those who had everything. See, Frankie wanted me with him. If your dad wants you nearby, it makes the things missing from your life seem unimportant.

A few months in Adelaide and Dad decided that it was time to go get Davy. By this time we'd found an empty and it must have seemed to Dad that he could get his kids back together under one roof. He took the train to Melbourne, another train to Ballarat, went to the house in South Ballarat, grabbed Davy, brought him back to the empty in Adelaide. He opened the front door, nudged Davy ahead of him down the passage to the lounge room where I was waiting and said: "Here's your brother." Davy was always as happy as I was to be with Dad. And just like me, he accepted as natural that he might be in Victoria one day in the care of Mum, and in Adelaide the next, with Dad. All good. A bit later, Dad thought it was time for Lynette to join us, so off he went to Melbourne by train, to Ballarat, off to Uncle Ian's place, spotted my little sister, picked her up and carried her back to the station. A day after he left Davy and me in the empty, he opened the front door, nudged Lynette down the passage. "Here's your sister." Big smile on the face of Lynette. All good.

Frankie saw nothing wrong with grabbing his kids and heading off with them on an expedition, but he drew the line at grabbing anyone else's kid, so Judy was never snaffled. I can't recall that I ever asked the old man why he always left Judy behind. Maybe I thought that because she was the eldest, and a girl, she wanted to stay with Mum. But maybe she wanted to be kidnapped too. I do know that she was heartbroken when someone finally told her that Frankie wasn't her true dad. She loved Frankie, and it took her years to recover.

So Judy missed out on the sort of education that Dad gave us at those times when he enjoyed sole control of us. Education in striking the right tone with the milk bar lady, for example. Frankie taught us how to ask for tick, or credit. Outside the milk bar, a little way down the street, he'd tell us to recite the script.

"Now, what yuh gonna say? Stannie, you first. What yuh gonna say?"

I was ready. "Gonna say, 'Missus, can we put this on tick until Thursday when Dad gets paid?' Just like that."

"No, no, that's not right. Say, 'This is on tick, missus. Dad'll be in to pay you Thursday, no worries.' Okay?"

"This is on tick, missus. Dad'll be in to pay you Thursday, no worries."

33

"Yeah, but when you say 'Thursday', say it strong. So she believes yuh. 'Thursday'. Like that."

"Thursday!"

"Not too strong, Stannie. Don't want to spook her. Okay, in you go. Bread, milk, sugar, Benson & Hedges."

Missus in the shop was more likely to give me tick than Frankie, maybe because he could well have been pissed, and I knew how to say what Dad wanted me to say, but here's the truth: I hated it. Hated it enough to make me sick in the guts. I could have scurried around in that milk bar and come out with biscuits and Mars Bars and a can of baked beans down my jumper without any problems at all. Wouldn't have felt guilty, wouldn't have felt scared. It was the pleading that upset me. Back in Ballarat, asking Stella for a fiver – that wasn't pleading. I knew Stella would give me the money, and she never tried to make me feel as if I was telling porkies. She *knew* I was telling porkies, and she was happy to overlook it. But the lady in the milk bar, she always looked at me in this serious way, no hint of a smile, as if I was making her shop filthy just by standing there, a beggar boy.

Anyone's soul can withstand a bit of thieving. A few fibs – that's okay. Your soul just says: "Deary me." But pleading, begging, that's something your soul hates. You can hear it saying: "For fuck's sake, Stannie, have some self-respect." And I know why that is. It's because it takes away your pride. I had pride. Frankie gave it to me. When I walked down the street on my way to mischief, I kept my chin up and I smiled all over my black face. I thought: "Sneer at me and I'll job you, if you're my size. Sneer at me and you're too big for me, I'll have Frankie onto you. This street, I *own* it, okay?"

Eventually, Frankie found work in a chicken factory, then a little bit later, in a chocolate factory. Never short of chickens while Dad

34

was at the chicken place, never short of chocolate while he was at Cadbury's. Ideal situation. Both the major nutrition groups covered, chookies and chockies. If Dad'd had a job at Philip Morris, would've been no need to ask for tick at all.

Yeah, it was a pain in the arse asking for tick, but it meant something good about me. It meant I had my pride. I've made my journey in life with my pride to guide me, and without it, where would I be?

# CHAPTER 5

# PIMPING

After a few months in one spot, Frankie would get restless and want to move on; the road was calling him. I liked it when Dad became restless. "Super duper," I'd think. "We could go north, south, east or west. Can't wait." I don't know why I thought hitting the road was certain to be an adventure. Wherever we went, it was the same thing – an empty maybe, a bit of larceny, other types of mischief. But just the buzz of being on the road, that was the great thing. The whole country spread out, Frankie and Stan and Davy on the highway, maybe Lynnie too, Dad's thumb out. Could be going anywhere, Dad looking satisfied, Stan smiling his head off.

After one of our stints in Adelaide, this would have been when I was about ten, we headed back to Victoria and Staffer House. Good old Staffer, rundown sure, but a place and a neighbourhood I knew so well. Only there for a week or two before Dad moved us down to Oslo House in Grey Street, St Kilda, I think because he was running some sort of scam on that side of town. Oslo was a big mother of a rooming house, been there in Grey Street for ages, not far up from Fitzroy Street. That intersection had the George on one corner,

37

the old St Kilda railway station on another, a seedy as hell milk bar on another, a bank in a big fancy old building on the other. And down Fitzroy Street from the bank, the Gatwick, a nightmare rooming house, with murders and punch-ups and dope and gear. Fitzroy Street used to be the wild west in the south, but it wasn't in its glory days when I was at the Oslo.

Frankie had a bright idea one day while we were at the Oslo: "Stannie, Davy, want you to go up to Shepparton and bring back Lynnie." He'd learnt that Mum, Judy and Lynnie had taken themselves up to Mooroopna near Shepparton to stay with Mum's sister.

"How do we do that?" I said.

"Like this," said Frankie. "You go up on the train to Mooroopna. You go to your aunty's place and tell Mum you've come for a visit. Your mum says: 'My lovely boys, my darlings.' Stay maybe ten days. Then you sneak out with Lynnie to the station, get your tickets back to Spencer Street. Okay?"

"How do we get our tickets? Y'gonna give us the money?"

"Stannie, Stannie, you'll find a way to make a few bucks. 'Course you will. Clever little bloke like you."

So off we went on this kidnapping mission, or sister-napping mission. Caught the train to Mooroopna at Spencer Street, me and Davy; there were a few suspicious looks from other passengers but we just said: "Oh, yeah, our dad's meeting us up the way, no worries." Took about three hours from the city to Mooroopna, and out we got, found our way to the address Dad'd given us. Mum gave us a big happy hug. "Oh my lovely boys, my darlings!" Judy whispered to us: "Y'gonna take Lynnie, aren't yuh?" And me: "Take Lyn, no way, what're yuh saying?" Lyn assumed that we'd be sister-napping her and was okay with it. And Mum, you'd think she would've been on

38

the look-out for mischief, but no, she kept thinking: "Oh my darling boys!" I don't say that I saw nothing wrong in snatching Lyn, but Dad had told me to do it, and I suppose I'd seen Mum crying so many times that I could think: "She'll get over it." I loved Mum like crazy, but loving her never made me think that what she wanted measured up to what Dad wanted. And Mum, she never asked much at all about Dad, never said: "What's your old man up to?" She knew without being told what Frankie was up to. He was up to no good.

It was comfy up there in Mooroopna. A real house instead of a rooming house. Wasn't much to look at I suppose; I'd have to say the house was 'on the wrong side of the tracks', an empty yard on either side, but, yeah, it was good to be there with Mum. Met my cousins, uncles, aunties again – heaps of them, big mob. Sunny weather. But there was the sister-napping mission to focus on. I needed money for the train fare back to Spencer Street. Couldn't let Dad down. I wasn't about to pinch money out of Mum's purse, though. For one thing, she hardly had a zack to her name, and for another thing – pinching money from Mum? I was a bad boy, but not that bad. No, I'd have to earn the money. And I'd noticed a tomato farm down the way a bit run by Sammy Coco, an Italian guy. Sammy was advertising for pickers, so Davy and I wandered in through Sammy's front gate and made ourselves available.

Sammy said: "You know how to work?"

"Sure."

"All day? You don't go home after two hours, boys. None of that rubbish."

"All day," I said.

Sammy put his hand to his jaw and had a think about it.

"Dokey-doke," he said. I didn't tell him it was 'okey-doke'. "I pay you end of each day."

"No worries."

Next day we turned up at Sammy's, were shown the rows of bushes we'd be picking, threw ourselves into the job. If I get going, I keep at it, whatever the job. Same for Davy. The more we picked, the more scratch we earnt. It wasn't the worst sort of picking. Beans, a bastard picking beans. Tomatoes, okay. You don't get spiders much in the tomato vines, or snakes. Maybe they don't like that tomato bush smell. But hard yakka. The sun goes up the sky and the sweat runs down your chest. Had to go to the taps and get a mouthful of water about every half-hour.

I didn't think about it at the time, but years later when I was picking somewhere or other when I knew more about my Indigenous heritage, I realised that this growing of big crops of one sort and another was something my people never bothered with. We grew enough for a few people, yams for example, harvested them, ate them, moved on. Whitefellas grew huge crops, sold them to people who sold them to other people, put the stuff on trucks and shipped it all over the country. That's commerce. Never had any use for it, mostly, my people. We let nature do all the work of planting, then we harvested it, bush tucker, atwakeye, quandong, alangkwe, hundreds of different fruits and vegetables. And what about grazing? The whitefella gets himself 10,000 head of cattle, keeps them for two years, sells them to the slaughter-house. Blackfellas, we let the bush do the grazing, then when we're hungry (all the time) we spear a wallaby that's passing by. I can hear things from the land around me that the bloke who grows fifty thousand peach trees, pear trees is never going to hear. Once the land becomes a business, there's no going back. And once the world becomes a business, your life becomes a business. Hard to listen to your soul once your life becomes a business.

We made our dough, Davy and I, and planned our next step. I'd checked the train times when we arrived at Mooroopna, and I knew that we'd have to be up early to wake Lynette and catch the first train. But it was a fair sort of hike from Mum's place to Mooroopna Station. We needed transportation. I noticed a bike parked just over a fence a little ways from Mum's and took informal possession of it, as you might say. Hid it in the long grass of the empty paddock next to Mum's.

At dinner that evening, Mum said: "Good to have the two of you around. Worked hard all day, you and Davy. What're you gonna do with your money? Gonna buy your mum a trip to Paris? Whadya think?" I laughed, maybe with a bit of a hollow sound. "Yeah, Mum, yeah, trip to Paris."

Early in the morning, still dark, I roused Davy, snaffled Lynette, and we were out the back door without a sound, onto the bike. I had Davy on the handlebars, Lynnie on the crossbar, pedalling like a madman, Stan's midnight express. Down at the station, three kids by themselves caught some attention. One bloke asked me: "Where's your mum and dad?"

I said that my dad was meeting us at a station further along.

"Yeah?" he said. "You sure about that?"

"Yep. Dad'll be there."

"What station would that be?"

"Seymour."

"Seymour? Your dad's meeting you at Seymour?"

I thought: "Who the hell is this guy? The chief inspector of kids on trains?"

We got aboard, a clean getaway, or almost clean. Because when we reached Seymour, where the train in those days stopped for about fifteen minutes, the cops were waiting. We'd gone to the station café for a packet of chips and some Coke, and we were grabbed. Two cops, both acting as serious as if we'd robbed the bank back in Mooroopna and got away with a million bucks. I thought: "Oh, shit. Think quick, Stannie."

One of the cops said: "You'd be young Stan Dryden. That right?"

If a cop asked me if I was such-and-such a person, I always had a think before speaking. I might just keep my mouth shut, or I might say: "Could be." Or I might give another name altogether. Not too hasty, okay? Now, on this occasion, I couldn't see any alternative but to admit that I was Stan Dryden. Otherwise these deadly serious cops would have taken us to the cop station to check things out. And I'd already nutted out a strategy to get us back on the train, back to Dad.

"Yep, Stan Dryden," I said. "And this's me brother Davy and me sister Lynnie."

"Had a call from the police station in Mooroopna. Officer there's heard from your mum. Said you'd made off with this little girl."

"Yeah, I did, officer." (I always called a cop 'officer'; it made them feel I respected them, which I didn't, but better if they thought I did.) Then I went on: "Had to, officer. We was being knocked about, 'specially Lynnie. Davy, too. Now we're trying to get to Uncle Archie. He looks after us real good, you bet."

"You mean you were being abused?" said the cop.

I had a pretty good idea of what 'abused' meant.

"Yeah, abused bad. Lynnie, Davy, me. Mum's drunk all the time. On our way to Uncle Archie. He looks after us proper."

I was banking on the cops not wanting the grief of following up a complaint by an Indigenous kid. A white kid, sure, they would have taken the whole thing further. Three black kids? Nah. But I was wrong. The cops had a bit of a nattter with each other, wrote something on a notepad. By this time the warning whistle had blown, meaning the train was leaving in a couple of minutes.

"Okay," said the cop who'd been doing the talking. "Let's have the address of your uncle Archie. We'll take you to him. Might need to have a word."

The train pulled out. So that was the end of the option of getting to Dad at Oslo House under our own steam. But I did actually have an uncle Archie in Fitzroy, so if the cops wanted to drive us there, sweet. I was impressed with the trouble they were taking. We piled into the back of the cop car, Davy glancing at me nervously, Lynette happy as a lark. And off we sped down the Hume Highway, listening to the calls on the cop radio.

Uncle Archie's address was a rooming house in Napier Street. I'd been to visit with Dad a few times; I knew how to get there. Archie was older than Dad, not actually a true relative but close enough. The cops took us to the front door and asked for Archie. When Archie appeared, he looked at us and the cops and said: "What the hell?" But the cops were content to hand us into Uncle Archie's care. "The kids will have to go to court, though. Get things sorted out with the mother. This one says his mother is a drunkard and that she abuses the three of them."

Archie said: "What? Charlotte?" But anything else he had to say, he managed to keep to himself.

We hung about with Archie until, in the middle of the afternoon, I heard a low whistle from outside. That was Dad's special whistle, and it meant: "Coast clear?" Uncle Archie had somehow got word to him that his kids were around at Napier Street. I sprinted outside, and there was Dad, peering from behind a big clump of mirror plant.

"How'd it go?" he said. "All sweet?"

We went back with Dad to Oslo. He was good and cheerful, having his three kids with him. The whole business with the cops, that didn't worry him for a second. Dad thought of the law, any law, as a nuisance, or as nonsense; meant nothing to him. He'd spent his life dodging and scooting and ducking around corners. All cops were bad guys to him, and he was the good guy. It was second nature to him to ignore anything the cops wanted from him. And as his son, I was pretty much content to say anything I had to say, do anything I had to do to keep the cops out of my hair. I'd told the cops that my mother was a drunkard who walloped us all day long, which was a rotten lie, I have to admit. But I knew if the cops went to interview Mum, saying that her son Stan had made 'certain allegations', she'd blow her stack and tell them to fuck off. And it would only take them two minutes to see that it was Mum who was telling the truth, and her son Stan who was telling porkies. She wouldn't hold it against me. She knew who it was down to, and that was Frankie. She'd married a scoundrel. Couldn't be helped.

While Frankie was away doing his thing, I'd sit at the window at night looking out over Grey Street towards Dalgety Street, noticing things that puzzled me, such as a woman standing on the footpath doing nothing except smoking one fag after another. Then a car would stop and she'd get in. Half an hour later, she'd be there again. I thought: "Huh?" I asked Frankie one time what was going on, and he said: "Hookers. Prostitutes. Have sex with blokes for money." I knew what sex was, up to a point. You can't live half your life in rundown rooming houses without seeing stuff. But it was news to me that girls might have sex with a bloke for payment.

I thought: "If you had a few bucks, why would you give it to a girl for sex? Makes no sense. Just ask her."

I needed to know more about this woman on the corner of Grey and Dalgety. One night, I left Davy and Lynette in the Oslo and slipped out and went over to her, smiled, said howdy. She was friendly enough, smiled back. She wasn't beautiful, but she was pretty, maybe in her mid-twenties.

She said: "Whatcha doin'?"

"Nothing."

"Over at Oslo, are yuh?"

"Yep."

"Good-o."

I asked her: "Are you a prostitute?"

"Does that bother you?"

"Nope."

"What's your name, well?"

"Stan."

"Veronica, Stan. Want to do a little job for me? Earn yourself a few dollars?"

What Veronica had in mind was for me to stand a little way up the road wearing a coat she had with her, the hood over my head, and pretend that I was her pimp. She explained that a pimp looks out for a hooker, and takes some of the money she earns. She wanted blokes to think that she had a pimp, which she didn't, so that they wouldn't mess with her, refuse to pay, give her a whack on the face.

"Think you can do that, Stan?"

"Yep."

This was my first paid job as an actor – Stan Dryden in the role of junior pimp. I kept the hood pulled snug over my head and face,

45

hands shoved into pockets, an especially menacing look on my face just to show I was into the performance. Loved it. I thought: "Stan the Man." And I went further in the role, fully believing in myself as a tough guy. "Don't fuck with me!" I thought. And: "I've done five years in the clink for biffing guys, I'm small but mean!" A car stopped and took Veronica away, and I kept to my post until she returned.

"Here you go," she said. "Five bucks. You did good. Hang around."

I did hang around, you bet. Veronica chatted away while we waited for another punter, just this and that, how hungry she was, what she'd eat if she could knock off now. "Big burger with the lot. Except for onion. No onion. Sticks around on your breath, doesn't it? Strawberry malted. Yum! What about you, Stannie? Burger from down on the corner of Barkly and Carlisle, you think? Good place. Know me there. Ronnie Sugarlips. Ha!"

Another punter, another five bucks. I was thinking: "Stan, you genius. This is the life." I had a bit of an idea that pimping was maybe against the law. I didn't care. My whole life was against the law. And I also had a shrewd idea that the cops were not about to put a twelve-year-old kid in the clink. The cops would say: "Good Lord! Twelve! We have to have a word with your mum and dad, so we do." Yeah? Frankie'd say: "Pimping? Deary me. I'll give him a biff and that'll fix it." There'd be no biff. Frankie'd say: "Gotta get outa here."

The pimping went on for weeks. Me and Ronnie Sugarlips. A team. Sometimes Veronica looked a bit green about the gills, as they say. Most of what she earnt probably went on gear. I knew about gear. Wasn't tempted. Nor Frankie. Grog was his escape, same as most people who needed a buzz.

When I wasn't pretending to be a pimp, I looked out from the windows of Oslo House onto the life in Grey Street. Not so many hookers in the daylight hours, but a few, some very young. They puffed away on their fags quick, threw the butts in the gutter, lit another one straight away. If they saw a customer cruising up in a car, they popped a mint and produced a big smile. They were hanging out, as I came to realise, needing a client and a payday so that they could meet with their dealer and shoot up down in Neptune Street, or in the toilets at Sacred Heart. I didn't have a big enough picture of their lives to feel sorry for them; I was just interested. Fact was that most of these girls would be dead within a few years – overdosing, mostly.

I wandered down Fitzroy Street with Davy at times, looking for trouble maybe, two skinny black kids swaggering along, afraid of nothing. We'd stop and look in through the windows of restaurants at people eating, always excited when we saw someone burrowing into a dish that we liked, like spag bol or chips. Used to look at cars on the highway and think: "Gotta get me one of those big flash things when I'm rich." When we watched people eating, we'd say: "Gonna have chips every day when we're rich." Trams rattled up and down Fitzroy Street, heading into the city and back. Could've jumped on board if we'd liked, and we did sometimes. Never bought a ticket – didn't even occur to us. Gives you a terrific feeling of freedom when you can think: "Might go here, might go there, see how I feel." We went all the way along Fitzroy Street to the Esplanade, where we could look out over the sea, yachts tied up at the jetty, smaller boats bobbing on the water in the marina and the sound of the sail cables jingling on the masts. Big palm trees – Canary Island Palms I think they're called – down in Catani Gardens. Then the Palais Theatre, big mother of a thing, and next door to it the Palace, where they had concerts.

And then what do you think? The best place in the world: Luna Park. Oh, man, so fabulous, so exciting. I'd have fivers in my pocket from pimping for Ronnie Sugarlips and we'd dive headfirst into the fairy floss and ice-creams, line up for our tickets (didn't bother with tickets on the trams, but couldn't avoid buying tickets at Luna Park) and head off for the Fun House – you know the Fun House? Mirrors that made you look super fat or super skinny, stretched you out or squashed you down, and this bridge you had to cross that wobbled and lurched, then the slides, strip of carpet under your bum and down you go, over the bumps, have to stop yourself before you crash into the barrier at the bottom. And as you go down, you scream – man, do you scream. Moved on to The Hornet, bloody fantastic gizmo, whizzed you round and round and up and down, everything flying past in a blur and your ice-cream and Coke about to get spewed everywhere. The Big Dipper! Best ride ever invented. When the carriage reached the top there was a couple of seconds before it roared down the slope at about a thousand miles an hour and in that two seconds I thought: "Oh poor Stan, you're gonna die." But I didn't, and when Davy and I got out at the end of the ride I just wanted to laugh my face off and get back on. The Rotor, too – best thing after the Big Dipper. You go into this thing that was like being inside a giant barrel and it spins around faster and faster until the floor under you drops away and you're pinned flat against the wall, all the girls shrieking and reaching down to stop their skirts hiking up and showing their panties. More than anything – more than the Big Dipper, even – what I loved about Luna Park was that it made me feel like a kid, like a little kid, and it was only in Luna Park that I ever felt like that. I was paying for our rides with my pimping money, but deep down I was still a kid.

# GOLDEN LIGHT

A nother bright idea from my old man: "Going to Sydney. Gotta move on. Change of scenery, good for yuh." Davy and me, we just said: "Yeah, sure, anything you say, Dad." Nobody ever overruled Frankie. If he wanted to go to Sydney or Darwin or Paris, France, that was it. Useless to argue. So off we went on the train, with all of our belongings (meaning, nothing). Frankie headed straight for Redfern. There's an old church there, don't remember who runs it, Methodists, Baptists, could have been the Catholics or the Presbyterians or the anyone at all, it didn't matter; what mattered was homeless people like the Drydens were allowed to camp there for a few days. Lots of boozers at the church. The minister didn't ban boozers because (I think) he knew that any pisspots he turned away would curl up in the cold somewhere and maybe croak. (Frankie told me one time that if you're pissed out of your brain, you can't tell if it's cold or hot or in between. Could be running around bare chested at zero degrees and freeze yourself to death.)

They were good guys, the people at the church, had a special soft spot for Aborigines. In the past, they used to think blackfellas like the Drydens were better off on settlements, well away from white people;

now the church folk were trying to mend the damage. Also, they could see the spirit life of black Australians, and church people love that stuff. These ones were what you'd call 'non-judgemental'. They'd say a few words from the Bible to you if you asked for it (some did) but they never came over all monster religious. You could get yourself some tucker from the church, too, orange juice, bottled water, but not grog; they drew the line at handing out XXXX and Tooheys and VB.

Couldn't kip at the church forever, so Dad found us a rooming house in Buckingham Street, Surry Hills, up the road from Redfern. Buckingham runs north and south beside Elizabeth Lane, with Prince Albert Park over to the west. That whole area is full of people sleeping rough, not all of them boozers, some just kids making the best of it. The rooming house Dad found wasn't a palace, pretty much a dump with the usual fleas and rats, but good enough for Frankie and his kids. Once we moved in, I filled in the time in the usual way, sitting at the window and gazing at the life in the streets, trying to dream up scams that would earn me a bit of dough, a criminal genius at work. Nothing much occurred to me except bag snatching, but women in this part of the city had learnt to keep a good strong grip on their bags, and also how to give you a bloody great whack on the noggin if they got half a chance. Could end up in hospital with a cop guarding you. So I gave high-risk bag snatching a bit of a holiday.

We met Uncle Watson while we were mooching down by the Redfern church one morning. Uncle Watson was Dad's good mate, a big powerful man just out of Long Bay after serving twelve years for killing a bloke with his fists. Frankie had a hell of a punch, by God, but Uncle Watson's fists were lethal.

He called out to Dad before Dad had noticed him. "Brother! Good to see yuh!"

Dad wrapped Watson in a huge hug and slapped him on the back. "Watson the killing machine! Long fuckin' sentence, bro!"

"Tell me about it. A third of my life in that shithole. Brother, you got somewhere for me to stay? Haven't got a zack."

Dad said: "Rooming house up in Buckingham Street, that'll do yuh. You can roost with us."

So Uncle Watson moved in with us. Most of the things he took an interest in were the same for Dad – boozing, crime, stirring things up with his dukes. But one thing was different. Uncle Watson was a Casanova of sorts, and Dad, he wasn't. Didn't take all that much interest in the ladies, my old man. It wasn't because he was married and wanted to stay faithful – hell, no. It was just that he never got excited by the female form except every now and again. Uncle Watson – he was a chick magnet. He didn't depend on sweet talk or charm, all that gear you get with your usual pants man. It was something in the way he carried himself, something in his eyes and the shape of his jaw. Girls, women, they fell in behind him and couldn't wait to get their arms around him. Can't say he treated them bad, but he did move from one woman to another without any sort of apology. It was as if he was saying: "Here I am, ladies, break your heart when you're ready."

Maybe it was the danger in him that attracted women, because Uncle Watson, I have to tell you, had a big capital D for Danger printed on his forehead. The fact that he'd killed a man with his fists, I think that just excited the ladies even more. I saw him one time in an argument with Tony Mundine's niece Carol, right there in the street – Redfern, it would have been. Can't remember what it was about but perhaps: "Told me I was the only one, and now I hear you're shagging every woman in Redfern!" And who should poke his head out of a window a couple of floors up but Tony Mundine himself. Wanted to see who was giving grief to his niece. When he saw it was Watson, he ducked his head back inside. Tony Mundine, middleweight champion of Australia, apparently no interest in going a round or two with the killing machine.

He didn't stay with us for long, Uncle Watson. Well, he didn't stay anywhere for more than a week or two. Except for Long Bay. He'd made enemies, and they always came looking for payback. Watson accepted it as part of his life, blokes wanting to smash his face in, maybe put a blade in his guts, shoot him through the noggin. We were down the pub this one time, me and Davy and Lynnie with Dad and Watson, when these four blokes appeared in the bar and made straight for Uncle Watson. No weapons on show, so they must have been under the impression that odds of four to one gave them an advantage with their fists. Uncle Watson, he just needed a half-second to ready himself. As soon as he saw these four assassins he squared up, belted two of them. Dad said: "Better get out of here, brother." Watson disappeared. Dad stayed where he was at the bar and finished his schooner.

Me and Davy and Lynnie, we'd watched on with wide eyes. The violence that I witnessed in a regular way, it never left me what doctors call 'traumatised'. Uncle Watson's fists smashing into the faces of those two guys – I just accepted the whole thing as a natural part of life. And I suppose I must have believed that the time would come when I'd be whacking blokes in bars, as if that was part of growing up. My old man never said to me: "Now, Stannie, there's more than one way to settle an argument, best you try talking it through before you raise your dukes." Dad's use of his fists was a way of continuing a conversation that had gone beyond words. Same for Uncle Watson.

I came to hear of people years later who held dear a philosphy of non-violence – admired people like Gandhi in India, and Martin Luther King in the United States. Well, my Dad had a philosophy of pro-violence, just the opposite of Gandhi, but not madman violence. He had no interest in belting blokes just for the fun of it. I think he believed that the sensible way to get to the end of an argument was a right hook. End of discussion. Like the time I recounted earlier, when he smashed Uncle Darryl's face into the jukebox at The Champ in Gertrude Street. Dad could have said to Uncle Darryl: "Now, that was rude behaviour, whacking me in the kisser like you did. I want you to apologise." Instead he stuck to his philosophy of the fist and left Uncle Darryl bleeding on the floor of the pub. Uncle Darryl had learnt the lesson Dad wanted to teach him better than any number of words on the subject.

My own career as a master criminal wasn't taking me anywhere in those first few weeks in Sydney. I needed a scam, or a heist, or something. Because I didn't go to school, I was desperate for things to occupy my clever little brain. The way ahead appeared one morning in the rooming house when Dad had the idea of robbing the electricity money.

Each room had an electricity meter fitted with a coin box, and you stuck your one-dollar coins, your twenty cents and so on into the box to make the power work. The coins would gather in the box until the manager came around and emptied it. The coin box wasn't all that sturdy, and Dad figured he could get to the dough with a can opener. But he could only do that when we were ready to move on because the manager would find the wrecked coin box and throw us out.

The old man's plan got me thinking. I kept watch on where the manager put the money from the coin boxes, and glimpsed him stowing the bag of coins in an alcove off the office behind the lounge area. "You beauty!" I thought. I found a chance to unlock the window that led into the lounge area so that I could slip in when I was ready and sneak along the passage past the guests and the manager. Then I thought: "Hold your horses, Stan, my friend. They'll hear you as you're walking along the passage." I needed something that'd muffle my footsteps. And this is where being a criminal genius paid off. I'd seen an old foam mattress that'd been chucked out in the lane at the back of the rooming house, and I went out at night and tore some hunks off it. Took them back to our room, used a carving knife to fashion some footwear. Dad wasn't home just then, but Davy and Lynnie watched me with fascination.

"Hey, Stannie, wotcha doin', well?" Davy said.

"Big surprise for yuh a bit later."

I tied a hunk of the foam to each foot with some string we happened to have on hand, then out I went and found the unlocked window, raised it, slipped in. I crept down the passage dead silent, then into the office, found the bags of coins, crept back like a panther, out the window, back to our room. What with stopping and waiting and being cautious, this had taken half an hour and Dad was back from wherever he'd been by that time.

"Where you been, matey?"

I held up the bags of coins, big proud smile all over my face.

"What's that? The electricity money? Woo, you little monkey! How much we got?"

I emptied out the bags and Dad counted it up. Came to more than fifty bucks.

"Did good, Stannie. Did good, mate. But now we'll have to ske-daddle, won't we? Only one person that manager will be looking for, eh? Be looking for a little monkey with funny lookin' slippers, eh?"

We packed up and flew the coop, went down to Central Station, the four of us, heading God knows where, maybe Brissy, maybe back south to Melbourne – no, maybe not Melbourne because the cops were hunting us down there.

On the way to the station we came across an old lady we knew a bit pushing a supermarket trolley full of every sort of thing you can imagine. She was about eighty, stooped and half-crippled but still doing her rounds with her trolley, picking up stuff she found here and there: almost-fresh food from the back of supermarkets, empty aluminium cans to take to the recyclers, chucked-out clothes. There were a few of these bag ladies about in the Surry Hills area, nobody to look out for them, somehow coping by themselves. Redfern, Surry Hills, they were like a jungle in those days, people living wild out-side of society, junkies, boozers, scammers, hobos, and then these bag ladies. Funny thing that you can have people living like cavemen and cavewomen right in the middle of a big, rich city like Sydney. Because they *were* like cavepeople, except the caves were bus shelters and empty lots and huts made out of newspaper and cardboard and the back seats of abandoned cars. But there was kindness in some of these people, and we got some kindness from that old lady.

"Wotcha doin' out in the cold?" she said. "No good for yuh."

"No good for you neither, missus," Dad said. "We're just moochin', you know?"

"Those little kids, what about them?"

"They're good, missus."

"Come back to my place. Keep warm."

The bag lady – her name turned out to be Doris – had a room in a boarding house in Redfern, big enough for the five of us with a bit of squeezing. Didn't have to skip town after all. If we did some dodging, we'd keep out of the hands of the manager of the Buckingham Street rooming house. But I could see that the old man would eventually run out of places to hide. The cops wanted us in Melbourne; the Feds wanted us everywhere; the Buckingham Street manager would have called for the cops as soon as he noticed he was a bit light in the meter takings; and we were being looked for in Adelaide after a scheme or two not strictly inside the law.

And something else I was beginning to realise at the age of twelve: the old man didn't have any plan in life other than to keep his kids close, booze himself crazy, and nut out ways to scam a few bucks from the public every now and again. It didn't bother me, Dad having no plan. Like I say, just being with him was the only plan that I cared about. But something was going on in my brain; some idea that the booze would one day do my dad in, leaving Davy and Lynnie and me to fend for ourselves. I didn't want to think about that day, but part of me knew it was coming.

Meanwhile, it was pretty comfy at Doris's place. She had a few pieces of furniture to loaf on. A lot of the space was taken up by the stuff she collected, some of it too nice (in her eyes) to sell. And she was friendly enough. Fussed about us kids. I had no interest in Doris's past while we were living with her – kids can't even imagine a past for a person of Doris's age – but I do now. She might have been married, she might have had children before she ended up in a rooming house with a shopping trolley. People, not all of them can fit in, can they? Most can, but some can't. What I think now is that their lives – the ones who can't fit in – matter as much as the lives of the people who make a big success. They have dreams. They probably hope for a bit of love and respect. Would've been people who looked at me when I was a kid and thought: "What hope is there for a tearaway like that? Clothes he's in, not much better than rags. No schooling, alcoholic father, where the mother is, God knows." Yeah, but I had stuff in my head and my heart that would one day give me a different life to mooching and boozing. And Doris, maybe she imagined something different, too. Maybe she thought: "One day I'll be pushing my trolley and picking through the rubbish and I'll find a bag of gold as heavy as a house brick, buy a place in Bellevue Hill, have cakes at morning tea." I make sure these days that I don't sell people short.

We found a dog on the street a few days after we moved in with Doris, a big hairy mother of a thing dangling a leash. Must have been tied up somewhere, maybe outside a shop, and got itself loose. It was a super-friendly pooch. We brought it back to the rooming house and showed the old man. "I want to keep it," I said, and Dad said: "Yeah, well, if that's what you want."

I named him Roger and fed him proper on cans of dog food I liberated from the supermarket. Between the three of us, we patted him half insane, smothered him with love. Roger was the first addition to our family in years, and it gave me a warm, happy feeling to take him out for a walk. I thought: "Whadya think? We've got a dog!" Yeah we did, for a bit. Then I saw a notice taped up on an electricity pole offering a reward for a lost dog. Fifty bucks. And a picture of Roger. Now, a dog is a dog and fifty bucks is fifty bucks. Had a tussle with myself, then decided I'd take Roger back to the address on the notice and score the fifty. Bloody shame, but there you go. As for Roger, I don't think it mattered to him who was doing the feeding. He was happy with me, and he was happy when I gave him back to the bloke who owned him.

That was a fifty easily earnt, but another fifty came my way a couple of days later, and that one was even easier. I had a buddy down in Redfern by the name of Darren Homer, a kid of my age, but I have to say, not brilliant. No, Darren was – not exactly naïve. Dumb? Could I say Darren was dumb? Okay, a bit dumb. Nothing wrong upstairs, just hadn't learnt the same lessons in life that I'd learnt. We were mooching along in Redfern one arvo and Darren suddenly stopped and bent down and picked up a twenty and a ten caught in the weeds.

"Stannie, look at this!"

I took a squiz. "Bloody hell, two notes, just lying there."

But what I mostly noticed was another note, a fifty, still in the weeds. It was in plain view, but Darren ignored it. Then I realised that Darren, he'd never seen a fifty in his life and didn't know that it was money just like the twenty and the ten. I scooped it up and stuffed it in my pocket. Then Darren, bless his heart, wanted to share the twenty and the ten with me – the red note and the blue note. He didn't know that the twenty was worth twice as much as the ten, so I plucked the twenty from his hand and stuck it in my pocket with the fifty. Any trouble with my conscience? Nah. I didn't have any real conscience in those days when it came to moolah. If I saw a way to make money, I just grabbed it. Would've been years down the track before I'd stop and think: "Hold on, this isn't right." The way the old man brought me up, pretty bloody difficult for conscience to develop at all. I told the story of the old man following that bloke into the gents at The Champion and coming out wearing the poor mug's suit; when Dad's mate told me that story, I just thought how brilliant my old man was. But if I was with a mate in the pub now (drinking lemonade, of course; I don't touch grog these days) and he said: "Stannie my man, I'm gonna track that bloke over there into the dunny, biff him and take his duds," I'd say: "No, no, brother, you can't do that, forget it." Your conscience is like your soul: it matures.

Speaking of the soul, around this time I had an experience with the spooky side of life – good spooky, not madman spooky. Good spooky is when you get a peek behind the scenes and see the patterns in your life. Most of the time, with your schnoz right in it, you can't see these patterns, but every now and then – yeah.

I was mucking about in Surry Hills with Darren and the pooch, when Roger was still with us, and we came to a big old building that had a sort of promising look about it. Kids like us, we could tell just by glancing at a building that a window was open somewhere or other, just a matter of finding it. We skirted around two sides, and yeah, there's the open window at the back, no worries. In we climbed and pushed Roger in, too. We'd seen the sign out the front of the building, Nimrod Theatre, the big posters advertising shows out the front of the building, but it was only when we were inside looking down at the seats in rows and the stage at the front that I understood where we were. I thought: "You beauty!" I loved the place. It was dead silent in there, except for Roger scratching himself and panting. I said: "Daz, you know what this is? This is a theatre. You know, for plays and all that gear." And Darren said: "Huh?"

I said: "Stay here with the mutt," and walked down the aisle to the front, and up some steps to the stage. The curtain was up, and the whole stage was waiting for me. I can't even remember how I guessed that this building was a theatre. What the hell did I know about theatres? I'd never seen a play in my life. And acting – what about that? Never met an actor. But once I was on the stage, this great surge roared through me and I thought: "Stannie, you're going to be an actor. You're going to have a big picture of your handsome face out the front. People are going to clap something monstrous. You're going to be famous, yeah."

I started my acting career right then and there. I made my hands into six-shooters. "Stop right there, buddy!" I said. And when he didn't stop: "Pow pow pow!" I blew the smoke away from the muzzles. "Told you to stop." I holstered the six-shooters, gave the audience a huge grin. "Told him to stop, didn't I?" I strolled about the stage, thinking of other scenes I could act out. I said: "Baby, baby, baby," and gave a smooching sound with my lips. "I love you, baby." Darren laughed like he'd wet himself. Roger was woofing away. Man, I felt like I was floating, surrounded by a golden light.

I now know this is what happens to me when I somehow stumble into the future. It only lasted for maybe a minute, but the 'me' of the present and the 'me' of the future were together in the one moment, both on the stage at the Nimrod Theatre, in that golden light. Because in the years to come, I'd be on this same stage in a play called *Stolen*, written by Jane Harrison, directed by Wes Enoch. By that time I'd be a professional actor, appearing in movies, on the tele, and of course, on the stage. But man, before that time, lots of bad shit, lots of strife. Better let me forget that for now, and just concentrate on Stannie up there on the stage at the Nimrod (which later became the Belvoir). When this sort of thing happens – the 'you' of the present and the 'you' of the future together in the one moment – that's when I knew somewhere way deep inside that the world was so much more than what I could see with my peepers. And telling my own story now, it gives me the chance to see the patterns.

# CHAPTER 7

# END OF THE ROAD

The Feds were well and truly on Frankie's case. Charlotte had dobbed him in as a kidnapper a second time. She knew that Frankie would go to the clink if he was found guilty of running off with me and Davy and Lynnie, but she'd had enough.

What the Feds did was this: hunkered down in a rooming house in Campbelltown where the old man had taken us to stay after we left Doris's Redfern rooming house. They figured – the Feds, this is – that Frankie would come back to the rooming house sometime, and they'd nab him. Most of the day, Frankie and me and Davy and Lynnie were off in Redfern, looking for trouble, but we'd come back to the Campbelltown place at night. Frankie had developed a terrific sense of danger – an intuition – and sometimes he'd say: "No, not going back there tonight. We'll find somewhere in Redfern." But this one time, intuition let him down. He'd phoned the Campbelltown rooming house to ask if his unemployment benefit cheque was waiting for him there. That's something he had to think about those times he was on the dole, which was most of the time – an address. He couldn't say: "Out the back of Sacred Heart in Grey Street." He had to have a letterbox. Frankie called up and the rooming house manager said: "Yeah, yeah, Frankie, my man, your cheque's here, no sweat." But what Frankie didn't know, and what his famous intuition didn't tell him, was that a couple of Feds were standing beside the manager to make sure he told Frankie what he'd been ordered to say.

Off we went, me and Davy and Lynnie and the old man, straight into the grubby paws of the bloody Feds. The old man knew the game was up. Didn't go the knuckle. It was almost as if he was exhausted. I don't mean in his body, but in his mind. A year earlier there was that time when I'd grasped that Dad couldn't go on like this forever. Well, on that day in Campbelltown, Dad grasped the same thing. He was punch-drunk from his battle with the world and maybe he didn't want to go another round.

The Feds held us in their Redfern station. They let Dad go, but with the understanding that he'd appear before the beak somewhere down the track. Yeah, sure. He phoned us up that evening and spoke to each of us. Me, he spoke to in code. He asked me if I was with a crowd, meaning: "Are the cops listening?" And I said: "Big mob here." He went on in code to say that he'd get us back. I just said: "Yeah, could be." The truth was, I didn't think Dad had another kidnapping in him. And I didn't know that I wanted to do any more kidnapping on Dad's orders. Something had changed in me.

A week or so earlier, me and Davy and Lynnie had been sitting in the park in Redfern watching an old bloke feeding bread to the pigeons. We hadn't eaten for a few days and we were bloody starving. All at once, Davy jumped up, chased the pigeons away and began picking up the pieces of bread and stuffing them in his cakehole.

The pigeons tried to sneak back but Davy snarled and chased them and they kept their distance. I didn't join in, but Lynnie had a go. Watching my brother and sister scrambling about for bits of bread – they even picked up the crumbs – made me sick at heart. I thought: "This isn't right. This is bad." In the whole of Sydney, no three kids were worse off than we were, fighting birds for food. In past times, when blackfellas lived all over Australia and the white people of Europe had never even heard of us, no kid would have gone without proper feeding. Mothers fed their kids on a hundred different things they found in the bush, fathers would drop a couple of blue tongues on the fire or crack open eggs from the nest of a magpie goose. Yeah, sure, there would've been times when tucker was scarce, but Lynnie and Davy fighting off bloody pigeons – no, that was poverty, that was as bad as it gets for human beings, anywhere. I didn't have the words to explain what I was feeling, but I knew that something was changing in me. How much longer would I look at Frankie and think: "Follow you anywhere, Dad – anywhere"? My old man had owned my heart. Now, although I didn't realise it, I was taking it back.

Mum had told the cops that it was only Lynnie and Davy she wanted returned. She said I could stay with Frankie. She knew that if she took all three of us back, Frankie would be crushed. She was being kind, in her way. So I stayed with the old man when the cops took my brother and sister up to Mooroopna. And what did we do together, the old man and me? Just the usual, mooching about, me trying to get enough food into my stomach to stay alive, Frankie boozing himself silly. But eventually, one way and another – I can't remember exactly how – I ended up back with Mum, too.

I know I was at Mooroopna in August 1977, aged thirteen. I came into the kitchen one arvo and there was Mum at the sink preparing something for dinner, and the radio was playing and tears were running down her cheeks. She kept brushing the tears away with one hand while she chopped up vegies with the other. I thought: "What the hell?" I went over to Mum and put my hand on her shoulder – I was as tall as her. The light coming in through the window above the sink showed all the lines in her face. The song playing on the radio was 'Can't Help Falling in Love', and it was Elvis singing it.

"Elvis is dead," Mum said.

"Yeah? Elvis? No way!"

I knew all about Elvis. He was Mum's favourite. Aboriginal people, they all loved Elvis. Also Hank Williams, Slim Dusty, Jimmy Little – even Cliff Richard for some strange reason. But Elvis more than anyone. The King.

"Dunno how," said Mum. "Sad business. Sad, sad business."

I stayed there with my arm around Mum's shoulders and watched her face as the tears tumbled down. I loved Elvis too – who doesn't? – but no one loved him like Mum.

All my life Mum had carried the weight of her family on her back, never any proper help from Frankie, not a lot in the way of love and affection – a bit, maybe – but I'd never seen her as a teenage girl with dreams and pretty dresses. Just a glimpse now and again, singing along with someone on the radio, maybe Elvis himself, swaying to the music. People's dreams disappear. Women's dreams more than most. Looking at Mum's face that day, I was watching her remember not just Elvis but the girl she once was. I loved Mum, but all that sisternapping and brother-napping – I couldn't say I brought that much joy into her life. When she looked at me, I knew what she was thinking: "His father's son. Frankie over again."

I was wrong about Dad not having the will and strength to kidnap us again. And I was wrong about myself, too. He met me up in Mooroopna, told me that he wanted me to get hold of Davy and Lynnie, and I did what he asked. Within a half-day, we were back at Oslo in the same stupid situation: living on scraps until pension day when Frankie brought home tinned sardines as a treat. Oh brother, did we love those tinned sardines. We'd pick them out of the tins with our fingers, all wearing these big, dopey smiles of happiness. Frankie'd say: "Whadya think? Pretty good, eh?" We'd shake our heads and say: "Mmm, yum!" Not so many times in his life when the old man could look at us three kids munching away and smiling our heads off, thinking what a great dad he was. I think his dream, his big dream, was about his kids and his wife and all his rellies and friends sitting around in a big, comfy lounge room munching away on tinned sardines and telling him that he was a top bloke, a great dad, a good provider, a terrific husband. Husbands, fathers, I know what their fantasy is. It's not sex. I mean something that reaches down into a bloke's guts, deeper than sex. It's this: everybody happy at the one time – wife, kids, the whole family, mates as well, all of them happy, loving you. I'm a husband, and I know. I know something else, too. Can never happen.

The time came when Frankie had to agree that he couldn't take care of us. The child welfare people were looking into his case. Child welfare didn't want to send us back to Mooroopna with Mum, because they doubted we'd be any better off. So they took me and Davy and Lynnie and shoved us into a sort of Christian foster care holding centre out in Collingwood. When we were rounded up, about to be driven to the Collingwood place, we grabbed hold of Dad by his arms and legs and screamed as if our throats were about to be cut. "Don't let 'em take us, Dad! We don't wanna go!" But Dad, blue down to his boots, just shook his head and told us we had to go. "Getcha back one time," he said. "Don't worry 'bout that." So we had these whitefellas ripping us from the arms of our father. That was 1978, well before the Stolen Generations stuff got into people's guts. They wouldn't do it these days, take us away from Dad, but they did then.

But here's the thing: the foster care place wasn't all that bad. At least we knew where our next meal was coming from, and we got three of those meals a day, starting with cornflakes and toast and orange juice. Man – breakfast every morning! Even when we stayed with Mum, you couldn't count on brekkie *every single day*. Talk about fancy. And the people at the clearing house, they were okay. No paedophiles. Pretty decent. And something else that was just monster fantastic – proper beds, real sheets, warm blankets. We'd come in from the Third World to the First World where most white Australians lived. It didn't take much comfort for us to feel like we were in paradise. Cornflakes for brekkie, then lamb chops for dinner.

But the luxury got better still. At the foster care place, people would visit and choose kids to take home for the weekend. The way it worked was like this: Friday arvo, various couples came knocking at the door; "Hidey-ho, got any kids who need a bit of love and affection?" And the couple would cast a look over the kids all bunched up there. "Okay, we'll have you and you, jump in the car." Now, this is bound to sound suss. For the past twenty years the news has been full of stories of kids being abused by adults – priests, vicars, bishops, clergymen of every brand, people in charge of hostels, orphanages, what have you. And it would be natural to think that foster care gave dodgy blokes the perfect opportunity to go gaga. Many other kids from the shelter maybe came up against bad experiences, but not me, and not my brother and sister. The husband and wife who picked us out to take home for the weekends were kind to us. The bloke was a doctor. This doctor and his missus, they took a gander at me and Davy and Lynnie looking super pathetic (we knew by instinct that we needed to put on an act, trembling lips, maybe a few tears, in the same way that dogs and cats in animal shelters try to look sweet and sad) and said: "We'll take that little Aboriginal kid," meaning me, Stannie, because no kid on earth knew how to look as appealing as me.

I said: "Oh, mister, missus, you gotta take me poor neglected sister, Lynnie, and me poor miserable brother, Davy, as well as me, otherwise I'll cry and cry and wet the bed."

And this lovely bloke and his lovely missus said: "Oh, of course, we'll take the three of you, we won't break up the family, you dear little fellow." Words like that, pretty much. And off we went with Mister and Missus Doctor in a white Rolls Royce to a mansion in Camberwell. Bloody hell! You should've seen it. These days I have a fair bit to do with buying and selling houses and blocks of flats and all that sort of caper, and I know a bit about styles of architecture. I'd say the mansion was Queen Anne. Lots of those Queen Anne houses in Camberwell. Bloody beautiful. A tiled roof, big bay window at the front, what's called a dormer window on the upper floor, garden full of trees and flowers. When we reached the house, Davy and Lynnie and me, we looked at each other, thinking: "Pinch me, I'm dreaming!" Had our own bedroom, our own bunks, toys to muck around with. The whole inside of the house, Jesus Christ, gorgeous – paintings on the walls, ornaments everywhere. Might've crossed my mind that a lot of this stuff could be shoved into a sugar bag and flogged off at the second-hand places in Smith Street. I don't say it *did* cross my mind. Just saying it *might've*.

Mister and Missus Doctor, they had a couple of kids of their own, Karen and John, both a bit older than me. They were as kind to us as their mum and dad were. Must have been Christians of some sort. Missus Doctor, she'd say: "What would you like for breakfast, dear little kiddies?" We'd say: "Oh, missus, how about bacon and eggs and toast and Weet-Bix and jam and crumpets and orange juice and apricots out of the can?" And Missus Doctor would say: "Jolly good!" See, you've got your dodgy Christians, the priests and so on, and you've got your nice Christians. The dodgy ones – you don't want to know about them. The nice Christians – whack-o-the-diddle-o! They'll give kids like me damned near anything they ask for, if they've got the dough; take them anywhere. Mister Doctor, one time he took me out on his boat. First time I'd ever been in a boat, scooting about on the waves. I'm like: "Mamma mia!" Ecstatic. Also a little bit spooked. I knew how to swim after jumping into the Murray at Swan Hill a thousand times, but I wasn't sure about the ocean. Bloody long way back to the beach.

Mister and Missus Doctor, they loved to see us foster kids having fun. They'd stand there with soft, kind smiles on their faces as we enjoyed ourselves with the toys, or watched the telly. Karen and John, too – they were always smiling at us. The good Christians, they're insane, but nice.

We had four weekends with Mister and Missus Doctor, and with Karen and John. Each Sunday evening, Mister Doctor would take us back to the foster care place, where we'd remain until the next weekend, when Mister Doctor picked us up again. If he'd wanted to, Mister Doctor could have chosen two or three other kids, but he always chose me and Lynnie and Davy. We were becoming part of the family, and we couldn't wait to get back to that big, beautiful Camberwell house.

On the fourth weekend, Dad picked us up from Camberwell. I think there must have been some sort of limit on the number of times kids could be taken from the foster care place on weekend visits, and probably the Dryden kids had reached the limit. I didn't want to go back with Dad. I was hoping that something would happen to prevent him picking us up. I felt guilty about it, but the truth was that I could see clearer than ever that the old man wasn't offering us anything. If Mister and Missus Doctor had said: "Well now, Stannie, dear little fellow, how about you and your brother and sister join our family permanently?" I would've said: "You bet!"

That was a sad thing, leaving Mister Doctor and his family behind. But there you go. Life isn't one happy time followed by another. I mean, sure, you get happy times, but you're going to have more disappointment than crazy happiness, so get used to it.

Disappointment didn't destroy me that time, but Jesus, it hurt. Dad took us up to Mooroopna to stay with Mum. Or not to stay with her, but to live with her. And you know, this time it was different. That spirit of adventure that came over me every time I thought of hitting the road with the old man had worn itself out. I began to feel once I was back with Mum that Frankie had just about used himself up. When I was younger, I believed him completely when he said: "Gonna have fun, Stannie. Gonna see the world." He didn't even believe that himself any longer. He wanted me with him because he loved me, and that was it. He didn't have any place to take me that was different to all the other places we'd seen. I turned sixteen up in Mooroopna with Mum, and it'll sound funny if I say that I was getting too old for the open road, but it's true. I was too old. I wanted to have adventures with kids my own age, not with my father. And I wanted to drink with kids my own age, too. I was well into the frothy stuff up at Mooroopna.

It made me happy, made me want to laugh, flirt with girls. I couldn't be happy in the way I wanted to be with Frankie. When he drank these days, he was on the nod after a single bottle. Charlotte was different. I could be on the couch boozing with my hand up a girl's blouse and all she'd say was: "Take it somewhere else, Stannie." Girlfriends weren't put off by a mum in the way they were by a dad.

Dad came up to Mooroopna by train and bus in the summer of 1981. Gave me a huge hug before he said howdy to anyone else. Mum, she just looked up for a second from what she was busy with at the kitchen sink. She said: "What do you want?" Frankie gave Lynnie and Judy a kiss, enjoyed a bit of a wrestle with Davy.

Once upon a time, Frankie could walk into a room and all eyes turned to him. That swagger. Duke Wayne. His friends would call out to him: "Frankie! How are you, champ?" I'd be thinking: "This man, he's *my dad*." Back then, he still had that feeling of danger. But now the grog had got to him. The amount Dad put away, Jesus, it would have killed ten men.

He stayed overnight in Mooroopna, just the wreckage of what he once was. And in the morning, he said to me: "C'mon buddy, let's hit the road." I was standing there by the bus with Davy and Lynnie and Judy and Mum and a few other rellies. At sixteen I was as tall as the old man and I could stare him straight in the eye. Which I did. I said: "Not coming, Dad." And Frankie frowned, looked puzzled, as if he must have heard wrong. "Nah, c'mon, Stannie. C'mon. Great times, buddy, gonna get a job down in Benalla. You and me, yeah?"

"No, Dad, I'm staying."

I could see as clear as day the pain in his face. Maybe he'd been telling himself that nothing had changed, that all he had to do was say: "Let's go," and I would be right there beside him. Maybe he didn't even see that he was not the feared Frankie, the adored Frankie, of years gone by. Or maybe he just thought, you know, that because he loved me, I'd always be there for him to put his arm around my shoulders. So me saying "No" was like a voice telling him that time was running out, that it was soon going to be all over, red rover. The legend of Frankie was fading away.

He climbed into the bus with tears running down his face. I was standing on the road behind the bus. Dad sat on the back seat. There was a knot in my guts but I wasn't crying. My mind was made up. Dad said: "Bye, cobber," and the bus drove away.

I never went on the road with the old man again. Never felt his arm around me again. Jesus, that's a sad bloody thing to remember. Say what you like about Frankie, he was a man. He didn't have it in him to change his life, get away from the grog, give up throwing his fists about, build something new. He had just the one way of making his way in the world. But he was a man, and I loved him.

# CHAPTER 8

# THE WARRIORS

Once the old man was gone, once the knot in my guts untied itself, I set about creating my own legend. I wore my hair long, slicked back with Brylcreem – talk about handsome, my oh my. I was around to all the dances and discos, gorgeous Stannie, the daydream of every chick in Shepparton. Might've been one of the reasons I wouldn't go on the road with Frankie. Hell, what can I say? If you're going to turn down an opportunity to make out with a city's worth of beautiful girls, what hope is there for you? At sixteen I was seething with energy, my sex drive off the scale. But I was ambitious in other ways, too.

I wanted to be as big as my dad. If people saw me somewhere, in the street, wherever, I didn't want them to say: "That's what's-his-name." I wanted them to say: "That's Stannie Dryden, you must've heard of him." And man, I had this big life to lead, I could feel it inside me. I wasn't the old man's offsider any longer, I was Stan. I was full to bursting with confidence. The others kids in Shep and Mooroopna and Ardmona – all those towns up there in orchard country – they'd lived their lives in the one place. Me, I'd seen everything; I'd been all over the place, seen bad guys and crooks and hard men and drunks and people with powers that came from their ancestors, people who could look you in the eye and read your whole story in ten seconds. My life with Frankie up to the age of sixteen had taught me stuff I would never have known a damned thing about if I'd spent those years in school. People who've been to university and come out the other end with a certificate are called 'graduates'. Well, I was a graduate myself. A graduate of the whole of bloody Australia, of pubs where they threw sawdust on the floor to soak up the blood, and of toilet blocks where I'd slept on the concrete floor. Monster stuff like that. Man, it made me tough, and that was part of my confidence. Wasn't spooked by anything. The other kids in Shep (Shepparton was the biggest town up there; where you made your rep) were in awe of me, I'm happy to say. Because I needed to be in charge; I couldn't be a follower.

There was a movie called *The Warriors* that came out in 1979, a few years before I started hitting the discos in Shep. It was set in New York City, all to do with these gangs: the Warriors, the Rogues and the Riffs, the Baseball Furies, and a girl gang known as the Lizzies. All the gangs were rivals, and the gang at the heart of the story, the Warriors, their leader was called Swan – super cool dude, good-looking – and he was the guy I loved. I had the movie on video; I'd be on Mum's sofa saying Swan's lines along with him, had them memorised, and Mum'd say: "Wotcha doin', Stannie? You've seen that film over and over." Yeah, I watched it ten times, and that wasn't enough. Swan, he had me in a spell. He became the new hero in my life. I studied the way Swan moved, the way he smiled. What I was looking at was an exhibition of cool. I was already known for what I could do with my fists, but being cool was something different. It meant that you kept your head, never panicked, smiled at danger, let chicks go crazy over you without ever going crazy over them.

It said a lot that my first new hero after Dad left the scene was a criminal. Other kids, maybe they wanted to be Robin Hood or King Arthur or Wyatt Earp or Audie Murphy or even Mark Ella or Michael Long, but for me it was Swan. Growing up with Dad had given me a different take on criminals and what they did to make a buck. I saw it as doing what comes naturally, with some craft added. Dad had trained me to live outside the law in the way that other dads trained their sons to become carpenters and motor mechanics. It was a trade, with its own set of skills. Another dad would say: "Watch closely, this is how you get a nice, even bevel on a length of two-be-four." My old man said: "Watch closely, this is how you lift a bankroll out of a punter's pocket without him knowing a bloody thing." Something that straight folk never understand is that the criminal life isn't all brutal and dirty; it has its enchantments. That bankroll I lifted, once I'd shuffled over to a corner and counted the windfall, I'd think: "Oh man, that was a thing of beauty."

I showed *The Warriors* to all my mates, three or four at a time. Sat them down on Mum's sofa, gave each one a can of Vic. When they'd seen the movie – and boy, they loved it – I'd say: "Which one's like me?" And the answer always came back: "Swan, he's you!"

I'd say: "Swan, that's right, the leader. And who am I?"

"You're the leader, Stannie."

So I set up my gang in Shep, and I called it the Warriors. It was a gang of misfits, of outsiders, kids who'd never been part of a tribe and wanted to feel that they belonged. I had Greek kids, Italian kids, Turkish kids, none of them ever likely to get rich, but that wasn't what they were looking for. Just excitement – that was enough. Difficult for a kid of sixteen to find excitement inside the law. We needed the thrill of knowing we could go to prison.

The gangs in the movie had rules, such as never saying a thing to the cops, and never questioning the leader, and I made sure my boys understood that we'd have the same rules. And we'd know how to fight. That was a big thing, knowing how to fight. In the movie, Swan and his gang fight their way from one side of New York City all the way back to their home turf on Coney Island, busting one rival gang after another. Terrific scenes of the Warriors fighting the Baseball Furies gang. The Warriors are outnumbered two to one when they run into the Furies, and they hightail it, but eventually they have to turn and fight. The four Warriors bust the arses of the Furies, mostly because of the moves that Swan has mastered. My boys knew that I could do the same thing – fight my way out of it when the odds were against me – but they also knew I had something else, and that was imagination. My boys could fight, wouldn't back off, but, nah, no imagination. They knew they had to leave the whole vision thing to me.

In the movie, each gang had its own uniform. The Furies wore striped Yankee uniforms and had their faces painted something like the guys in Kiss, and carried baseball bats. The Warriors wore leather waistcoats, open at the front. I took my boys down to the op shops of Shep and bought each one a waistcoat, not leather but fabric, worn without anything underneath. The gangs in the movie also had 'insignia' – badges and that sort of gear. I wanted my boys to have their own badges, so I drew a picture of a skull and crossbones, with the word 'Shep' above and the word 'Warriors' below, took the design down to a printing shop and got the guys there to screen-print it on the back of each waistcoat. The boys loved it. Then I went further. Each Warrior was tattooed with the letter 'W' on the back of his right hand. The tattoos were homemade: a Redhead matchstick was encircled again and again with white cotton thread until a bulb was formed on the head of the stick, then the back of each gang member's hand was pricked over and over with a needle to make the letter 'W' for 'Warrior'. The matchstick with the bulb of thread was dipped in ink, and the ink was dripped into the raw flesh, and that was it – a homemade tattoo. My boys were proud of their tatts. Putting up with the pain of being pricked with the needle was important. No tears.

We had all our gear, uniforms, insignia, but what we needed was a ceremony to announce ourselves to the world. I got all the boys down to the lake in Shep one night and made a big circle, each Warrior holding a candle. A few onlookers: girlfriends, brothers, sisters. We swore loyalty to each other in the Shepparton darkness, stars above.

What I should've called my gang was not the Warriors, but the Dukes, after Frankie 'Duke' Dryden, because it was his philosophy of 'Take it easy – but take it' that made a foundation for the gang. Frankie's rules were our rules: 'No weapons but your fists. Never hit a woman, never hit a girl, never hit a kid.' We didn't carry blades, didn't carry guns. The gangs they have in the big cities, especially the bikie gangs, they're built around weapons, murder, torture. My gang was built around the idea of having fun.

Looking back, I have to admit that my need to start the Warriors was also about insecurity. At the time, I didn't know what 'insecurity' meant, and if anyone had explained it to me and told me I was insecure, I would've biffed him. I needed to be loved, still do. I don't have to be adored, just loved and recognised for the things I do well. What I was doing with the Warriors was building a family. Frankie, Charlotte, they loved me, sure, but we weren't a family except for now and again. When I lived with Mister and Missus Doctor in Camberwell, that's when I got an idea of what a family was. They filled up the inside of that big house of theirs with warmth, not just for ten minutes but all day, every day. We'd sit down to meals together, all of us around the table, Mister and Missus smiling across at the three of us as if we were gifts from heaven. I wasn't about to get the Warriors around a big table for a festival of love, but I wanted the warmth of us all belonging together. Any arguments, I'd soothe the boys, just about kiss their cheeks and pat them on the head: "Hey, hey, hey, we're all in this together."

Recently it dawned on me that I was also acting out my Aboriginal heritage when I was building the Warriors. In 1982, I had only a blurry idea of that heritage. I knew I was black and Indigenous, and that was cool, but I didn't know anything deep. Yet there I was, building from scratch a tribe with rules and rituals and initiation ceremonies. I didn't want to be crime lord; I wanted to be a tribal leader. It was in my blood. The Aboriginal Stan had become blended with the Stan who was the son of Frankie. I'd set up a tribe that made its way in the world not by hunting and fishing, but by knocking stuff off.

We Warriors were heavily into burgs. Find a window that's not too difficult to open, doors with dodgy locks, hinges that can be unscrewed, walls that can be scaled – that was us. Down at Shep station one night – having a bit of a squiz – we came across this warehouse full of cartons of beer. All the beer for Shepparton came up on the train from the breweries in Melbourne, mostly from Carlton & United, and it'd get stored in the warehouse until the pubs of the town sent trucks to pick it up. Never been a crook in Shep who'd had the brains to rob the warehouse, but the Warriors, oh yeah, we were onto it. Made off with two hundred and forty cartons of VB, Melbourne Bitter, Foster's, a king's ransom in grog. Ferried it all back to Mum's place in various cars, worried all the time that we'd be pinched for driving without a licence. Stacked it all eight cartons high behind Mum's shed. Fantastic feeling of triumph for the Shep Warriors. I looked at the big smiles on the faces of my guys and said: "You'd think we'd robbed Fort Knox." We stood gazing at those cartons stacked up to the roof of the shed shaking our heads in wonder. "Oh, man, two hundred and forty cartons, get the hell outa here!"

Now, all of us knew how to do justice to the noble product – but two hundred and forty cartons? Too much even for the thirsty Warriors. But with Christmas coming up, it meant a big chance to play Santa Claus. We took five cartons around to all the struggling families in Shep, knocked on the front door, huge grins: "Whadya think? Merry Christmas, brother!" Man, were we popular. But maybe not so clever, because the cops came looking for us. Well, they would, wouldn't they? We'd begun to get a rep; we were seen all over the place. One morning a couple of coppers turned up at Mum's place and collared me in my Warriors vest.

"Now see here, Sonny Jim, you're the leader of this Warriors mob, right?"

"Me, sir, no, sir, dunno who the leader is, sir."

"Then why is everybody pointing the finger at you, matey?"

"Dunno, sir, big mistake, sir."

"'Zat right? We think you're leading us up the garden path, we think you and your boys knocked over the warehouse down at the station and buggered off with a hundred cartons of beer."

"Was two hundred and forty cartons, sir. That's what I heard, sir. Wasn't us, but."

The coppers didn't think to look behind the shed, where all the cartons were stacked. They thought the Warriors were probably involved in the whole thing, but the truth was that they didn't know how to deal with us; we baffled them. We looked so cheerful, we had no weapons, didn't show any aggression. My story was that we were a basketball team out to enjoy the open air, the Shep Warriors shooting hoops and doing nobody no harm. As soon as the cops went on their way, me and the boys stepped up the Christmas deliveries. Didn't want Mum to see what was behind the shed. She'd never lag, but surrounded by crime most of her life, what with everything Frankie was up to, and then me, deep down she wanted law and order. Had to protect Mum from the truth for her own good.

Any bloke who leads a gang has to deal with people who want to take his job. It's natural, same thing for kings and prime ministers. The leader says: "I'm on top, I'm here forever." Some kid hears and says: "Yeah? Well, cop this!" I was a bit different. I told the Warriors never to tell anyone I was the leader. I went further than that. I said: "I'm not the leader. I'm just one of you, the same. Johnny's the leader." Johnny was my best mate, sharp and tough. The boys listened to me, but they didn't believe me. And everyone outside the gang, they knew I was the leader. Had this one kid, Robert, a rough nut; down the pub one time he shuffled up to me and said: "Heard you're telling everyone you can beat me. You saying that? Saying you can beat me?" Well, I hadn't been saying that or anything like it. Wasn't the Stan style to go about bragging. I said: "No, I never said that, bro. Never did. But as a matter of fact, if you want to try it on, let's go out the back." So out we go, and pop! Floored him. Thanks to Frankie, I knew every punch in the shot locker. I didn't brag because I knew I could sort out anyone who wanted to give it a go with one punch, two punches, three at the most.

Here I must mention another kid who wanted to knock my block off, not a Warrior, a karate champ, also a Nazi-loving white suprema-cist, total arsehole. He'd be out on the footpath, hanging out, slagging off every Aborigine who walked past. "Hey, you black bastard, get off the fucking footpath, hear what I'm saying?" Me and my boys were outside the Star Bowl tenpin bowling centre in Shep when this halfwit, the karate champ, starts in with the slagging, and I'm like: "Listen, fuzznuts, let's you and me go out the back and have a chat." Down the alley beside the Star Bowl we went. Halfway down, I turned, grabbed Adolf by the shoulders, chucked him against the wall, pop, pop! All over. It was one of Frankie's tricks: "Make sure you land that first punch."

We were all under eighteen in the Warriors, meaning that we couldn't go to the bottle shop and buy grog. It was a problem because the Warriors ran on grog. We only came fully to life after a couple of VBs. I didn't grasp it at the time, but I was an alcoholic. You can get away with being an alcoholic for a good long time before you fall to pieces. Healthy when you start, yeah, you'll be okay for years, at least on the outside. Inside, different matter. I was turning my liver into a fat, black sponge and destroying my brain. I'd started drinking at fourteen, so I had about another fourteen years of okay health. This is what I tell kids these days who want to take up booze in a serious way: it's not the grog that does you over; it's the rotten diet, bad sleep-ing habits, also falling over and whacking your noggin. If you eat well three times a day, get eight hours' kip, clean your teeth top and bottom morning and night, scoff down a few vitamins, you're going to be fine, for a while. Same with smack, same with coke, amphetamines. Live healthy, you've got years of mischief in front of you. The thing is, if the kid's in deadly earnest about the grog, he won't be bothered eating proper, won't be bothered sleeping proper, cleaning his choppers. But that's my advice, all the same. "Mate, you want to be an alcoholic or an addict, have to show a lot of discipline, have to look after yourself."

The Warriors weren't worried about any of that; we just needed a stooge to buy grog for us at the bottle shop, an adult. And we found a stooge in Jimmy the Greek. Jimmy, he had a thing for Aboriginal girls of about the age of sixteen, which is to say about half his age, but the girls didn't have a thing for Jimmy. I said to Jimmy: "Mate, I can fix you up with a few gorgeous chicks, but you have to do something for me." And Jimmy was excited. He had a car, and he'd drive in to the bottle shop with me and maybe six of the Warriors, buy four or five slabs, and off we'd all go down to the river and booze away for hours. Paradise. But Jimmy wanted to get with the girls, the other part of the bargain. I took Cathi and Maureen aside and coached them. "Now, you don't have to do anything with Jimmy, right? All you have to do is give him a smile, let him kiss you on the cheek, say something nice to him. Then disappear." The girls understood. They led Jimmy a merry dance, as they say. A few smiles, and Jimmy was hooked.

Man, that was a time, it really was. The Warriors were high on fame, high on grog, girls going berserk for us. We were the kings of Shep. And not only Shep, because I'd get Jimmy to drive us down to Melbourne so we could mix it with other gangs in the City Square – Sharpies, Broady Boys, any gang that wanted a taste of what we could do, yeah, down there in the square throwing our fists about. It didn't matter to the Warriors what the other gangs believed or didn't believe, whether they were racist or not, whether they hated everybody who didn't go for their particular taste in music; that was just surface stuff, rubbish. All the boys in all the gangs, what they believed in more than anything else was fighting. Me as much as anyone. Great feeling, throwing your knuckles around. Didn't want to kill anyone. Just wanted that terrific surge of adrenaline when you see a face and sink your fist into it. Primitive, sure, but monster exciting.

# CHAPTER 9

# REAL LIFE

I was sixteen and a half and ready for anything when I met Sophia. Down by the Goulburn River in Shep, me and my buddies, just mucking around, trying to dream up genius plans that would make the Warriors a legend for all time. Burgs that would go down in history; scams they'd write about in books. I looked across the river and saw something that blotted out everything in the world for a minute or more – the most beautiful girl on earth riding a bay horse bareback, her brown hair flying. I came out of my trance when the girl and the horse disappeared from view, and stood there muttering things like: "Bloody hell, jeez, God almighty ..."

My offsider Johnny was staring at me. "'S'matter?"

"Johnny, you saw that girl on the horse? I'm going to marry her."

And Johnny's like: "Yeah, yeah." But I was deadly serious about it. It wasn't just a fantasy. I've always had this thing whenever something like destiny comes along. Everything goes quiet, not a sound, and it feels like I'm not breathing. When the world comes back, it's as if I've been on a long, long journey.

I met Sophia again when my mate Normie asked me to come along on a date with his girlfriend, Michelle. I said: "What do you want me along for, you idiot?" Normie explained that Michelle's mum wouldn't let her go out with him by himself; had to bring this other girl along to keep Michelle company. "Yeah," I said. "If it helps you out, bro." As soon as I saw Michelle's friend, I knew who it was. "You ride a horse?" I said. "Nice little bay?" And oh man, this was the clincher – she was shy. A blushing girl like that, so gorgeous – who can resist? We got chatting, of course we did, and I let her see that I thought she was something special in a huge way. Brown hair, big eyes, the sweetest lips on earth, fabulous shape to her body, and yeah, all of that's good, but it was the way she had about her that got into my heart and my guts: quiet and shy like I said, but at the same time bursting with life, so many smiles. From that night on, it was Stan and Sophia, Sophia and Stan, you and me, babe.

She was still in high school, Sophia, and doing well. Younger than me. Her mum, Bev, and her stepdad, Steve, they didn't approve of me one tiny bit. If you were an Aboriginal kid in Shep, no one had very high expectations of you. Steve and Bev looked at me and thought: "This kid's on the highway to hell." They advised Sophia to think again before teaming up with a tearaway Indigenous semi-hoodlum. But like I said, Sophia was nuts about me, monster stuff, wanted to be with me twenty-four hours a day forever. Wasn't long before we were living together at Mum's place. And Mum, she accepted Sophia without a single word of criticism of me, and nothing about Sophia being too young. It was as if she thought: "Stannie wants Sophia, Sophia wants Stannie, that's the way it has to be."

And she accepted it when Sophia became pregnant. Maybe more than I did. Nothing's going to be easy for two kids with a baby on the way. Mum thought: "That's the way it is." I thought: "Dunno about this. Good in some ways, bit of a problem in others."

86

Meanwhile, the Warriors, we kept busy. Sixty burglaries in three weeks. A crime wave. Well, what could we do? Doors were left open, windows left unlocked. Had to take advantage. I had this thing going with wristwatches. If you're in and out of people's houses looking for loot, a watch is one of those glittery things you always grab. May not be able to sell them for much, but you grab them. I liked to collect a watch from every place we did over – a sort of souvenir. And if I wasn't along on the burg, I'd tell the boys to bring me back a watch. Ended up with so many that I kept them in a Sunshine powdered milk tin. Another day, another watch. After a bit, I didn't even have to tell the boys to bring me back a watch; they knew the drill. As the Sunshine tin became heavier and heavier, I could use its weight as a measure of success. But naturally, heaps of other stuff came our way. Getting rid of it, not always so easy. Only a certain number of pawnbrokers in Shep and Mooroopna, and even then, you had to have a story to tell the guy behind the counter.

"Yeah, got a nice set of silverware here for you, buddy. Used to be my grandma's."

And the guy at the counter: "Your grandma? What, she's given up using knives and forks, has she? Gave all her cutlery to you?"

"Gone into a home for oldies. Said to me, 'Stan, you can have me silverware.' Deadset."

"And the candlestick holders. She told you to take them, too?"

"Yeah, them too."

"And the bicycle. That was your grandma's, I suppose."

"Yeah, that was grandma's. Too old to ride it these days. No use for it in the oldies' home. Told me to keep it."

"Interesting that your grandma was riding a man's bike."

"Huh? Oh, yeah, yeah. Sorry. That was grandpa's."

Only so many stories you can spin. Different if you've got a decent fence, because a fence knows it's all been lifted, whatever you offer him. But a fence wants jewellery; he isn't about to take a bike off your hands, or a jaffle iron, a toaster. And after sixty burgs, the cops were on the warpath. See, for the coppers, it's all about paperwork. A citizen calls the station, says: "Somebody took my bloody jaffle iron!" The cops have got to write it down. And the same thing when the next citizen comes in to report that the toaster's missing, and so on. It doesn't look good if sixty citizens have had their goods lifted – it's like the Shep cops aren't doing their job. Somebody higher up in Copworld sees the figures – somebody in the city, maybe – and calls up the local cops: "What's going on? Catch those scoundrels!"

The cops came after the Warriors because for one thing, we stood out: the vests, the skull and crossbones, the cheeky attitude. They hauled a dozen of us down to the station, including my old man, who was up in Mooroopna on one of his visits. They weren't about to charge Frankie with anything, he was just along to look out for my interests. He said: "Don't say nothin', Stannie." The cops questioned all of us and came to the conclusion that we were genuine bad boys. They fingerprinted us and took the others away to charge them with illegal entry, burglary, being smart-arses, all of that rubbish. The old man and I were left to ourselves in an interview room. We'd been fingerprinted on a strip of paper that had five squares on it for the fingers of the right hand, and five for the left. Frankie, he wasn't looking so good. Hadn't had a drink for hours and was in that sorry state of alcoholics who are getting close to madness. He said: "Change of plan, Stannie. You'll have to give 'em one or two burgs just to shut 'em up. Gotta get out of here, buddy. Need a drink bad as."

I was thinking: "Okay, I give the cops something, that'll be a year in juvenile detention, don't like the sound of it." At the same time, I hated to see Dad suffering. Then I noticed the bottle of meths that the cops had left behind – it was meant to be used for cleaning the fingerprinting ink off your paws. Big bottle. Now, the old man had swallowed more meths in his time than most people had swallowed water, so there was no harm – or no worse harm – in telling him about the bottle. Why he didn't see it himself, that might have been to do with his eyesight, not as good as it once was; the meths and the grog pretty much destroy the vision out of your eyeballs after a time. "Hey, Dad – bottle of meths on the desk there."

And Dad: "What? Fuck me!"

He grabbed the bottle, tilted it up, the whole lot down the hatch. Did him good like you wouldn't believe, came back to life ten seconds after draining the bottle. "Don't tell 'em a bloody thing, Stannie. Nothin'!"

One of the cops, he came back to us. I was thinking: "Here we go." But instead of charging me, he stood there with his hand on his chin just sizing me up. Dad said: "My kid never done nothin'! Never!" And the cop said: "Yeah, yeah. Shut up, Frankie." Then he nodded his head. "Something special about you, Stan. You know that?"

And me: "Huh?"

"Something a bit special. Not going to charge you. But I'll tell you what I want you to do."

What he wanted me to do was front up for footy training. "Want to redirect your energy into something that'll do you good. You turn up, and keep turning up, I'll keep you out of the clink. Deal?"

As I said, I started the Warriors for the fun of it. If the cop wanted to give me something else to do, just as much fun, okay by me. I shook his hand. Dad was watching on. "Never did nothin'!" he said.

My boys ended up in juvenile detention – Parkville, Malmsbury, Beechworth. Four of them – Johnny, Abraham, Blackie, Dean – I'd trained so well in the Warriors that they were practically running the prisons they served time in after a few months. They knew how to stand up for themselves, mongrel stuff like that, and to show loyalty to each other. The most important skill they had was organising. They knew how to keep things running, and not just for themselves but for the prison altogether. Prison staff all over Australia have to rely on the cooperation of the prisoners. Unless they can do that, the prisons turn into concentration camps. Nothing pleases the prison staff more than to find a few guys they can trust to make the porridge thicken and the custard set, in a manner of speaking. They want these guys to be intelligent, and my Warriors, all of them, had genuine intelligence, genuine savvy. All that I'd learnt on the road with the old man I passed on to my boys, and they used it to make the system inside work for them. Funny thing, but with the same set of skills they could have run BHP Billiton, or any big company. As it was, they had to settle to running the slammers. You could do worse.

In the natural way of things, Sophia grew and grew until it became impossible for me to ignore that I was about to become a dad. Sort of exciting, but also ridiculous. I was only a kid myself, and so was Sophia. What the hell?

I went down to the city to see Dad at Oslo. He hadn't been up to Mooroopna for a while and I wanted to tell him about the baby, for one thing, and for another, take a look at his face since I might not be able to do that for much longer. It gave me real pleasure, just looking at the old man's mug. The whole story of his life was written in lines and creases. And a good part of the story of my life. When I looked at Frankie, a festival of memory started up. That time when he came to get me in Ballarat, and we were out on the highway hitching to Adelaide, sleeping under the trees on a bed of pine needles, and me thinking: "This is the best, this is me and Dad." So often on the move. Any place we stopped, it was always temporary, the road calling us. The way that Frankie was never tied down, it meant that he had some Aborigine in his blood. I don't know how, but he did. Because Aborigines, we're still the great travellers of this continent. We are, yeah. We wake up one morning in Fitzroy and think: "Know what? Gotta see Aunty Judy in Perth." A whitefella, he wants to go Perth from Fitzroy, two months in the planning. Blackfella, two minutes of planning, down to Spencer Street, buy a ticket (or not), jump on the train, thirty-two hours later: "Aunty Judy, great to see you." We like to keep in touch, sure, but another thing about the way Indigenous people are always hopping on trains or jumping into a Toyota or boarding a Boeing, or a six-seater in the outback, is that travel, even long, long journeys, is natural to us, no big deal. We get itchy feet. Me, these days I'm barely in one place long enough to cast a shadow. Gotta keep moving. Torture to me would be being chained by the ankle to a redgum stump. Nobody would need to jump on me with a length of rubber hose and a cigarette lighter to make me scream. Just lock me up, tell me that I won't be going nowhere for a year or two. These deaths of my Indigenous brothers (sometimes sisters) in custody, what that's about is being tied down in one small space. It tears us to bits. Okay, okay – I know there's more than one cause; I know about depression, coming down off the grog, racial abuse, a sense of the hopelessness of it all. But believe me, more than any white Australian, my people can't hack being tethered to the one spot.

Dad was at Oslo, a place that was as much a home to him as he ever knew. The old man could've written a guide book to the rooming houses of Australia, but Oslo was the one he knew best. I met up with him there, and boy! He looked crook. Every time I'd seen him over the past couple of years, he was just that bit frailer. Imagine Frankie looking frail – what the hell? Frankie, who ruled the land with his fists? It made me weep, just about. We sat in his room and I told him about the baby. And he teared up, this wild man of the highways. "Yeah? Stannie, that's terrific." These hard men, they melt like chocolate on a sunny day when a new baby comes into the world. "A baby, Stannie. Gonna be a dad, eh. The best, Stannie, best of all time having a kid."

The way Frankie was, the tears and so on, that was genuine. But it was Mum who did most of the real work of raising us kids. I have to remember that. Frankie loved being a dad, but all the hard slog, no, he never even noticed that. It was a tribal thing with him – he was the chief, his kids were bound to him by love; the rest of it was women's business.

That was the last time I saw my father alive. The last time. I drove my old bomb back to Mooroopna. My plan was to drive down to the city after the birth with Sophia and the baby and show Dad his new grandchild. A postcard came from him four days before Sophia and I and baby Kylie were due to make the trip. "Dear Stan, you know what? I can die a happy man knowing I have a granddaughter. Thank you, son. Thank you, Sophia. Love, Dad." The picture on the postcard showed a Melbourne tram.

After months and months of him looking so crook, and Frankie himself saying that he was on the way out, I knew it'd be a bloody close-run thing, getting Sophia and the baby down to see him before it was too late and I was like: "Come on, come on, gotta get moving!"

But my old bomb, all the windows were broken, and Mum said: "Just forget it, Stan! You're not driving that wreck down to the city with no windows and a baby inside." I could see her point – would have been like a hurricane inside the car at 120 kay on the highway – but I wanted to try it. Still, this was one of those times when Charlotte got her way.

A few days later, I was in a telephone box down the street from Mum's place in Mooroopna, yakking to someone or other, when I saw a cop car pulled up at the house. Okay, when I say I was 'yakking to someone or other' I'm not being dead honest. I know who I was yakking to. It was another girl I was seeing, best not mention her name. Anyway, that's just for the sake of being honest. I saw the cop car and the thing I naturally thought was that the wallopers had come for me. Might have been an incident or two or three in Shep that the cops might've thought I *might* be able to help them with. *Might.* Even after the intervention of the officer who suggested I join the footy team, I wasn't a completely reformed character, I have to admit. What can I say? I was trained for a life of crime from the cradle, and it's a bloody hard thing to put aside what you're good at.

I waited a bit, out of sight. Saw the wallopers climb back in the patrol car and drive away. When I walked in through the front door I could hear Mum crying her eyes out in the kitchen. "Mum, what's this? What's going on, well?" And Mum said: "He's gone, Stan. Frankie's gone. The police were just here telling me." Now, I thought I was well and truly prepared for Frankie to die. I should've been ready. But I wasn't. A huge wave crashed over me and dumped me down and turned me over and over. I ran straight out the front door and kept going and crashed full bore into the fence. Picked myself up and threw my head back and howled. Man, it was the worst feeling that I'd ever had in my heart, in my guts. Stood there and howled to the sky. But this is something truly weird. At the exact same time I was howling my head off, I was also feeling relief. I didn't realise that I'd been carrying around this huge weight of worry and pain, expecting to hear that Frankie was gone. And when I knew he was gone, I thought: "I don't have to worry anymore." Can you imagine that shit? My heart ripped out, and at the same time, terrific relief.

They'd found him in his room at Oslo. He'd been dead three days. It was said that his ticker gave out. I don't know who told me – somebody. There must have been an autopsy. All of Dad's family were told about him passing, lots of his friends. Dad's brother Siddie stumped up the dough to get Frankie's body sent up to Mooroopna, and it was Siddie who paid for the funeral. I'd met Uncle Siddie barely twice in my life; he came from the well-behaved side of the Dryden family, and the Good Drydens kept a space between themselves and the Dodgy Drydens. The Good Drydens had steady jobs and proper houses. Dad was the black sheep, along with Uncle Darryl. Well, Dad was the black sheep and Uncle Darryl was the grey sheep – not as far down the Lost Highway as Frankie. In the days before the funeral, rellies and friends would come knocking at Mum's door, and they'd always single me out because I'd loved Frankie so much. Everyone knew that it was me who had that special bond with him. "Well, Stannie, you're going to miss your dad, hey?" And: "Your old man, Stannie, what a legend."

Frankie was buried at Shepparton Cemetery on 5 August 1983. I was eighteen, old enough to ache but too old to stand at the graveside howling. I kept to myself at the head of the grave, looking down. People sort of knew to leave me alone instead of calling me over to join hands. Uncle Darryl was there, Uncle Siddie, Uncle Watson (from Mum's side of the family, not Uncle Watson the killing machine). Lynette and Davy and Judy, of course. A minister from one church or another spoke the words that are always said at a Christian burial, even if, like my old man, the person being buried is not a Christian, and we all said: "Amen." The minister told us to take a handful of soil from the heap of earth and clay beside the grave and throw it onto the lid of the coffin. When Davy threw his handful, I heard him say in a quiet voice: "Thank you for being my dad." He had tears in his eyes. How good it would have been if we'd been able to give Dad a traditional, Aboriginal send-off, too, because there was something in his spirit, in the way he was never tied down, that meant he had some Aborigine in his blood. I don't know how, but he did. I've been there at traditional ceremonies in the years after Frankie's burial – ceremonies that can go on for two weeks – and I think of my dad at those times. I hope he's managed to team up with the ancestors on Mum's side of the family. That's where he should be, in the dreaming.

As for me, I was numb with grief, and at the same time still feeling that weird relief because I wouldn't have to worry about the old man any longer. I reckon I'm not the only person who has felt wacky stuff like that at a graveside, gladness and pain, then neither, just numbness. What can you say? It's a passing, and one of the people in the cemetery while the service is going on is never going to be in the world again, never going to laugh and cry and sit down to a square meal or pour a glass of beer, never going to light up a smoke, never going to give anyone a kiss, or a biff. It's mysterious, the whole thing. I can say this, though. If Dad had come back to life and thrown open the lid of the coffin and scrambled up the walls of the grave, I would have said: "No, Dad, you go back down there, I can't bear the pain of you drinking your way to a second funeral." Yeah, a passing is mysterious, but love – that's twice as mysterious. Insane.

Frankie maybe didn't do enough to earn the love of those closest to him, but who cares? I loved that man. Not everyone gets his or her due when life's over. Sure, we always make nice when someone's being buried. But what I mean is the truth. And the truth about Frankie – bigger than all the other truths – is that he lived the life he was born to live, brawling, boozing, loving and losing. It was a real life.

# CHAPTER 10

# NINE TO FIVE

A second baby was born a year after Dad's passing, a boy. We gave the little bloke my name, so that was two Stans under the one roof, more than any woman could cope with. Mum helped out every day with Kylie and Stan, as everyone knew she would. Mum had a huge heart, and terrific stamina. Never too tired to take the babies off Sophia's hands when needed. I look back and think: "How the hell would we have got by without Mum?" Just as Charlotte was a born mother, she was a born grandmother, too. I was some use to Sophia, but maybe not as much as I could have been. There were other girls in my life. And as a matter of fact, other babies that became pretty much the responsibility of one mother and another. I can't say I covered myself in glory at that time. In my community of family and friends, the men pretty much got away with murder. I wasn't the only father running around on a merry spree. Settling down with a nine-to-five job, devoting myself to wife and kids – no, I couldn't give myself to it. I was too young to say goodbye to adventure. The days of the Warriors were all over, but what made me build up that gang and what gave me such a buzz when I strolled around in my skull-and-crossbones vest – that was still there.

Not a man in the world who can put that hunger for adventure aside and say: "Oh, looks like I need to be a good boy from now until the end of my life, well, that's okay."

But at least I understood that I needed a job and a steady income for the time being. I couldn't put down 'career criminal' on my tax return, under 'occupation'. And it happened that Steve and Bev, Sophia's olds, were moving down to Melbourne for the sake of Steve's work, which was bricklaying. Not that much to keep a brickie occupied in Shep. Steve said he'd take me on as his labourer if I wanted to go with him. He was trying to be helpful. He thought that getting me the hell out of Shep and Mooroopna would put a gap between me and my life of crime, also between me and the girlfriends, give me a good taste of adult responsibility, make a man of me and so on and so on and et cetera. And Sophia was in favour of a fresh start. I didn't keep the girlfriends completely hidden from sight, but at the same time, Sophia had been enjoying a bit of mischief of her own. I'd made her miserable, and she'd given me a taste of my own medicine. There were times when we looked at each other and there was nothing in her heart or in mine but anger.

So, a fresh start. I said: "Sure, I'll be your labourer, let's go." Packed up everything we owned, which amounted to the clothes we wore and a couple of spare pairs of under-junders, and off we went, Steve and Bev and Sophia and the two baby Drydens and me, down to a house Bev had found for her daughter and Stan the Legend in St Albans, fifteen clicks north-west of the city.

This new life was okay. Not brilliant, but okay. Maybe just a bit less than okay. Up early each day to put in eight hours or even ten on building sites, pushing wheelbarrows full of mixed mortar across narrow planks above the ground, carting bricks. Bloody hell. They don't call it 'labouring' for nothing. It was labour all right, hard labour, you bet. But I was hacking it, putting in the hours, coming home each evening to the missus: "Hi, darlin', it's me, Stan the Man, working hard to support his family." Well, when I say 'coming home each evening', I mean most evenings. Every second Friday, I'd nick off with my mates instead of coming home. Sample the frothy stuff, then me and the boys might head off anywhere. "Okay, we're going to Adelaide, we're going to Sydney, we're going to Echuca; Yarrawonga; Timbuktu; Paris, France." We'd land on the doorstep of mates in any of those places (except Paris, of course – didn't go that far afield) and spend all the time until late Sunday arvo drinking ourselves mental as. Might wake up on the floor at somebody's dump in Redfern, look around in a bleary-eyed way, think: "Bloody hell, gotta get back to St Albans, be ready for work first thing Monday." I always found my way back in time for work. Sometimes I couldn't find the car, might have been anywhere, and I had to ring Sophia and tell her to buy me a ticket on the train from wherever I was to the city. Other times, all of us would pile into somebody's old clunker and roar down the Hume Highway, arriving back in Melbourne for two hours' sleep before getting my mitts around the handles of that bloody wheelbarrow. How did I do it? Couldn't say. Must have had the constitution of a bullock in those days. And yeah, I know – not the best situation for Sophia, husband off on the tear. I got away with murder for the simple reason that Sophia was so generous in her nature that she held up my end as well as her own, a huge burden.

I could get along with Steve, just about. He had to look out for Sophia, try to keep me working and earning so that there was less of a load on her. But every now and then, he'd get in my face with some complaint or other that came from Bev. One time I bought this big punching bag, hung it from a rafter back at the St Albans place, gave myself a chance to work out. And Steve – this is while we're sitting down to eat our sangers at lunch – he says: "Aw, I don't know about that punching bag, Stan, don't know you should've spent your money on that, Bev's not best pleased, I can tell you."

And I'm like: "What the hell's it got to do with Bev?"

Steve's shaking his head and sighing: "Aw, I dunno, Stan. Bev, she thinks you should be spending your money on proper stuff, you know?"

I could've just about given him one in the kisser. I hated that rubbish, being told how to spend my wages. I said: "Listen to me, buddy. It's my sweat that makes my wages, and I'll spend it any bloody way I want to. So tell that to Bev when you get the chance, hey?" Should've kept my temper; not good for family peace and quiet to go off like that. But family life – don't know that I was cut out for it. I was trying, my oath I was. I'd come home from work and give Sophia a kiss, cuddle the kids, sit down like a proper hubby and watch the telly; I never swore at the missus, never biffed her or any of that roughhouse stuff. I was being a hubby best as I could, but deep down I was still a Warrior. I still had a hunger for the open road. Me and a million other blokes in Australia, trying to be responsible, trying to obey the rules, bringing up the kids, taking the missus down the pub for a sherbert every now and then, putting money aside for a rainy day. Sure. But me and the million other blokes, what we really want is the wind in our hair and not a damned thing to worry about, no responsibility, freedom. Can't have it, I know, but that's what we want.

After a year or more with Steve – well into 1985 – I'd had enough of pushing that bloody barrow. I said: "Steve, buddy, I'm off." Had to find a new job, of course. And I found one, no problem, but it only lasted three hours as it turned out. The job was working in a shoe factory, Clarks, down there in Coburg. They had me on a machine punching holes for the laces, just standing there by the upright drill, ten eyelets in each shoe, over and over and over. After the first thousand holes, I thought: "Have to cut me throat, Jesus suffering Christ." I mean, come on. Punching holes in leather? What the hell? Is that what I was born for – me or any man, any woman, any human being?

Midday came around, a hooter sounded. The foreman told me: "Go and get yizself summat to eat, Stan." I walked around the corner looking for a sandwich shop or, even better, a building to jump off. There was this bloke with a truck, unloading all sorts of stuff at another factory – rolls of fabric, pillows wrapped up in plastic in big cartons. He was struggling with one of these cartons so I gave him a hand, stayed on and helped him unload everything. "Good on you, matey," he said. "Any time you need a job, come and see me." And I said – of course I did – "Buddy, I'm ready to start right now." Because this was outdoors, and I loved being outdoors. Also driving a truck; I loved driving.

I never went back to the shoe factory; I stayed with my new buddy, landed a job back at his place, Snuggle-Rite. This was a factory where they cut out patterns from rolls of fabric, and took the fabric to a hundred homes out in the western suburbs where women – mostly Italian – would sew the material into garments, like jeans and dresses, that sort of thing. It was what's called piecework. Then a driver would pick up the finished clothes and take them to wholesalers. Snuggle-Rite did other stuff too, like the pillows, but my job was all about driving the truck to the houses of the Italian ladies. Man, they loved me, those ladies. Don't know what it was about me, but they damned near all the time asked me to stay for something to eat, maybe a glass of vino, too. "Ohh, Stannie, you too skinny, here,

I make you a bigga roll of cheese and tomato, I give you a bigga kiss, okay?" And what did I say? Damned right: "All the bigga rolls of da cheese and tomato you can spare, Maria, all the bigga kisses you wanna to senda my way!"

I loved that job, driving along each day with the window down, sun on my face, singing Elvis songs. Stayed at Snuggle-Rite for three years, got to know every Italian lady in the west of Melbourne, so many lovely wet kisses and cheese rolls that I could have stayed happy for another ten years. But I got restless. Little itch, then the little itch became a big itch. I had Frankie's way of thinking about going to work each day: as soon as it weighs you down, get the hell out of it. For the old man, that was about two months. For me, a bit longer. I was thinking: "Okay, Stan, my friend, time to move on, the kisses and cheese rolls, terrific, but gotta find something new." That's the best thing on earth – something new.

I found what I was looking for at the MMBW – Melbourne Metropolitan Board of Works. I'd heard from someone or other that there was a job going at MMBW; I must have been telling people that I was on the lookout for something different. Now, this job, it was for a fitter and turner, a little outside my glorious fields of expertise, but obstacles like that never troubled me, and still don't. I grew up under my dad's rules, and inherited his self-confidence. "Kid, you do whatever the hell you want to do in this world, you got it?" I know people who say the same – you know, "Anything is possible", and that sort of thing – but they say it hoping it's true; they don't truly believe it. Frankie, he believed it. And what he told me, that's what I believed about myself. I was a prince.

So heading into the interview at the MMBW when I'd never turned and fitted in my life – no problem. I walked in thinking: "Stan, my brother, this job is yours." First problem was the long form I was given to fill out. Not that flash at filling out forms. I said to the receptionist: "Can you help me out, sweetheart? Hurt me hand yesterday, can't hold a pen proper. If I give you the info, could you fill out the form for me? Love yuh for keeps." She filled out the form. I contributed a few flourishes just to give the application a bit of sparkle: previous employment, Secretary-General of the United Nations, that sort of thing. The receptionist entered into the spirit of the occasion, gave a few giggles. I tried to give her the impression that she was a queen in her beauty and charm and it was only because we were in the open that I was restraining myself from making love to her on the top of her desk. With the completed document in hand, I walked into the interview: five blokes in a row behind a long table, all looking grave and no-nonsense. I said: "Glad to be here, my brothers, any questions just fire away." The first thing the chairman of selectors told me was there'd been more than a hundred applicants for the job. I said: "Brothers, look no further. I'm your boy. I've fitted and turned with the best in Australia and I gotta tell you, I'm hot to trot." They grilled me about my experience in the trade and I don't think I did too badly. A certain amount of invention, of course; never let the truth stand in the way of gainful employment. The five dudes – very impressed. The chairman said: "Mr Dryden, we'll be in contact pretty damned soon."

I said: "Here's the thing, my brothers, I have to nick away to another place to get the result of an interview from earlier today. That's in an hour. So not to put you under too much pressure, gentlemen, but I need to know your decision in, say, fifty-five minutes."

I wandered about on the footpaths for fifty-three minutes, then rang up the MMBW to get the result. "Mr Dryden, we're happy to tell you that you were the successful applicant. We look forward to seeing you at eight-thirty Monday morning." Good-o! Out of nowhere, I was a fitter and turner. Stannie Dryden, come on down!

The MMBW put me into the care of a redneck roughnut by the name of Mick. He had a sense of humour that was deadset toxic. Before I started working with him as his offsider, I had to endure his racist gags in the canteen. "You're an Abo, Stan, that's right? Had a house full of your mob living next door one time. Started a fire in the middle of the lounge room floor, bloody hell! Probably having a corroboree, wanted to cook a goanna on a campfire. No brains, you see. Failed to recognise they were indoors."

When I was a kid I barely paid any attention to racist shit like that, didn't even know that it *was* racist shit. But by the time I reached twenty-two, yeah, I knew what was racist, and I hated it. Because when people start up with jokes about this group of people or that, there's contempt at the base of it. People think they're being hilarious, and they're likely to say that there's no offence intended, but the offence is intended, all right. It pisses me off. Look, I've got a certain amount of time on the planet, and it's not a million years; same goes for everyone else. I want to say: "Mate, is this what you want to be known for? After your short stay, you want to be remembered for being a smartarse about black people, Asians, Muslims, women, gays? That's good enough for you? Not one generous thing in the ledger? No kindness, no understanding?" So when I heard Mick making out he was the funniest guy on earth, I felt my blood boiling. But just for the time being, I kept my temper under control. I'd only been at the Board for a week. Actually, I should have biffed old Mick right there and then, but I gave him a chance.

And as it turned out, I was working as Mick's offsider down at the Brooklyn pumping station when he asked me for the 'calibrated tension wrench'. Never heard of any such thing, so I asked him what it looked like. "It looks like a goldfish bowl, you goon, get it for me." He'd had one chance, didn't deserve it, and didn't profit from my lenience. I said: "Mate, you're ten seconds away from the emergency room at St Vincent's." Then I took out my phone – I had a mobile, supplied by MMBW – and dialled my mum. She answered, and I said, good and loud: "Mum, I need you to talk me out of murdering this bloke standing in front of me. You know I can do it. One punch. Talk me out of it, Mum, for God's sake." And I held the phone to Mick's ear so that he could hear Charlotte. "Don't do it, Stannie! Get a grip, for the love of Jesus! Your fists are deadly weapons, Stannie, you know that!" Mick went pale. My stare was boring into his brain. "Whadya think, mate? Listen to me mum, or do what I really want to do and that's smash your teeth out of your face?" He mumbled an apology, and I told Mum it was all good, and hung up. Never heard any examples of Mick's sense of humour after that. I probably don't need to say that this was in part just me being dramatic. Wasn't really about to destroy his face; just wanted to let him know that I had the weaponry.

Seeing the blood leave Mick's face when my mum was begging me to refrain from murder was satisfying, of course it was. But there was an even more satisfying episode involving Mick and me and a CLK-class Mercedes convertible ten years after the affair at the Brooklyn pumping station. By that time, my fortunes had changed, as they say. That Merc, beautiful piece of machinery, I paid over a hundred thousand for it and kept it sparkling. I was cruising along Nepean Highway in the gorgeous vehicle and happened to pull up at the North Road traffic lights beside a garbage truck. Who was hanging on to the back of the truck but Mick the comic genius.

I recognised him before he noticed me, but when he did, his jaw dropped. I gave him a smile, raised my eyebrows, then took off when the lights changed. It was one of those little dramas of revenge you dream about – fantasies, really – but which hardly ever happen in real life. Yet for Stan, yeah, this fantasy of revenge came true. Not a word spoken, but a big, big message all the same: "Don't underestimate the black man, my friend. Might just surprise you."

# CHAPTER 11

# THE CAPER

I got into acting without knowing how hard it was to find roles, to earn a living. Through sheer ignorance, you could say, which is actually the way most people get into acting. One day – this would've been around 1988 – I was watching television, surfing the channels, when I hit on an Aussie movie called *The Fringe Dwellers* that starred Ernie Dingo. I'd never seen an Indigenous bloke in a movie before that. I didn't think Aborigines could even be in movies. I didn't think there was any law against it; no, it just never occurred to me that this was something a black Australian could think about, being a film star. But there was my man Ernie acting his guts out in technicolour. I thought: "Bloody hell!" Then I thought: "Gotta get on the screen." The movie had been on the ABC. Next morning, I telephoned the ABC and told the woman who answered that my name was Stan Dryden, and that I was an Aborigine and wanted to be an actor.

"What do I do, missus? Who do I talk to?"

She was polite, very calm. "Perhaps you should come to Ripponlea and see our head of drama. Could you do that?"

"No worries, missus. What's the address?"

I'd taken the day off from the MMBW especially to contact the ABC and find out what was possible, full of optimism. If I think of something I want to do, I nearly always do it. It might be nuts, this confidence I have, because the life I led as a kid should've buggered me for good – sleeping in parks, in toilet blocks, with the old man, half-starved, fights breaking out all around me. That's the sort of thing that doesn't give you much confidence about yourself in the legit world, but with me, somehow it did. I grew up thinking I was special and clever and good-looking and charming – and I know why I thought I was such a gift to the human race, why I believed I could do anything I chose to. I was watched over. My ancestors told me: "Stannie Dryden, Stan the Legend, we've got high hopes for you." I don't have to explain this to any of my Indigenous brothers and sisters. They take one look at me and think: "Bottle tree." In the outback, those bottle trees store juice, never feel threatened by drought and heat, can survive anything.

So I found my way down to the ABC studios in Gordon Street, not so far from where I'd once lived in Elsternwick. Had my hair brushed, best shirt, polished shoes (polished with spit, which is a good substitute for Kiwi), maybe a bit crazy confident.

The drama guy at the ABC was one of these highly educated blokes, very suave, polite, interested in me. "Stan, may I ask if you've done any acting in the past?"

"No, mate, not a damned thing."

"So what was it that inspired you to come looking for work as an actor?"

"Saw my bro Ernie on the telly. Thought if he can do it, I can do it."

"Your 'bro' Ernie?"

"Ernie Dingo, mate. Aborigine. Top actor."

"Oh, Ernie! Of course! Wonderful actor."

I was given a couple of short scripts to read, the idea being that

I'd come back and act out a part, show my stuff. Yeah, but what stuff? Since I couldn't read that well back then, I had to get Sophia to read the scripts to me. Nothing too difficult for the Dryden brainbox. I learnt a couple of parts overnight and shuffled off back to the ABC the next day. The guy from the drama department heard me out as I waltzed around spouting lines. I didn't go overboard. I figured the drama guy would be turned off by shouting and stuff like that. And I was right.

"Stan, I have to tell you, I'm impressed. Very much so. I'm going to give you a number to ring. We haven't got anything that would suit you here, but try Reg Grundy. I think they'll be as impressed as I am."

I'd never heard of Reg Grundy but a couple of people I spoke to told me he was king of the castle. Said that if I got in with Grundy I'd be drinking champagne for breakfast and smoking Cuban cigars. Also, chicks knocking down my door, but probably the less said about that the better.

Grundy made *The Flying Doctors*. All these spunky doctor geniuses and fabulous nurses stitching people up and falling in love with each other. I tootled along to the studio, one person and another took a look at me, got me to do the lines I'd learnt, and yeah, signed me up for a small part in *The Flying Doctors*. Scene set on a cricket pitch, it was, not so many lines. Merv Hughes, with his doormat moustache, was in the same scene. One of the regular actors took an interest in me. "Get yourself some acting lessons, Stan. You've got something going for you there, just need a few tips."

I took myself off to the William Bates Academy down in Bowen Crescent, just off St Kilda Road, for acting lessons. A six-week course. Opened my eyes to a few things. It was: "Show me joy! Show me rage! Show me tenderness! Nice work, my man, but just a little more subtlety."

And I was like: "Huh? Little more what?"

The acting coach: "Subtlety."

"Subtlety? Who's he?"

"You can show rage without going berserk, Stan, my dear chap. Just use your eyes, only your eyes. Or tenderness. Don't collapse in tenderness. Just a small smile, my dear fellow."

So little by little, I began to see that acting was something you needed to think about. No good throwing yourself into every role like a madman. Subtlety. That word. Did me good.

You'd think that producers would be always casting me as a black-fella. But no. I had roles that could have been given to a white boy. I was a bank teller in *Bony* (all about an Aboriginal detective with a brain the size of ten of Sherlock Holmes's), got up in a neat blue suit, white collar and tie. We used a real bank to film the scene down at the corner of Victoria Road and Russell Street, Westpac could've been. When I saw where we were filming I gave a huge hoot of laughter. Frankie had been planning to rob the very same bank years earlier. I remembered him telling me: "Race in, make like I've got a gun in my pocket – 'Hey you, stuff this bag full of money or I'll blow your fuckin' brains out all over the wall!' – race out with the moolah, catch a tram down to Flinders Street, jump on a train, Bob's your uncle." He was completely pissed when he dreamt up this plan, and a couple of hours later when he'd sobered up, he began to have second thoughts. "Wait a minute. No trams in Russell Street. Could grab the Victoria Street tram down to Vic Market. Bit of a risk. And Stannie, almost next door to police headquarters, that bank. No, no, better give it more thought, whadya think?"

"Yeah, Dad, bit iffy."

And that was the bank where I was looking sharp in my suit ten years later playing the role of a teller.

There were a few little roles that interrupted my fitting and turning, a week off here, a week off there. If I ever thought of the injustice of manual labour getting in the way of the art of acting, all I had to do was remember the other actors on the set, some serving tucker in restaurants between gigs, some on the bar, some in call centres, and one changing tyres for Bob Jane. It's a bit of a heart-breaker, the acting racket. Can't be too sensitive.

I know what it was about acting that made me so excited, made me ring the ABC, get my skinny behind over to Grundy. My whole life is full of drama, not just when I'm on stage. I don't mean that I've got it in my mind to act my head off in real life. No, what I mean is that drama keeps coming my way, flooding over me. I've never had a time in my life when nothing was happening. Never a time when my mum or dad said: "Here, Stannie, sit down and relax and I'll tell you a story of a family that loved peace and quiet and found plenty of it." Peace and quiet? What the hell was that? What I saw in acting was an outlet for all that madhouse stuff that had built up in me. I wanted to show people what I'd felt, what had knocked me about or made me cry with happiness. I had all that stuff in me.

One of the things I had to know about if I was going to perform lots of different roles was trouble. Trouble taught me more about life than happiness did. There was a movie made years ago by some Italian cove, *The Tree of Wooden Clogs* – terrific story of hardship on the land. The director, they say, mostly used real working people, people who knew all about trouble and strife, and it worked perfectly. Okay, I'd maybe find it a stretch to play some roles, like maybe the part of an English toff or a Christian saint. Might be beyond me. But any role that's all about strife, I'm your boy.

And comedy. A bit of a knack for comedy as well. I had a mate on the set of *Bony*, a bloke with a fair bit of time in the caper, and he said: "Stan, the acting game, you know what the motto is? What we're telling the audience? 'You'll laugh, you'll cry, you'll damn near die.'" Ted Emery, wonderful bloke, he was directing a comedy sketch show for Channel Seven, *Full Frontal*, and he asked me to try out for it in 1993. He'd seen me in the *Bony* episode and *The Flying Doctors*. His idea was that I could take the piss out of the whole whitefella racist thing as an Aborigine. He had in mind a sketch where this smiling white couple stand outside their new home in Brighton gurgling with happiness, a 'sold' sticker on the board behind them. I arrive in a car, pull up, seem to be walking towards the house next door. The white couple just about wet themselves. The lady says: "Excuse me, are y-y-you our neighbour?" And I say: "Just here to take down the board, missus." Or I might play Desmond Tutu, might be Nelson Mandela, anything that called for a black face. Ted never had to worry that the writers might offend me in some way, unintentionally, because I'd never had any super-sensitivity about my race. Just the opposite. I went about thinking: "Pity the white man. No chance of showing off a gorgeous black skin."

These roles in *Full Frontal*, they only came my way now and again, half a dozen times in a season. Not enough income to live on, so I had to hold on to my regular job. Difficult to say whether I was an actor who worked part-time as a jack-of-all-trades, or a jack-of-all-trades who worked part-time as an actor. Earning a living was a decent motive for going to work each day, sure, but I also had this hunger to do some good, reach out a helping hand. I worked away at one thing and another apart from acting without feeling that I was helping anyone at all. Then in 1991 I found an opportunity to help out at ACCA, the Aboriginal Child Care Agency down in Fitzroy, a place where Indigenous mothers – mostly unmarried – brought their babies and littlies for a spruce up, bit of a birthday, advice on feeding, all that handy gear. I did a bit of lifting and shifting at the ACCA group house, not much but enough to make me feel my existence amounted to more than slurping the froth off a glass of beer. And that's where I was, lifting and shifting at the ACCA centre, when catastrophe crept up on me, threw me to the floor and stomped a boot into my guts.

A few years after Frankie's passing, Mum had moved down to the city from Shep, found a house in Werribee and a job at ACCA. She was born for that job. The ACCA clients might not have listened to anyone else on earth, but by Jesus, they listened to Sarge, and they respected her. Whenever I thought about Mum or visited her, watched her ruling the roost at ACCA (it was Mum who got me into the group house to help out), I never felt anxious in the way I had with Dad. I always thought: "All sweet, Mum's happy, relax, Stannie, my friend."

I was there one arvo when I was summoned to the telephone to take a call from Charlie, the ACCA boss. "Wanted to make sure you were there, Stannie. Stay where you are. Need to have a word with you." I'm thinking: "Fuck me, am I in strife?" Because maybe I'd done something dodgy in a drunken haze without knowing it, shuffled a typewriter from the office into a pawnshop, a bit of folderol with one of the mums. If only. When Charlie arrived, he told me he'd had a call from the Nagambie coppers: Charlotte had been in a fatal car crash on the Hume bringing a kid down from Shep to the city. I didn't know what 'fatal' meant back then – sounds nuts, but I didn't – so I said: "She's okay?" And Charlie shook his head. "No, she was killed, Stannie. The kid's okay but Charlotte was killed. It was instantaneous, the Nagambie coppers said. Happened in a second."

It took me a couple of minutes to grasp what Charlie was say-ing. I let out this terrific wail and all the mums and kids turned their heads to see what was up. I think this happens to lots of people when they hear that someone they love has died without any warning – they can't believe it's true. Must be some mistake. Mum had been in my life for twenty-five years, and now I was being told she'd gone in a second? How was I supposed to get my head around that? How can anyone?

What had happened was this, so said the truck driver who'd been driving in front of Mum: the spare tyre in the rack underneath the truck's chassis had come loose and went flying off into the path of Mum's car behind; Mum had swerved to avoid it, left the road, crashed into a tree. One second, gone. The kid in the passenger seat was okay – Mum had taken the impact on her side. I went up to Nagambie – the nearest town to the crash – on a mission. I found the crashed car in a tow-truck place, and I smoked it. Burnt gum leaves to smother all the pain and fear of the last bit of time Mum spent on earth. I'd spoken to the kid Mum was bringing down to the city; he said Charlotte was singing along with a tune on the cassette player just before the crash. I took the cassette out, put it in the player in my car and listened. It was 'Send Me the Pillow That You Dream On', the old Dean Martin hit, Mum's favourite and Dad's, too. I sat in the car playing that song over and over again, blind with tears.

At the funeral in Shep, where Charlotte was buried close to Frankie, I smoked the whole area of the grave good and proper and played the didge as Mum was lowered down. My sisters, Judy and Lynnie, and my brother, Davy, all stood close to the grave. Man, that's a lonely, lonely feeling, watching a coffin disappear into a hole in the ground. It's pretty much the same, no matter whose funeral it is. You go into the ground. I kept playing the didge, low and mournful as the family said goodbye. "See you, Mum," I said. The image of Mum I kept there in my head for the whole funeral, even as I played the didge, was of Charlotte and Frankie on a day they were happy together, singing 'Send Me the Pillow' in the kitchen of the Mooroopna house.

# CHAPTER 12

# BOOZE

I was making my way as a fitter and turner and actor, earning a salary, raising my kids – all good. On the other hand, I was an alcoholic. I'd followed Frankie down that path.

When you're an alcoholic, the thing you say to yourself all the time is: "I'm not an alcoholic." You know you drink a bit, maybe sometimes go off the radar, but you're convinced that you don't have any real problem. You say: "Might give it up altogether. I could, you know." But you can't. The truth is, you can't live without a drink, and once you have the drink you feel better about yourself, and why? Because you had a drink. If one drink makes you feel better, two drinks will be twice as good. Six won't hurt. Why not a good, round dozen? Do it, Stan! In fact, it's not quite right to say that booze makes you feel better. Booze *is* you. When you're not drinking, it's not you; it's someone else who doesn't enjoy life, a sourpuss. So who wants to be a sourpuss? Be the cheerful person you were meant to be. Get that stubby into you. Whatever you're doing, you can see that frosty bottle right there in your mind's eye, and you can feel the lip of the bottle against your lips, and that first big gulp. The world is the taste of booze, nothing's more important. You develop a fantastic ability to deceive yourself as an alcoholic, and you have to because the evidence of disaster is all around you, north, south, east, west.

Booze isn't evil. Neither is smack, neither is speed. Not any of it. And addicts and pisspots aren't evil, necessarily. What all this rubbish does to you is to make you feel that you've shrugged off the howling dog blues forever. The love life that's giving you grief, the bills you haven't paid – all of it's gone when you feed that good stuff into your system. Who wouldn't want to get some relief? But there's a catch, a true bastard of a catch. You end up wanting relief all the time. Once you've felt what it's like to get that blue shit out of your life, you never want to go back. Some of us, not everyone. Most people make a deal with themselves: a bit of relief every now and again; the rest of the time, Mister Responsible, Missus Good Mum.

Me, I was off with the boys on Friday afternoons, carrying on the booze-up tradition from when I was working for Snuggle-Rite. My life at home with Sophia and the kids was a crying shame; I couldn't be relied on for anything. This is where the alcoholic needs those terrific skills of deception. Sophia'd be sobbing, the kids'd be looking at me as if I were a stranger, but I'd be thinking: "Everything's good, I've put food on the table, kids've got a telly to watch, Sophia'll be okay when I get her a box of those Lindt chocolates from the supermarket, yeah, all good, and now I've gotta take off for an hour or so or maybe two days to meet the boys." The thing is, people do what they want to do, most times. They might do it in secret, super sneaky; they might do it out in the open. But people are bound to do what they truly want to do. If you want to do something that stinks rotten, you've got to have a good excuse ready, not for the people you're destroying, but for yourself. "An alcoholic? Get the hell outa here. Could an alcoholic play footy for Spotswood, like I do? Could an alcoholic put in time at the gym on the punching bag and the speed ball and the skipping rope? No way."

My drinking came to the notice of my boss, by and by. I was called in to the office. The boss said: "Need to talk to you about something, Stan. Need to talk to you about alcohol."

"Yeah? What do you mean, boss?"

"Think you know what I mean, Stan."

The MMBW in those days was like a great big family. This was at the time before everything was outsourced. If you had a problem, your boss didn't say: "Here's your first official warning. If you get another one, you're out." No, your boss said: "Gotta fix you up, my brother." I was sent to a dry-out place up in the north-east at Beechworth, Fletcher House. They were good to me there, gave me good advice, but it did nothing for me at all. I put in my week at Fletcher, came back, hit the grog with renewed enthusiasm, went back up to Beechworth.

I lost the job at the MMBW. The boss was patient, but his patience wore out. "Stan, we're going to let you go."

"Yeah? For what?"

"Because you're an alcoholic, Stan. Sorry. Can't keep your mind on the job."

Without admitting a damned thing, I took a mate's advice and turned up at the St Francis' jamboree of confirmed pisspots, two hundred people down at the church on Lonsdale Street and Elizabeth in the city, struggling to get off the booze. You think all pisspots get about in unwashed clobber? No, no, no. A good half of the turnout at St Francis' were suited up like businessmen or lawyers who'd wandered down from William Street. I went to these meetings week after week and got to know a number of my fellow booze hounds. Lawyers and businessmen, like I said; also motor mechanics, builder's labourers, shopkeepers, bankers, teachers. No matter what class you come from, what work you do, you can fall victim to booze. We had people up the front giving good advice to us, telling us to talk to each other, support each other, maybe sign up for the twelve-step program. The thing that was so interesting to me was that so many people wanted to get off the booze. I never met any fellow pisspot who said: "Nah, it's all good, my brother, I'm coping nicely." At the same time as you're pouring that stuff down your throat, you're thinking: "Gonna kill myself before long, gotta get off the grog." You love what you're drinking; you hate yourself for drinking it. Nobody wants to see ruin. That's when the denial kicks in. But you can get yourself to a place where denial can't help you.

The most miserable thing about being addicted to whatever it might be – booze, heroin, coke, speed – is that it makes something cheap out of something that should be precious to you, and that's your honour. You can't find a spot in your whole body and brain where honour is located, of course not; if it's sick, you can't rub some ointment on it and make it better. It only gets better when the whole of you is better. So what do you do when you're telling monstrous porkies to people who believe what you're saying? What could I say to my wife when she said: "Stan, my darling husband, stay off the grog today, can you promise me that?" What could I say to my kids when they said: "Daddy, come home tonight and play with us in the backyard"? What I said was: "Sure, sure. No worries." The lies roll off your tongue. But later, could be out of the blue, you feel a pain in your heart, and you think: "Jesus Christ, I'm bloody shameless, I'm a dog." You can destroy your soul that way, if you don't give up the booze, the heroin, whatever it might be before there's nothing left.

But if you're going to get off the grog, you have to be ready for it. I'm not saying there's this one moment among millions when you're ready. There are a number of moments when you can slip out of alcoholism and latch hold of the alternative. What has to happen is that the time must be right for you, and right for the world. It's as if time is revolving, and every so often you find yourself standing in front of a door, and you know that you can push that door and it will open. Might only be for a few seconds that the door is there in front of you. Maybe you stop and think, and you think a bit too long, and the door disappears. That's because it has to be all or nothing. You stand there at the door, and what's facing you if you walk on through is the end of drinking, forever. You can't think: "Okay, I'll get my boozing down a day at a time, go from twenty drinks a day to eighteen, then fifteen, then ten, and finally, nothing." Won't work. Has to be stone cold zero. That's what causes you to think a bit too long when the door comes round. Zero is terrifying.

There's a scene in *Indiana Jones and the Last Crusade*. Old Indy, he's looking for the Holy Grail, the cup that Jesus drank from at the Last Supper. He's frigging around over in the Holy Land, searching high and low. And he comes to this ancient city, gets his arse inside. Comes to a chasm, too wide to jump. He's got this little guidebook from the olden days, shows a crusader knight stepping out into the chasm, into nothing, just stretching his foot out into the air. Old Indy sees that he has to do the same thing, step out into the void, a leap of faith. So he does, and his foot comes down on something solid, a bridge that the human eye can't see. Takes another step and another and lots more, and he's across the chasm. Fabulous scene. To get to zero, you have to step out into the void. But each time that door came round, each time I was being asked to make a leap of faith, get that holy grail, I sort of thought: "Next time."

I wasn't ready to open the door and make a leap of faith. But I was ready to put in a couple of days' paid employment at Galiamble, a centre for Aboriginal addicts, including alcoholics, down in Grey Street, St Kilda, run by Richard Ambrose, a top bloke with a big heart and a sharp mind. The first time I went to see him he told me he had nothing for me, no job, see ya later, brother. But I persisted, as I do, and the second time Richard said he'd give me a weekend job looking after the guys, a live-in gig; a bit like putting the fox in charge of the henhouse, but there you go. It was proper rehab, and the message from Richard and the staff was always: "Mate, there's a shitload more to life than piss, believe it!"

I got along good with the Galiamble blokes. Cooked their tucker, enjoyed a natter with them, swept the floor, made sure there was a packet of fags or ten on hand for the weekend. Because the whole place was locked up from Friday night to Monday morning you had to have anything you needed before that Friday night lock-up. But the place wasn't just about food and shelter. Had all sorts of programs to offer the blokes. People came in and taught my lovely gang of pisspots how to paint, how to make pottery, how to cook – all that good gear. The clients were given health and dental check-ups, and boy – that was a monster task just by itself. We had guys in Galiamble with medical issues starting with gangrene at their feet and going up all the way to eczema on their scalps, heart problems on the way, lungs buggered, cuts and bruises from falling over that had never healed. And dental, Jesus Christ, there were blokes who hadn't looked a toothbrush in the eye for years. Each one of those guys could have used an entire hospital and all the staff to get him back into nick.

There were also self-esteem programs for the clients, because believe me, by the time people got to Galiamble self-esteem was something they could barely remember. We had experts working on it. They'd say to a client: "Ever expect to feel good about yourself again? No? Okay, what would it take to get back your self-esteem?" And anger management. Booze and hard drugs leave lots of blokes ready to erupt like a volcano at any hour of the day. Not all of them. Some addicts become pussycats, just want to sleep in the sun. We gave each client one-on-one counselling, worked out an individual plan for the way ahead. Sometimes all this intervention (as Richard called it) did some good. But most addicts and booze hounds need to go into rehab programs five, ten, fifteen times before they learn to stick with it. Lots of them die along the way. You might say: "Anyone heard from old Chooka lately? Haven't seen him for months." And you're told: "Gonna be a bloody long time before you do see him again. He's down in Fawkner cemetery."

The cultural programs were tied to the self-esteem stuff. Richard wanted all of our clients to learn about their heritage, get some tribe-pride in being a Wurundjeri man, Gunditjmara, Yorta Yorta, Gunai, Wathaurong, Boon Wurrung. Because when you grow up black in Australia, you've got damned near everything white around you trying to make you feel like rubbish. In 1967, the government held a referendum to get the say-so of white Australians to count Aboriginals in the population. What does it mean when the government does a huge count of all the men and women and kids in Australia but doesn't count the Indigenous people? It means the Indigenous people don't exist. After the referendum, sure, they counted black Australians. It took from Botany Bay to 1967 – one hundred and seventy-nine years – for the white people of Australia to stand up and say: "Yeah, okay, these blackfellas are living and breathing on the continent." In all that time, the worst of the white men could get away with murder.

We had government departments lording it over black people who didn't exist. Taking children from black families who didn't exist. Except that they did exist, and they bled when a white settler pointed a gun at their heads and pulled the trigger, and they screamed in grief when a couple of white coppers called on a black family and grabbed the kids. Bleeding, screaming – not good for the black soul, for black self-esteem. Might make a black man wish he was dead, especially if he's battling the booze.

Every day in the life of a pisspot like me there are a few minutes when you're stone cold sober. Your body takes you back there even if it's the last thing you want; your brain turns cold and you look around and think: "I'm a wreck, my life's rubbish." That's the worst experience, like looking over the edge of a cliff that goes down too far for you to even see the bottom. The reason Aborigines are so likely to take their lives in these moments of ice-cold despair is that the abyss is deeper than any white drunkard ever faces. A white bloke, a white kid, he may have disgraced himself over and over, broken his word a thousand times, pissed his pants in public, lost a dozen jobs, slept with his head in a gutter, but when he hits the cold zone and looks around, he sees a white world, he sees a place where he once belonged. When an Indigenous man looks over the edge, he sees where his culture, his heritage, his pride in being human has gone. It's down there. And he follows it down.

Richard and the other people teaching cultural awareness, I listened to them, sometimes more than the clients. I was a bit different from the guys who had to be dragged up to their feet from a kneeling position, made to see their worth. I'd had years of chipping away at my soul with lies and boozing, but I was still full to the top with confidence. No need to tell me that blackfellas were every bit as good as whitefellas – I knew that from Frankie. No need to tell me that the Aboriginals of this country had a fabulous culture reaching back tens of thousands of years – I'd heard that from Mum and my rellies on her side every now and again. I knew that my people were Charlotte's people, the Wathaurong. And I knew that my people were watching over me, especially Mum. I'd played the didge at her funeral. Our bond was forever. The spirit light was all around me. I enjoyed hearing what Richard had to say.

There was one thing I didn't pay enough attention to, though. A blackfella is just as good as a whitefella at lying to himself. Didn't listen to that. I thought: "Can get myself up to scratch any day I choose. Any day."

# CHAPTER 13

# GRAIN OF SAND

F ar from getting myself up to scratch, after a few months of cooking and cleaning in Galiamble, I had the brilliant idea of taking the minibus out on Friday nights to meet up with the boys for a monster piss-up, returning Sunday afternoon. Had to leave the place locked up while I was away, so I climbed out a window each Friday night. I left food for the guys, and was pretty sure they weren't about to dob me in. Not a good example for blokes who were being encouraged to accept responsibility for their lives, but that was something I put to one side.

After one of these highway to hell weekends, Richard caught up with me, sat me down in the office.

"Now, Stan, the bus was seen out on Hoddle Street the other night. Know anything about that?" The bus had the Galiamble name plastered all over it.

"Yeah? Out on Hoddle Street? No, don't know anything about it, mate."

"I was told a bloke who looked like you was behind the wheel."

"Nah, couldn't be me. I was here. I tell you what, must have been one of the clients got hold of the keys."

"Don't think so, Stan. Reckon it was you."

I didn't admit anything, but the game was up. Richard sacked me. Didn't want to do it, but he did. Real sorrow in his eyes. He was so used to hearing the sort of bullshit he was getting from me – heard it all the time from the clients. But that didn't make any difference to his disappointment.

Richard didn't throw me out with nothing. He could see that I had something to offer, and he introduced me to Andy Walsh, who worked at the Turana youth detention centre over in Parkville. There was a job going at Turana as a liaison officer with the Indigenous kids in custody, and Richard had told Andy that I had a knack for communicating with bad boys. The job title, 'liaison officer', worried me. It made me think that book work was involved. At the interview with Andy, I said: "Mate, I have to tell you up front that my reading and writing's not that flash." And Andy said: "So what? I don't need you for your reading and writing, I need you for talking. You get yourself into the heads of these kids, okay? See what you can do to keep them from graduating from dabbling in crime to a full-time life of crime."

And Richard was right about me – I did have a knack for talking to those kids. I'd say: "Listen, brother, there's such a thing as the future. And the future is made up of one day following another. If you want to spend all those days of the future in a place like this, or worse, keep to the track you're on. But if you want freedom, buy your ticket by keeping off the junk." Now, I knew that my own life pretty much made a mockery of everything I was telling these kids, since I'd been a genius of a criminal in my time, snatching ladies' handbags from the age of nine or ten. And I shouldn't have been telling these kids to get off the gear when I was still pouring booze down my throat at the rate of a dozen stubbies a day. All the same, I connected with the kids. One reason they listened to me was that my name was written in texta on a brick wall in the Poplar wing – the meanest section of Turana – written right at the top with my brother Davy's name just underneath and a dozen other members of the good old Warriors gang beneath Davy's. All the Warriors had been locked up here years and years back, with Johnny in charge, and it was Johnny who'd written the list, the honour roll. That list was good for my credibility as a liaison guy, but maybe not so good so far as the admin people were concerned. So one day I got a rag and some turps and scrubbed my name and Davy's from the top of the list.

It was a job that suited me perfectly. Might have been even better at it if it wasn't for the booze. As well as meetings at St Francis' I also went to meetings for smaller groups of addicts – ten, twelve – at St John the Evangelist, down on the corner of Victoria Parade and Hoddle Street, big mother of a church, Catholic. It's just over the road from a toilet block I used to sleep in with Frankie when I was a kid. I thought I was making progress at the St John meetings, letting a bit of light in. I'd look over at the toilet block and think: "Well, at least you're not sleeping there anymore, so that's an improvement." But the fact was that I was worse off than when I'd been on the road with Frankie. I'd had fifteen years to learn something worthwhile about life since those times, and I'd learnt nothing.

I'd met a dozen people, like Richard, who tried to make a difference in my life, held the door open for me. Like I said, I was ready, but not quite ready enough. The person who made that difference in my life was a stroppy, short-tempered bloke in his forties by the name of Jackie Chris. I'd met him at St Francis', and again at St John's. Powerful-looking bloke, big hands, big feet. He gave testimonies, spoke about his life as a drunkard, took us through all the disgraceful things he'd done. He spoke in a fierce way, as if he was stewing with anger about the wasted years. I listened to him this time at St John's, followed him out of the hall around to the little grassy area at the front of the church. I said: "Brother, your story, mine, damned near the same. Might be able to help you."

Jackie looked at me out of his black eyes with massive scorn. "Help me? You must be joking. You can't help yourself, you idiot."

"Whadya mean, Jackie?" I was upset. We were all meant to support each other, all friendly like. "Just saying, you know, could share our stories."

Jackie thrust his face at me. "Yeah? How many meetings do you go to in a week?"

"Dunno. Could be two, three."

"Listen, when you get up to a dozen, you might be worth listening to. This isn't amateur hour, idiot. You have to go twelve rounds."

And he stalked off, muttering to himself in disgust.

I was left stunned. When I went to the meetings, I was looking for sympathy, and Jackie wasn't in the sympathy business. But I couldn't get what he'd said out of my brain. "You have to go twelve rounds." As a bloke who knew how to box, that way of putting it meant something to me. I thought: "Am I ducking out after two rounds? Am I one of those blokes you see, jump into the ring, throw a few punches, use up everything they've got in a couple of minutes?"

I met another bloke at the meetings, Bill Byrne, who'd given up the booze three years earlier. Boy, what a personality. He was nothing like Jackie Chris, stern and hard. Bill was full of optimism. "Mate, you're gonna give it up, I know it. Take your time, but give it up.

It's rubbish." I listened to Jackie because everything he said was so forceful. I listened to Bill because every atom of him loved life; he gave up the booze out of his love of life. "Stannie, when I was on the booze I was miserable. Even when I was completely pissed, I still thought: 'I hate this, hate it, things are going on that I'm too pissed to enjoy.' I gave up drinking to get joy back into my life." And he said: "I'm not going away, mate. I'll be here every day singing the same song. The booze is garbage, that's the song." He was an accountant, Bill was, had a lot of clients with big, fat bank accounts. He kept coming back to the AA meetings at St John's to encourage blokes like me, tell his story of waking up in the morning and hitting the bottle even before he had a wee. He had clients telling him: "Bill, Bill buddy, this's no good, you're missing appointments, costing me money." Just like Jackie, Bill had a hundred different ways of telling his tale, never the same way twice in a row. It's a responsibility members of AA take on for life, giving their testimony at meetings. Bill's yarns were always full of comedy, just to show that you don't have to become a misery guts when you give up the booze.

I went to three more meetings at St John's after that talk with Bill before I met up with what was waiting for me on 5 August 1993. I was twenty-eight years old, just on, and I remember it was in my head that this was the day Frankie died, ten years earlier. It was the grog that did for him, and it was the grog that was stalking me. Is that what I wanted? Me and the old man, side by side in the graveyard: "Father and son, done in by grog." Something was happening in my head, a sort of vibration, just soft. I got myself along to the meeting at St John's, listened to the testimonials. When Jackie left the meeting, I followed him out. I needed something from him; didn't know exactly what it was. I called out to him, and he turned and looked at me as if the only thing I was good for was making a pest of myself. I said: "Jackie, mate, how do I do it? How do I get off this stuff?" I had a bottle of VB in my hand.

Jackie shook his head. "Ah, mate, mate. You're waiting for God or someone to pick you out from millions and say: 'Have to give all my attention to Stan.' There's nothing special about you. Nothing. You're a grain of sand, billions more just the same. That's what you have to grasp."

He wandered off, and I was left staring after him. That vibration in my head was getting stronger. I sunk down on my knees and closed my eyes. Something was coming. I thought: "Dear God, don't leave me like this." My heartbeat had slowed down to next to nothing. There was no light in my brain, just that deep abyss. I wanted to let myself fall forward and plunge down. It seemed as if I could fall for hours, for days, and never reach the bottom. But instead of falling forward, I opened my eyes. I don't know where the impulse came from. I opened my eyes and saw the feet of the statue of the Virgin Mary rising up in front of me. I didn't see the stone of the statue, but living flesh. When I raised my gaze, a golden light had formed all around Mary. In my heart, peace. Peace. I climbed to my feet, gazed about like a zombie. I noticed the bottle of VB in my hand. I upended it, and the beer ran out of it in a stream. I said aloud: "That's it."

From that day to this, I haven't swallowed a drop of booze. Nothing. That part of my life was over, as if it was always destined to end on 5 August 1993 at three in the arvo.

It was over, sure, but no boozer on earth can go from a dozen VBs a day to nothing without a boost from a buddy. When you say, "That's it," and empty the bottle on the ground, what you mean is, "That's it, hope so." It was Jackie who encouraged me, time and again, tough love, did everything but biff me to get me to listen. "Stan, you surrender to win, see what I mean? There's that voice calling you: 'You don't want this life, brother, you don't want to wake up with your pants smelling of piss.' That's the voice you surrender to, Stan."

I'd go to his place out in Oakleigh, meet him at the front door. He never invited me in, as if this part of his life, hauling pisspots back onto their feet, was separate from his home life with his wife and kids. He'd say, "Stan, we're off to a meeting in Carnegie, off to a meeting in Fitzroy ..." Seven, eight meetings a week in church halls, community centres. And often enough, I saw the same blokes at these meetings again and again. I'd say to Jackie, "Heard this fella yesterday." And Jackie would glare at me out of his big black Mediterranean eyes. "Yeah? Well you're listening to him today, too, and tomorrow if you need to. You think he gets himself down here to the Baptists for the fun of it? He needs your support, bird-brain."

What Jackie wanted me to see was that I had to change one community for another; the booze hounds who were married to the product for life, and the booze hounds who wanted a divorce. He didn't settle for getting me sober; he also wanted me to be honest and generous and hard-working. He had a program for me that put the Christian scheme for salvation in the shade.

Sometimes he'd shock me with what he expected of me. This one time we were at an AA convention in Adelaide, went out for a bite to eat at a café in Rundle Mall, Jackie and me and a couple of mates. We'd ordered scrabbled eggs on toast and while we were waiting, two gorgeous women wandered in and sat nearby, long blonde hair, boobs that broke your heart. Me and my two mates, we were in agony – exchanged a few comments among ourselves concerning the beauty of the women, may have boasted a bit about our own physical endowments. Jimmy listened in with a disapproving look, then he suddenly gestured to the two women: "Would you mind stepping over here for a minute?" They glanced at each other, shrugged and wandered over. "Now," said Jackie, "tell these ladies what you just said." We cleared our throats, coughed, looked every which way except at the two women. "Yeah, that's what I thought," said Jackie. "That's all ladies, thanks for your time." Then the sermon: "If you're going to talk about women, about anyone, you make sure you own what you say. Too embarrassed to say something to someone's face, then don't say it at all. You're as sick as your secrets, remember that."

So Jackie, he became my guru. It was important to me that there was someone I trusted completely. It might have been a tribal thing, a need that went way back to my Indigenous ancestors. In a tribe, you listen to the elders, the wise men.

It would be unnatural if I hadn't revisited that day further along. I wasn't a Christian and I'm still not, but I'm certain that I wasn't suffering hallucinations when I saw Mary become flesh, golden light floating all around her. Maybe it was my ancestors working with what was at hand. Sent me a sign through Mary, but those ancestors – especially Frankie – would have used a statue of Buddha if that was nearby, or even the dog on the tuckerbox at Gundagai, Ned Kelly at Glenrowan. I wasn't saved by Jesus Christ or his mum; it was an Indigenous rescue. And the date of my last drink was ten years to the day of Frankie's passing. To the day.

It was six months later that I became Stan Yarramunua. It couldn't have happened any earlier because I wasn't Yarramunua before I gave up the booze. I didn't choose the name for myself; I was given it as a gift by an old Aborigine, Mate Mate, down at Galiamble.

When Richard Ambrose heard that I'd got off the grog, he invited me back to Galiamble to lend a hand here and there with the clients, and I was glad to do it. One afternoon I was in the common area nattering away to a kid who needed a bit of advice and Mate Mate was sitting nearby watching and listening, huge grey beard, black eyes. When I'd finished with the kid, Mate Mate gestured for me to come over. I'd only seen him once or twice before, had never spoken to him. "What is it, brother?" I said. I'd pulled up a chair and was staring straight at him. Mate Mate nodded a few times, pushed his hand through his beard.

"Yarramunua," he said.

"What about it, brother? Yarramunua? What's that?"

"That's you. Yarramunua. Wise fella. That's your name. You think you're Stan Dryden, that's what Richard says you're called, Stan Dryden. But your name is Yarramunua."

"Is it?"

"Do you believe me?"

"Yeah, damned right. Yarramunua?"

"Yarramunua. From now on. Don't forget."

"I won't forget, brother."

It took me two days to find a way to wear that name. I said it over and over in my head but it wasn't settling on me proper. Then after breakfast this one morning, something came to life in my head, and I said aloud: "Yarramunua." It was there, like a cloak that had been draped over my shoulders from behind. I knew what Mate Mate had been trying to tell me. He'd found my name and sort of introduced me to it, but it took those two days for me to feel it settle. Yarramunua. Wise fella. I said to myself: "Hold on to it, Stannie, my friend. Yarramunua."

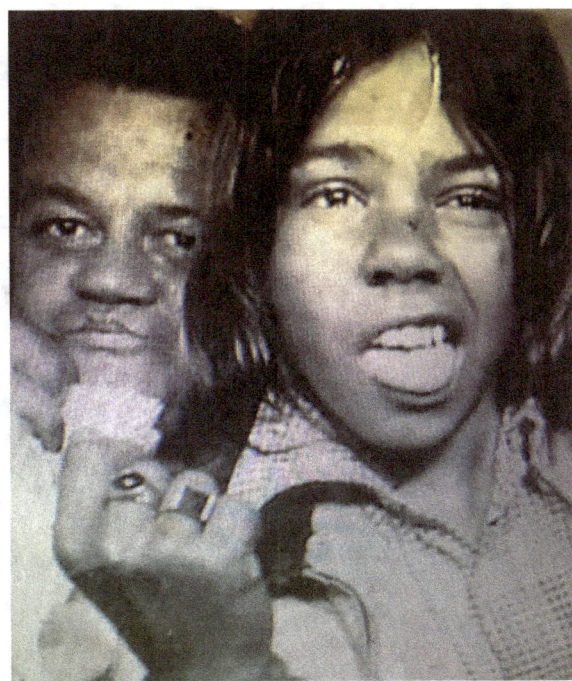

**Left:** Frankie and me in a photobooth at Luna Park when I was twelve. Those rings I'm wearing cost me two bucks each and made me feel special.

**Below:** Stan the Legend with my brother Davy – the time of the warriors.

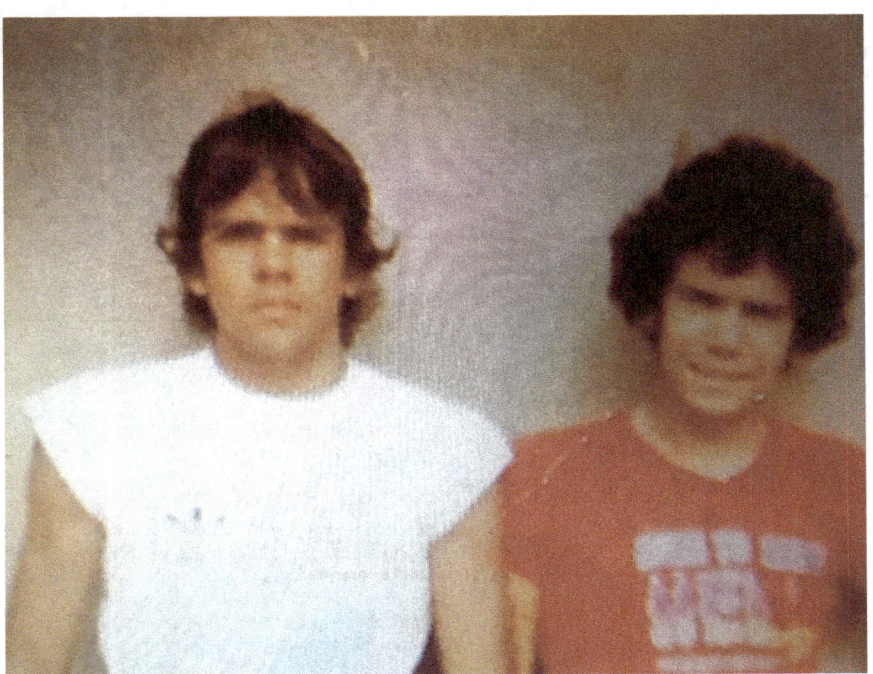

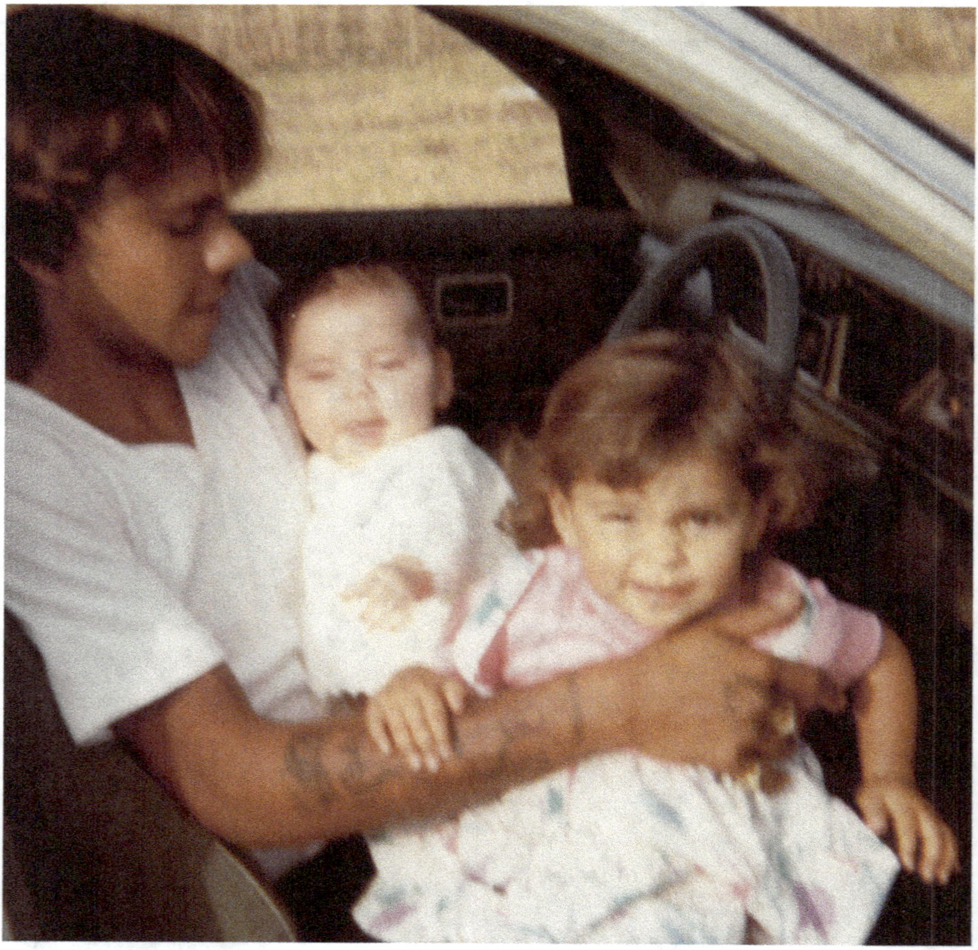

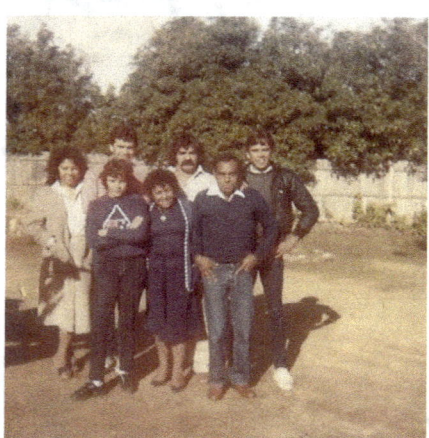

**Above:** With the babies, Stan Junior and Kylie, in the Commodore in 1985. Loved that car; loved the kids, too. Good old Mooroopna.

**Left:** In the backyard at Mum's place in Mooroopna around 1985. *Back, left to right:* my big sister, Judy; Davy; Uncle Watson, the most feared man in Australia for a bit; me, age nineteen, looking likely. *Front, left to right:* my younger sister, Lynette; my mum, Charlotte; Uncle Ian.

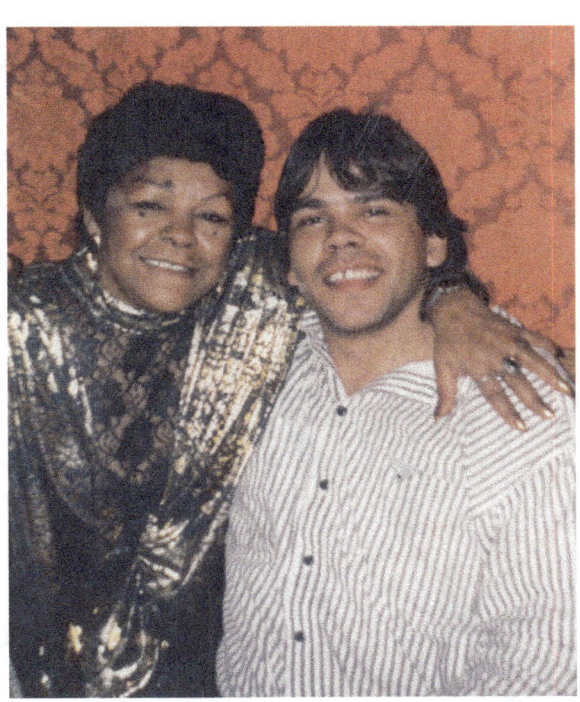

Mum and me at the Middle Hotel in Mooroopna in 1990.

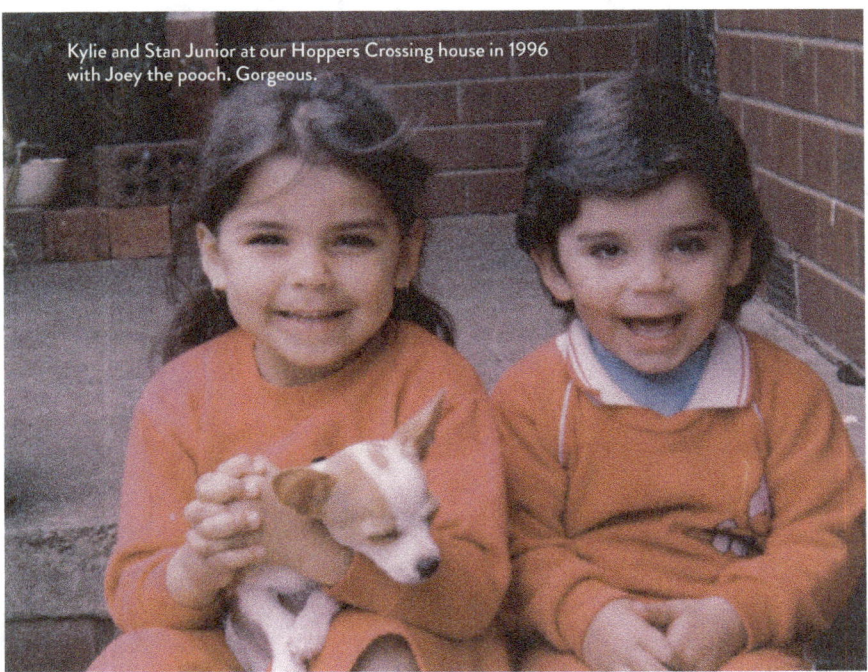

Kylie and Stan Junior at our Hoppers Crossing house in 1996 with Joey the pooch. Gorgeous.

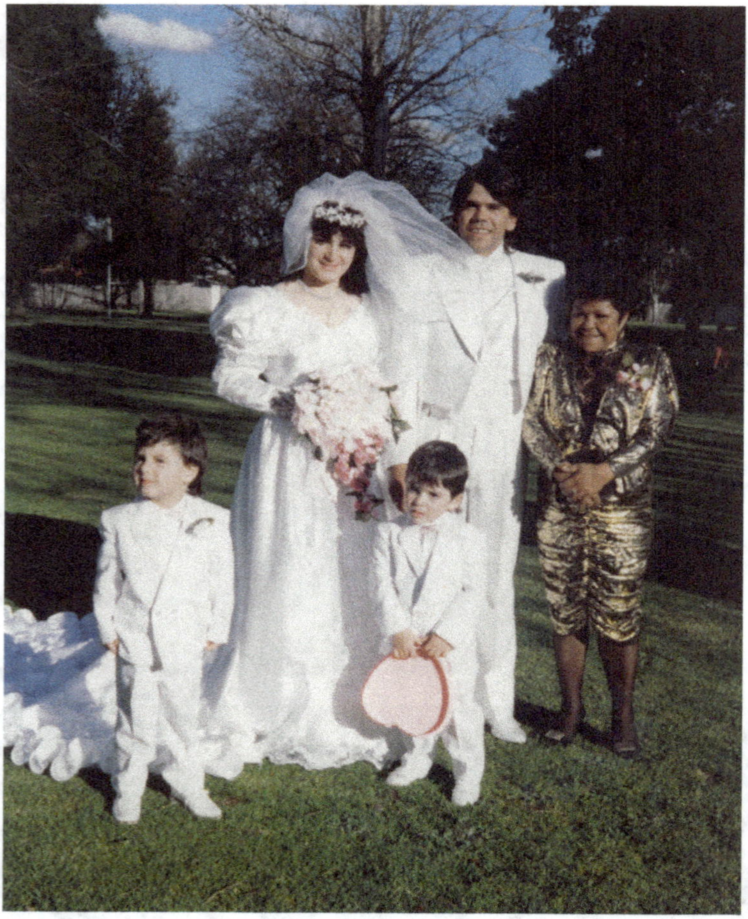

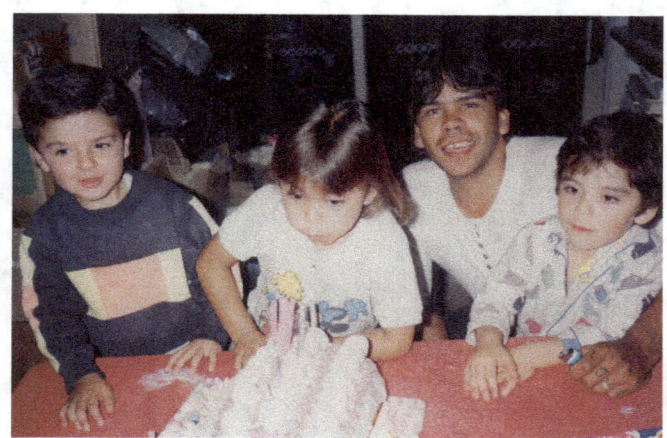

**Above:** Tying the knot with Sophia at a park in Northcote in 1990. Stan Junior's there, and a nephew named Joel.

**Right:** A birthday party in Hoppers Crossing around 1990: Joel, Kylie, Papa and Stan Junior.

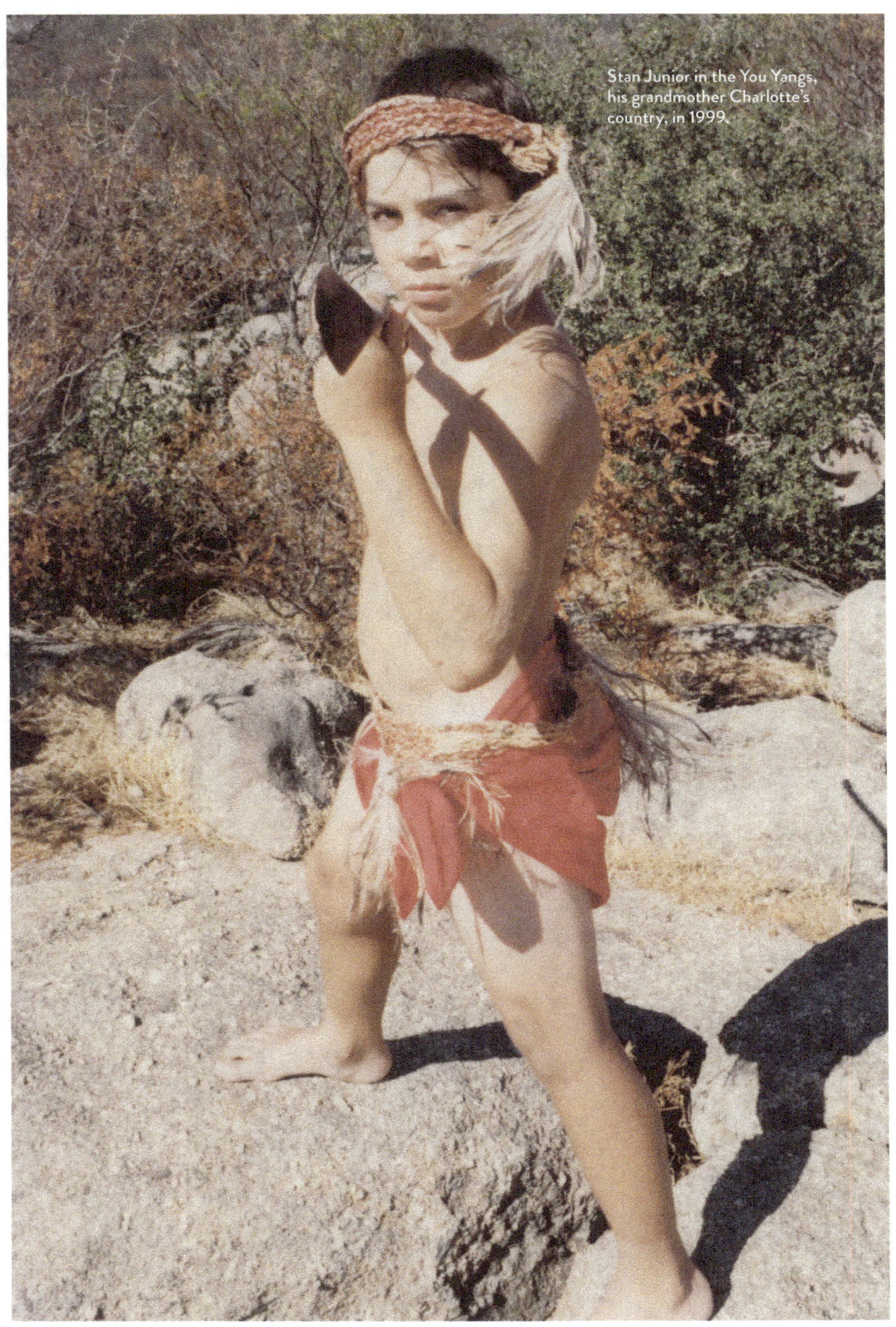

Stan Junior in the You Yangs, his grandmother Charlotte's country, in 1999.

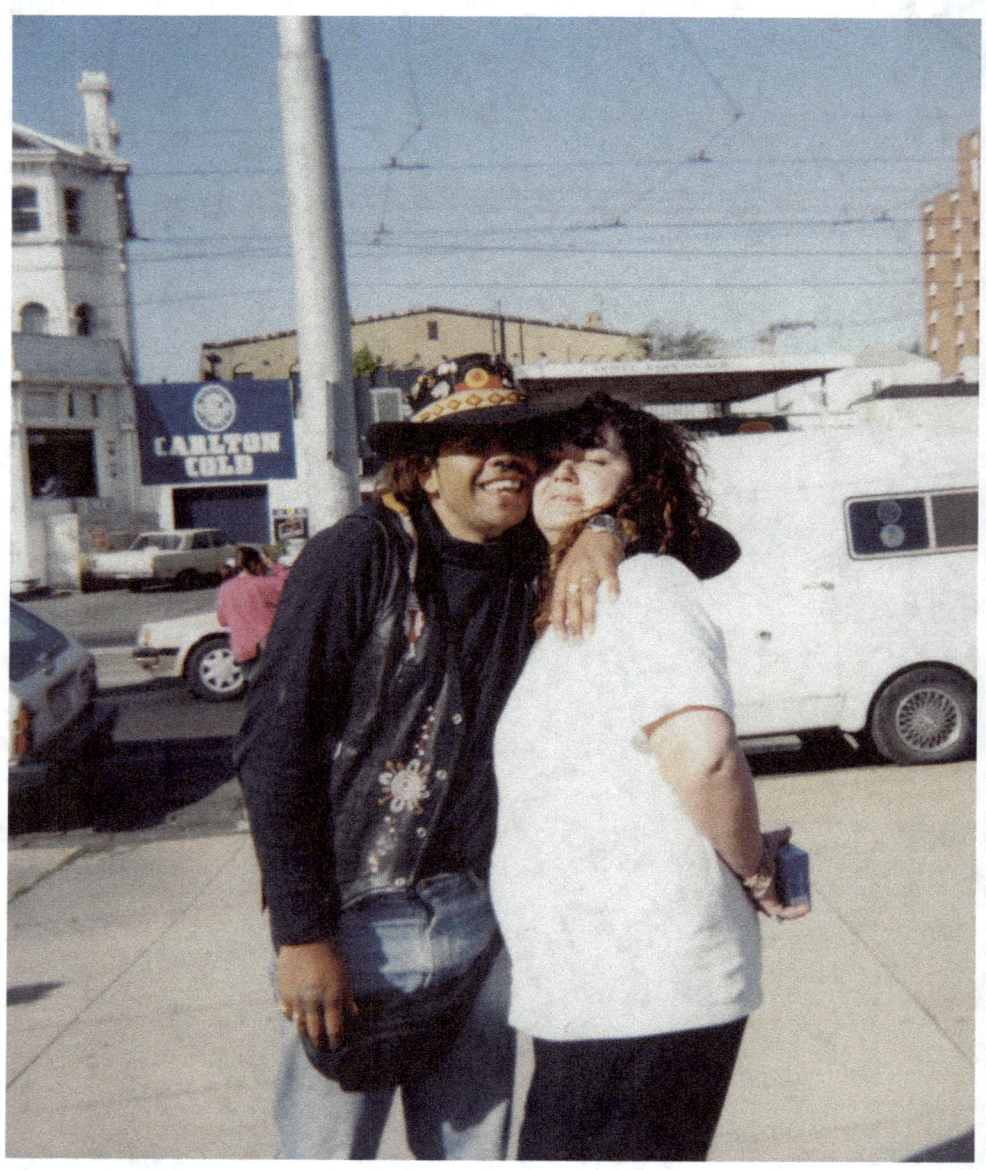

Sophia and me at the Esplanade Market in St Kilda in 1996. You can see the edifice of the noble Espy Hotel in the background – dear God I made some mischief there in my drinking days.

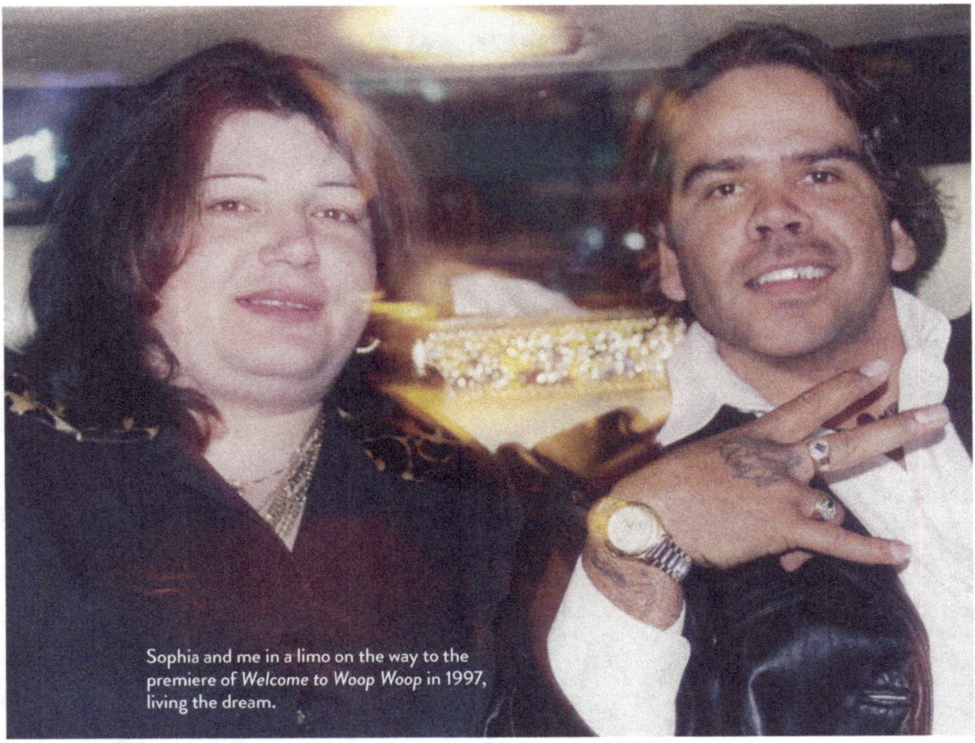

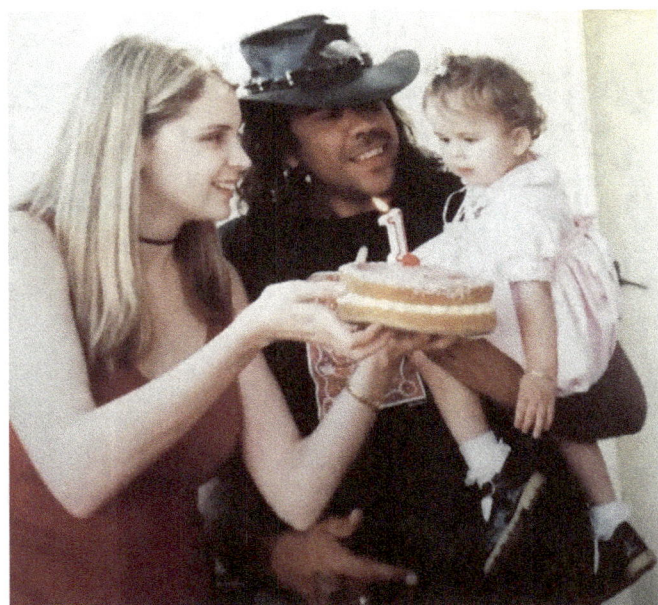

Sophia and me in a limo on the way to the premiere of *Welcome to Woop Woop* in 1997, living the dream.

Katrina, Aleira and me on Aleira's first birthday, at the Moreland Hotel in Coburg in 2002.

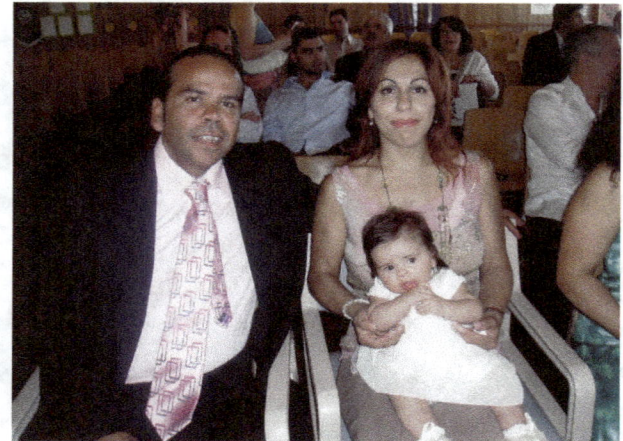

Lisa, Alkira and me at Alkira's christening in 2004.

Miss Australia 2007 Caroline Pemberton wearing a dress I designed. We're at the opening of an exhibition at my Collins Street gallery in 2008.

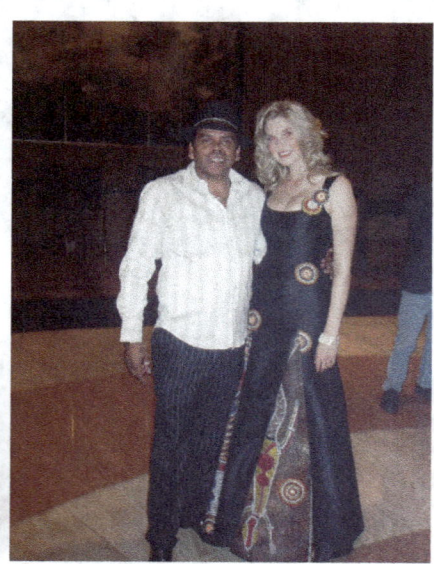

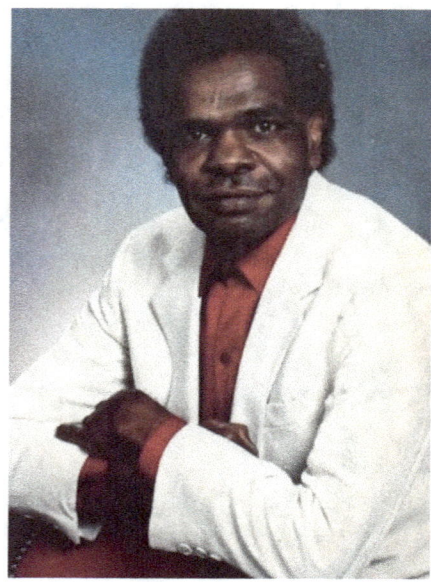

My buddy Robert Mate Mate, who gave me my Indigenous name of Yarramunua. Mate Mate was at Galiamble, where I started painting.

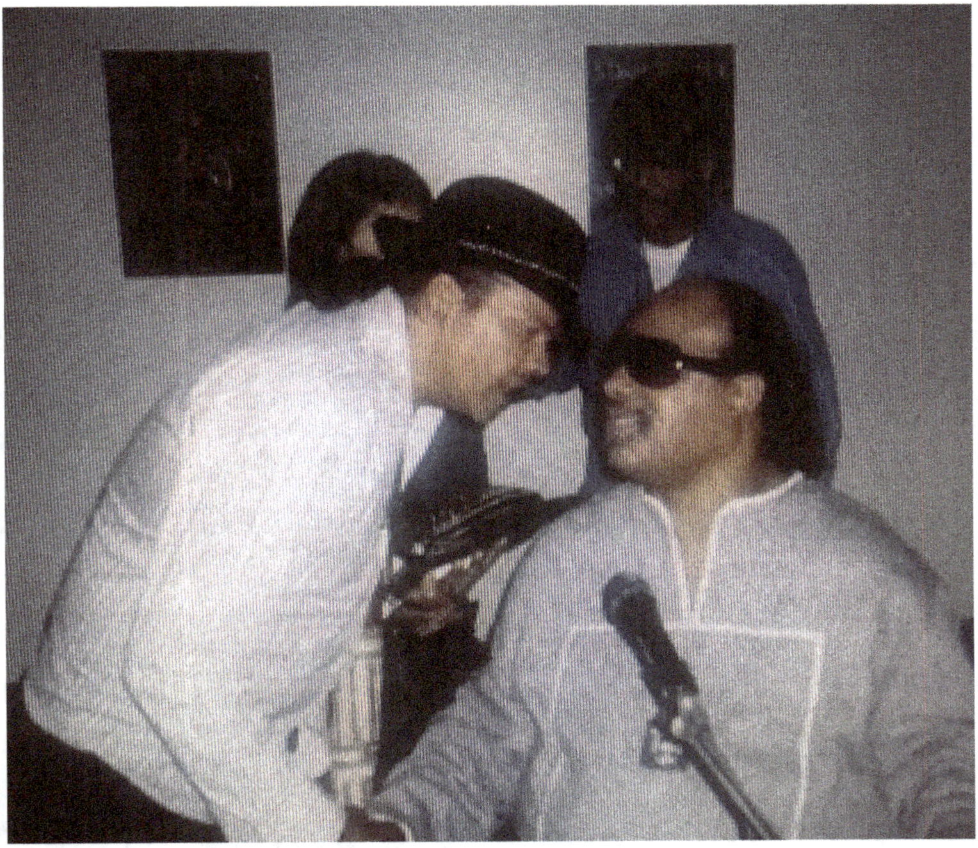

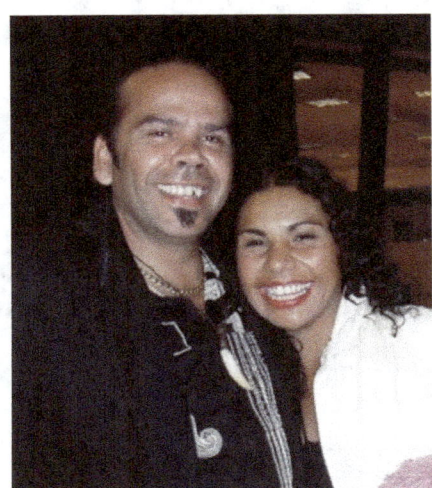

**Above:** Backstage with Stevie Wonder at the Sydney Entertainment Centre in 2008. I'd been playing the didge in his show, but at the moment this photo was taken Stevie was asking me about girls in the audience.

**Right:** Debra Mailman and me at Federation Square in 2010 for the opening of an exhibition about David Gulpilil. Isn't she gorgeous?

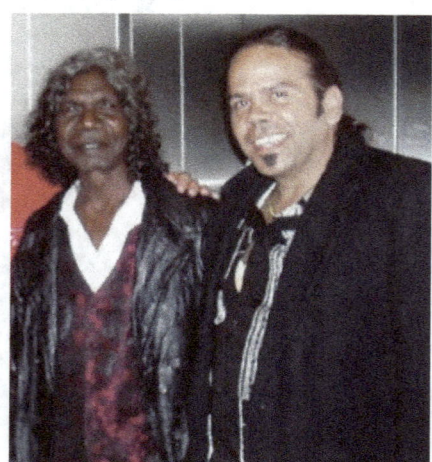

Legendary actor
David Gulpilil with
me at the exhibition
in 2010.

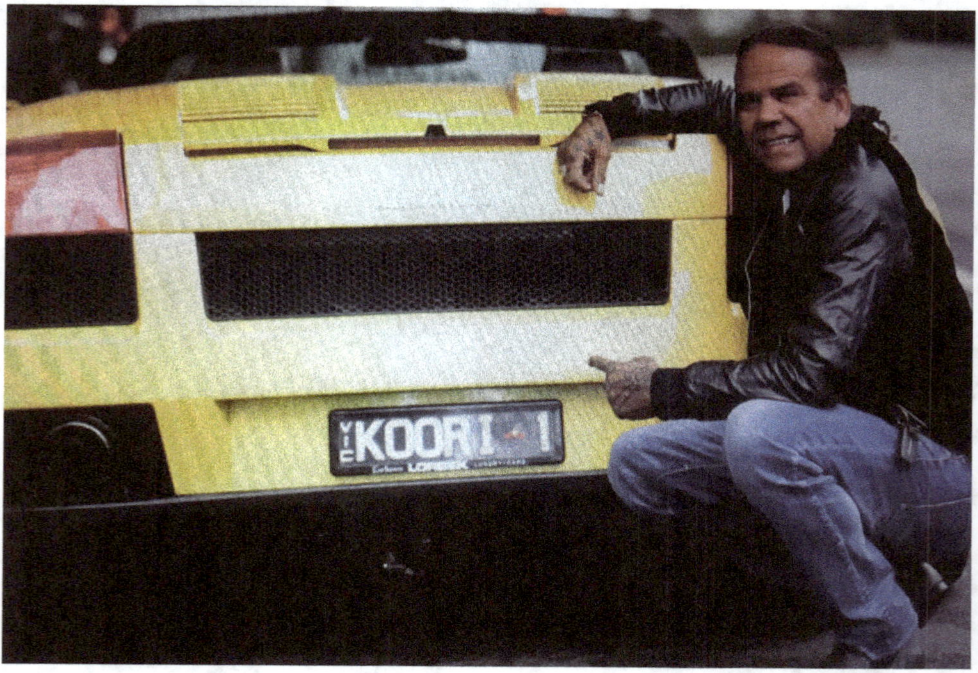

I might be the first Indigenous guy to own a Lamborghini – and a Ferrari. Mid-life crisis?
Man, all of life is a crisis. If you get a Lambor out of it, good for you.

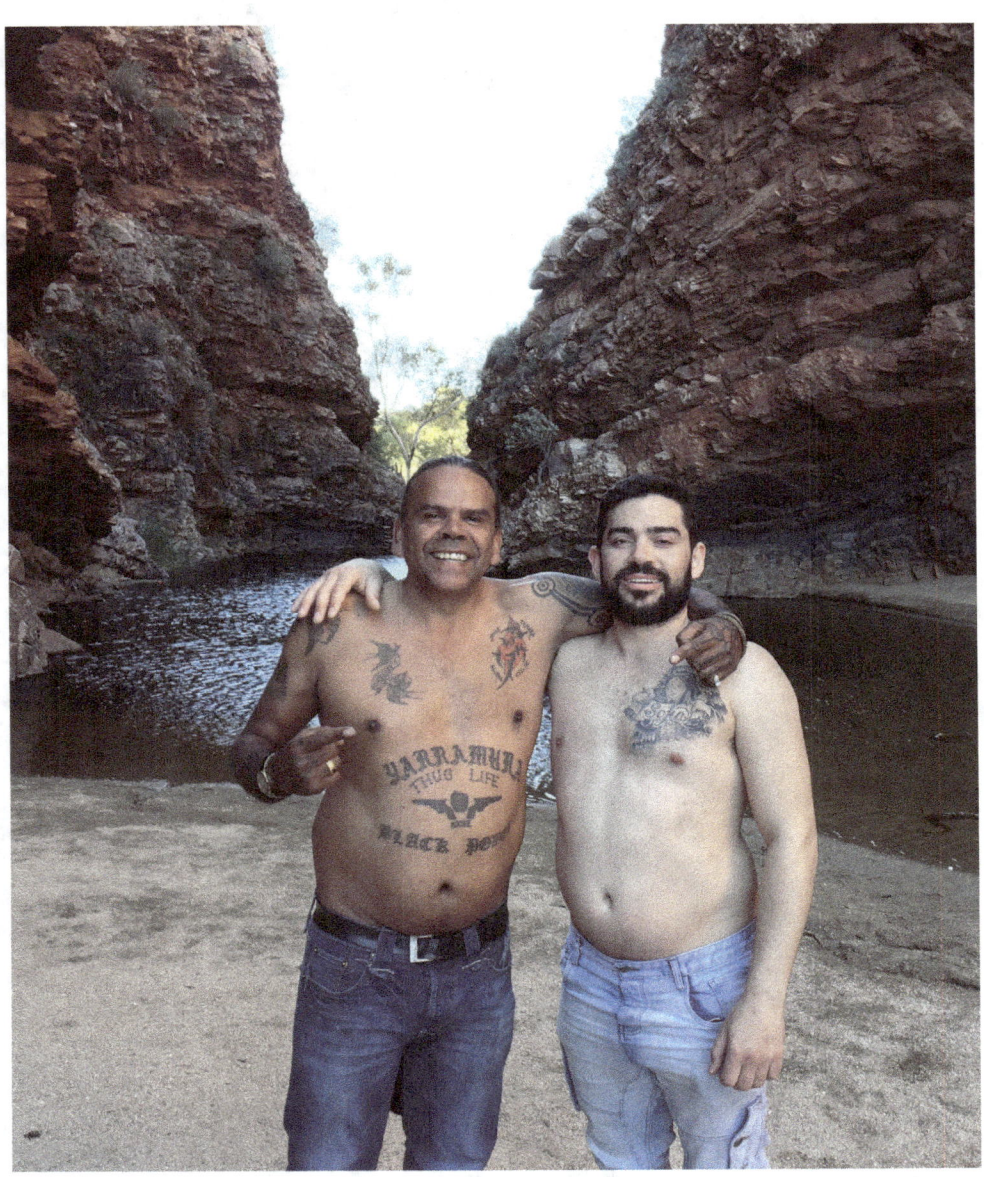

Stan Junior and his dear old dad up at Standley Chasm, near Alice, in 2016. Stan Junior is in full recovery from his addiction, and we're celebrating with some time in the heart of the country.

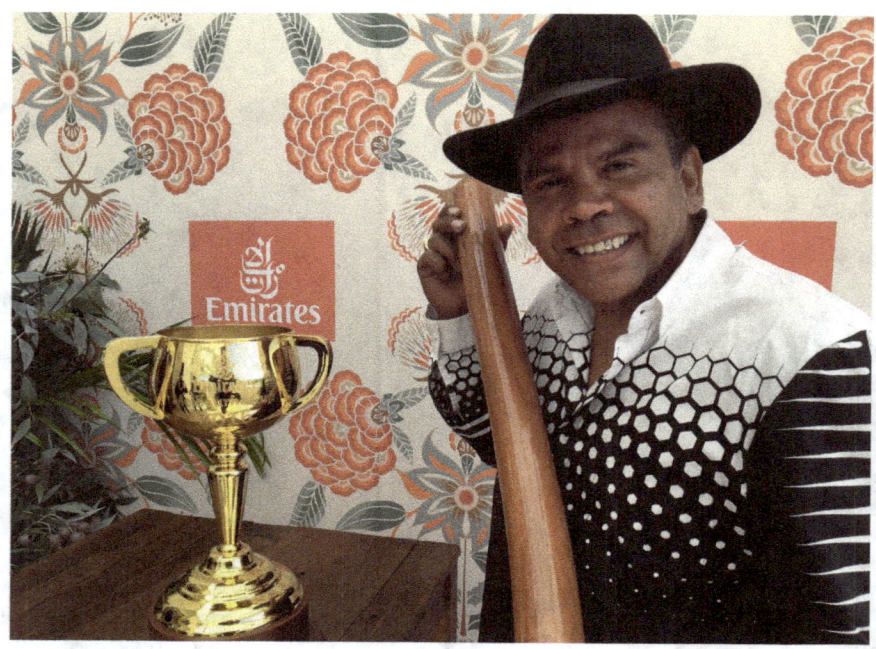

About to have a toot on the didge at the 2016 Melbourne Cup.

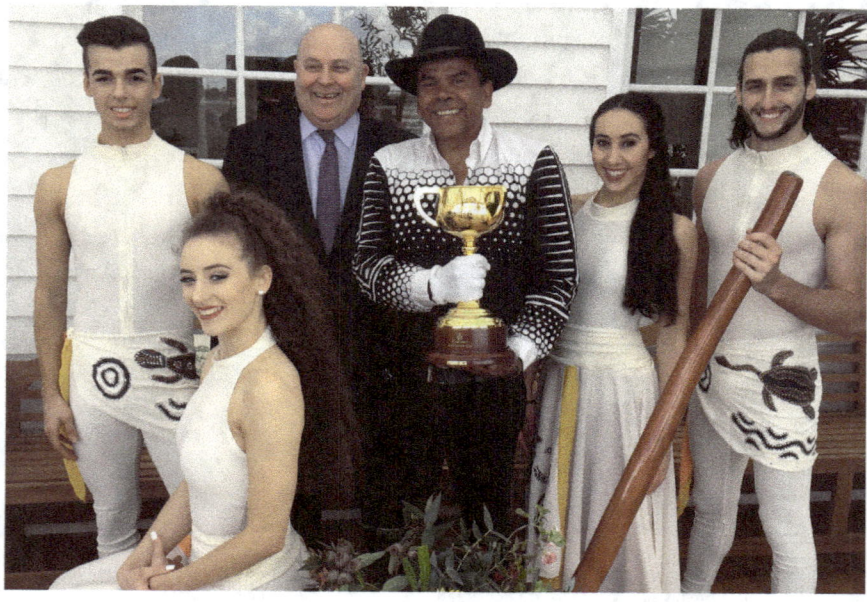

With Barry Brown, Emirates' Australasia Divisional Vice President, and some good-looking kids in outfits designed by me.

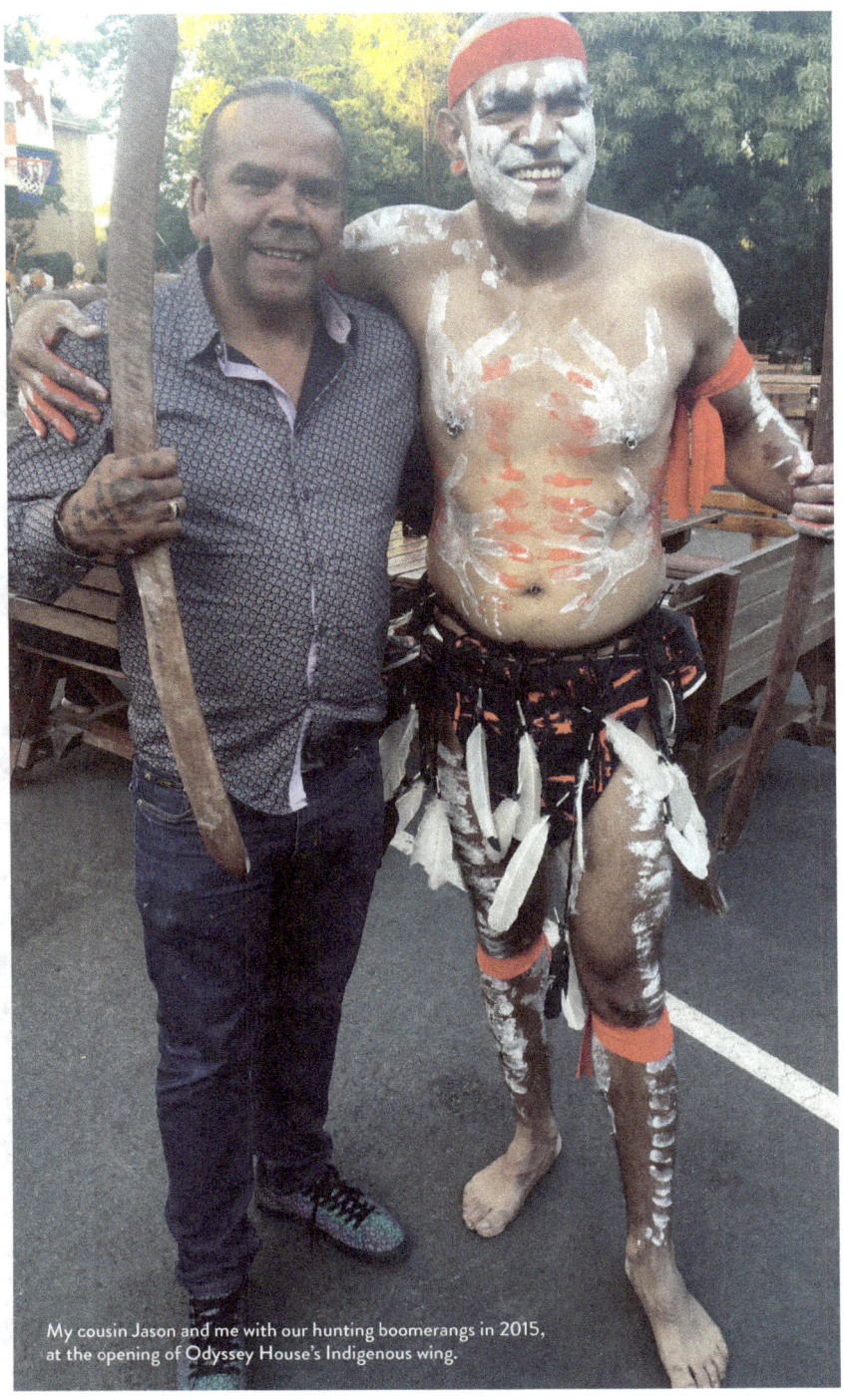

My cousin Jason and me with our hunting boomerangs in 2015, at the opening of Odyssey House's Indigenous wing.

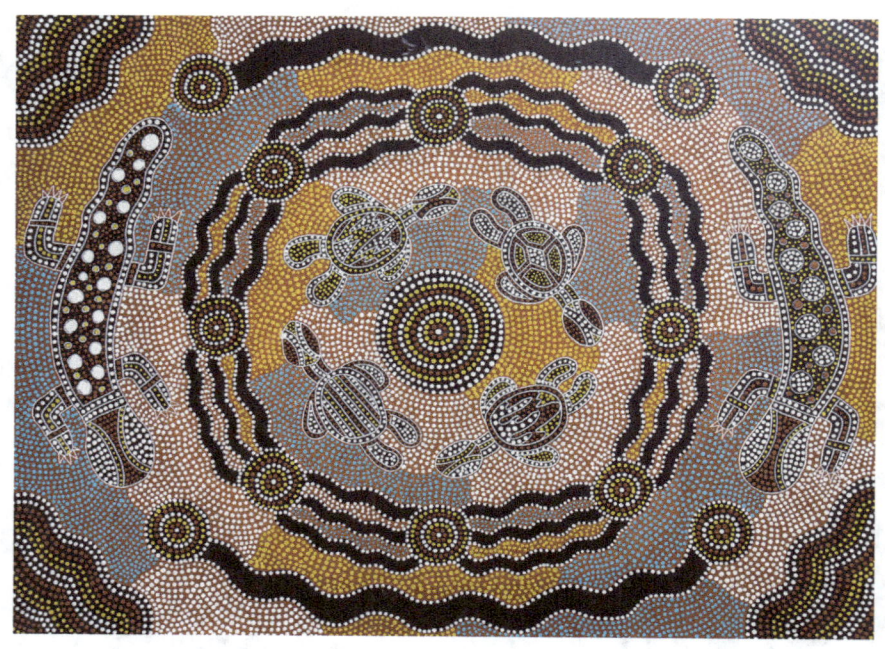

Here are two of my canvases. Painting gives me a high like nothing else. © Images Tobias Titz 2018

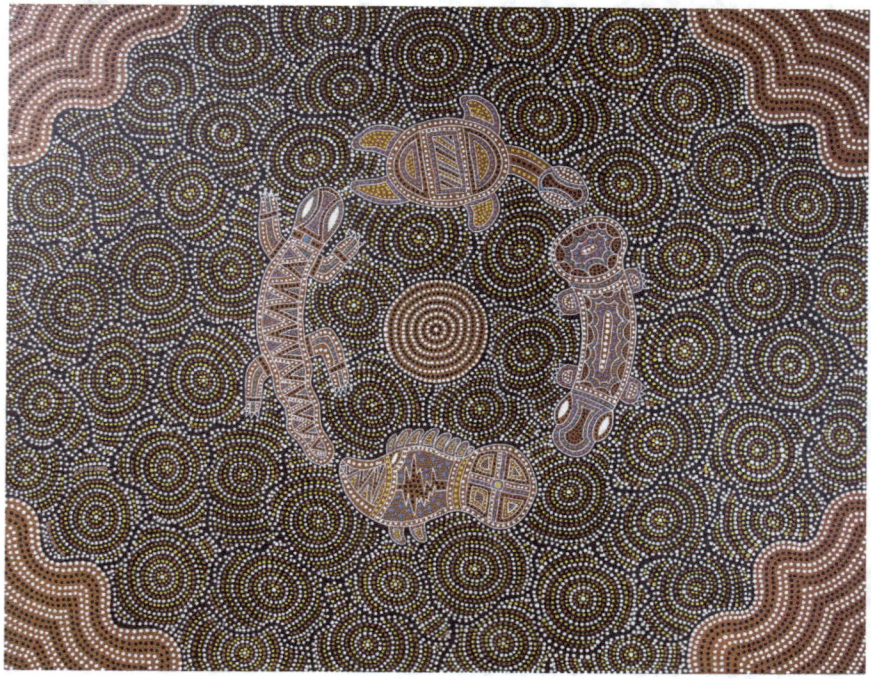

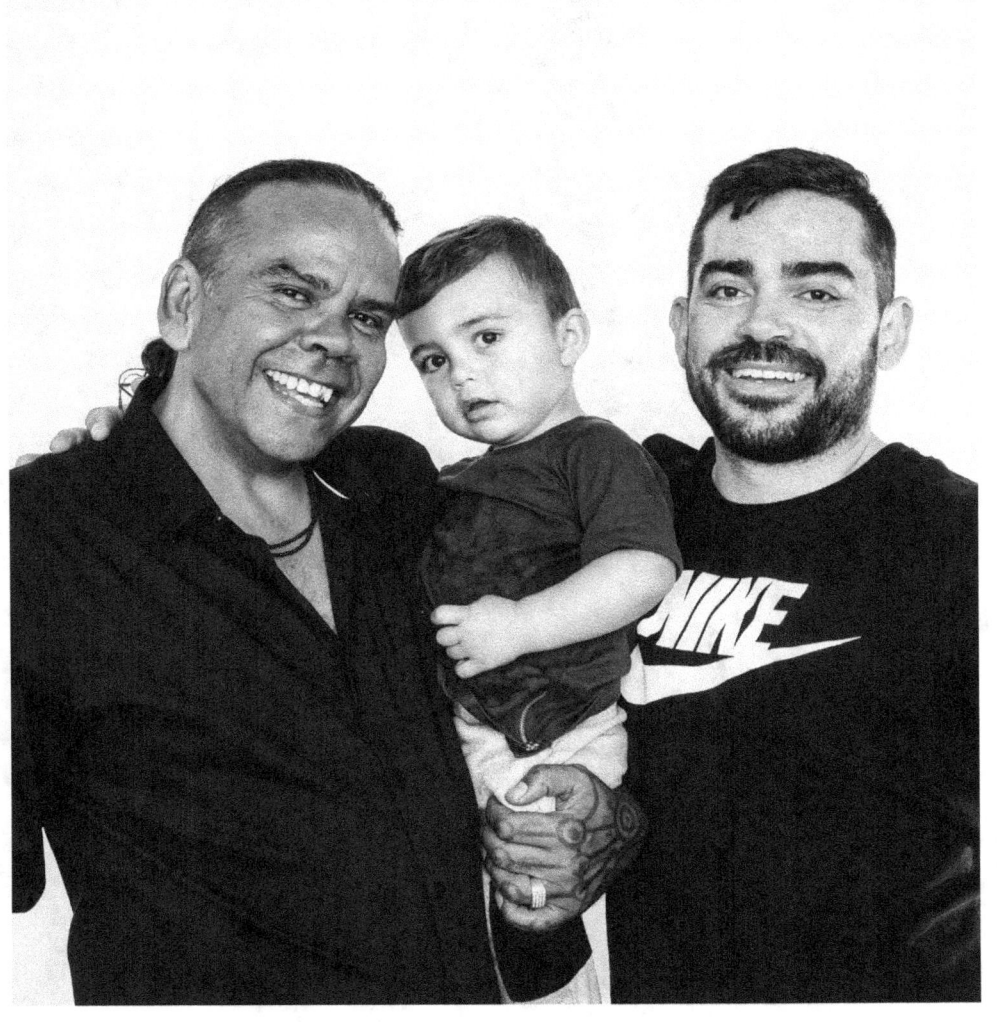

With Kylie's son, Anthony, and Stan Junior. I have to tell you, we're a good-looking family.
© Tobias Titz 2018

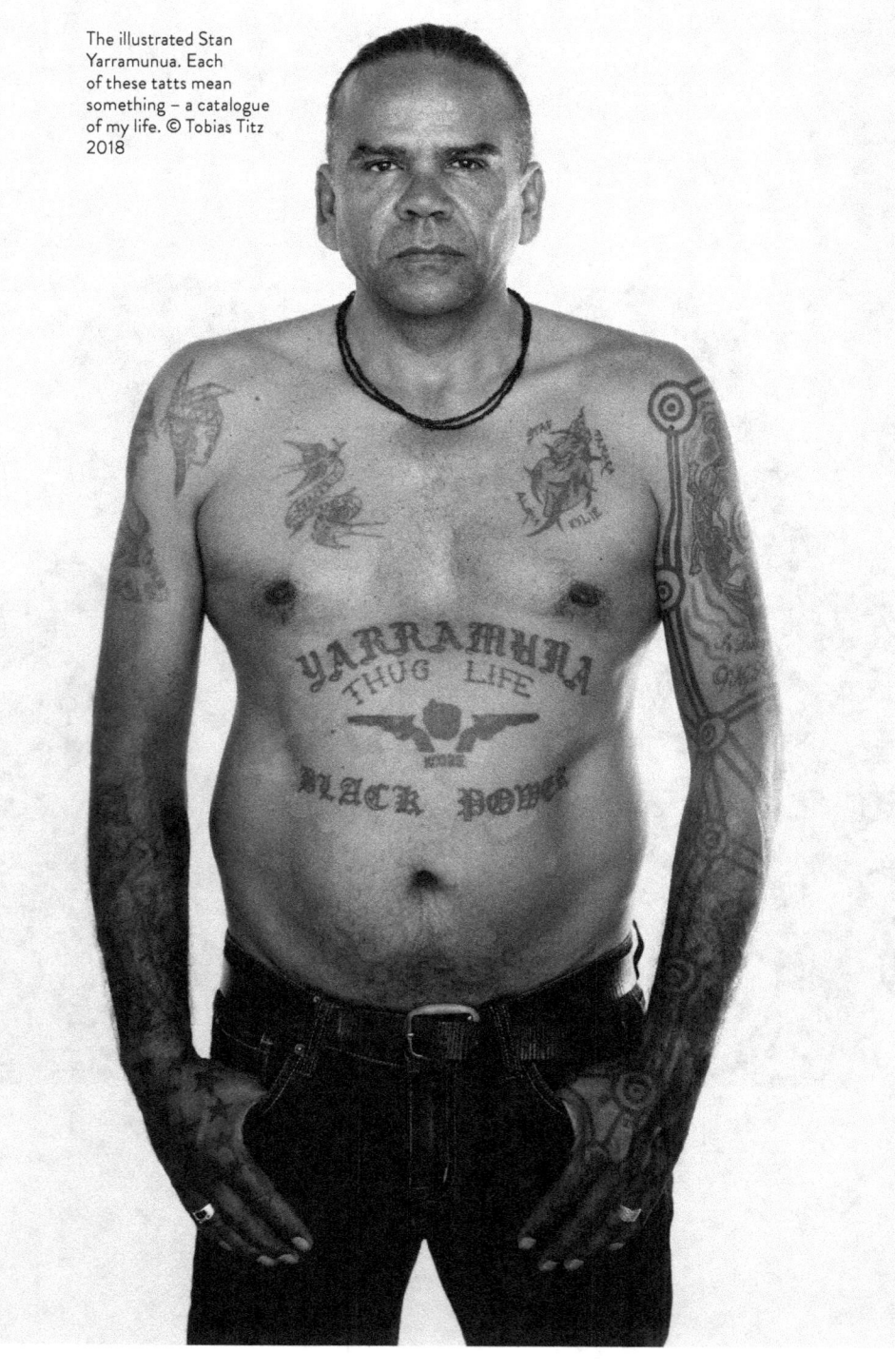

The illustrated Stan Yarramunua. Each of these tatts mean something – a catalogue of my life. © Tobias Titz 2018

# CHAPTER 14

# ART

I was lucky when I gave up the grog and accepted the guidance of Jackie Chris that I had something to fill the empty space left by the booze. This was another big development from my time down there in Galiamble, one that changed my life.

One of the programs Galiamble ran for the clients was an art class. A woman, Samantha, used to come to Grey Street and show the guys how to paint on canvas: the way you go about it, the sort of paints you use, how to mix colours. We had a special room set aside as a studio so that the guys could leave their paintings to dry, or work on them between sessions with Samantha. It happened one fine day that I was mooching through the studio and stopped to look at what the clients were up to. By the looks of it, didn't seem too hard to master, painting on canvas. The tubes of paint were sitting there on a bench, dozens of colours, and boards, which I later learnt were called palettes, for mixing the colours. There was a blank canvas on offer, too. I thought: "Stan, my friend, give it a crack."

I set to work squeezing out colours onto the palette. Loved those fat worms of paint bursting out the neck of the tubes. The paints were acrylic, no need to mix linseed oil to thin them – I knew that much.

I rested the canvas flat on the bench top and let inspiration take over. I had no knowledge of traditional designs, had barely seen Indigenous artwork before, but even without knowing, I began to create what was a true Indigenous painting. What came into my head was a time when I was sleeping under the stars, gazing up at the Big Dipper and another million stars glittering overhead. At that time, Frankie snoring beside me, I enjoyed my first experience of beauty. I thought: "So many! How can there be so many?" And I thought: "Stars are alive."

What I painted that day at Galiamble was the way an Aborigine sees the Milky Way: millions of living souls spread out across heaven, ancestors going back to the beginning of the Wathaurong. No one disturbed me. I filled one brush then another with colours from the tubes in a dreamy state, and my hands did the painting. I left the picture in the studio when I was finished, and it was still there the next day when Samantha returned. I happened to be there at the moment she caught sight of my picture. She picked it up in both hands, and stared at it in a puzzled way.

"Whose is this?"

"That one? That's mine. Sorry if I wasted a canvas. Just fooling round."

"Stan, this is terrific. Perfect. Do you want to sell it?"

"Yeah? You want to buy this?"

"Yes, I do. How much do you want?"

I didn't know anything about prices. Samantha said she'd give me a hundred bucks. I thought: "She's mad." But I said sure, sure, a hundred bucks, more than I made working the whole of the weekend at Galiamble, sure. That was when my life as an artist began.

When I was painting that canvas at Galiamble, I lost track of everything in the world but making a picture. Yet as soon as

Samantha handed over that hundred bucks, the world came flooding back. I thought: "I'll paint a hundred of these in a week, sell them for a hundred each, that's – here, let me see, one hundred by ten is one thousand, one thousand by ten is – well, whatever it is, a lot." I used Samantha's dough to buy tubes of acrylic paint and a few canvases. By this time we'd moved into a new house in Hoppers Crossing, bigger than our old place, room for a workshop. I set up my gear and went to work like a madman. The kids, Stan and Kylie, were watching me. "What you doing, Dad? What you painting stuff for, Dad? Can I have a go, Dad?" I told them that their old man was becoming an artist, and so I was, but not at the rate of a hundred pictures a week. That was impossible.

For one thing, I couldn't churn the pictures out as if I was turning a handle on a sausage-making machine, which was my original idea. As soon as I went to work on a canvas, I was in that state that made the world disappear. I couldn't say: "Okay, I'll give this one twenty minutes." I might have wanted to flip out a picture every twenty, thirty minutes but the truth was that the artist in me had a much bigger say in things than the merchant in me. I had to get the picture right. And I couldn't paint the same picture over and over. Each one had to have something special about it. What was happening to me as an artist was what happens to all the other artists in the world, that's my guess. I was being forced to accept a deal. I had inspiration, sure, I had ancestors looking over my shoulder, I had the spirit of my people running in my bloodstream, but my ancestors didn't give a damn about selling; they were only interested in the picture. So the deal was: "Get it right, or we'll bugger off." It's the same for all artists, Aboriginal or not, white, black. Your inspiration gives up on you and vanishes unless you're fair dinkum. That's the deal.

All this time, I was getting my arse along to meetings, standing up for my brothers and sisters in the struggle. Most every meeting, Jackie was at my side. Man, that guy never used up his commitment to the reformed pisspots of Melbourne. He sat beside me paying attention to the words coming out of the mouth of some jittery guy, some woman, and if I whispered a few words myself – just, "Gotta have a leak, old pal," or, "Forty-five this bloke is, looks about ninety" – he'd say, "Shut up, stay where you are."

But I took the chance to talk to Jackie after a meeting at the back of St John in Victoria Parade – the church where I had had my vision. I told him about my painting and my plans. Whenever I told Jackie about the plans I had, one thing and another, he'd listen with a black cloud hanging over his head, like everything he was hearing was a big fat fantasy – he wasn't convinced. This time he nodded his head and smiled. "I was waiting for this, Stan. This is what I wanted to hear. I see it in your eyes, my friend. You know the reason you found the strength to stop drinking? For this." Then he said something that I keep locked up in my heart like the crown jewels: "The best is yet to come."

Still, the paintings were piling up, and I needed a shop. I couldn't sell paintings from the kitchen. I knew about all the craft stalls along the Upper Esplanade down in St Kilda, hundreds of them, people selling every sort of thing: jewellery, ornaments, paintings, pottery, earrings made from Pepsi caps, hand-knitted toilet-seat covers. I phoned up the council and asked what I had to do to get a stall. Simple enough: I had to pay for a licence. I set up my stall on a couple of card tables and a display board – paintings, boomerangs, clapsticks, lovely stuff. I kept the prices low. From the first Sunday, I sold almost everything I had on offer. Out there in the open air with the sea and the pier and the blue sky – loved it. Crowds of people walking by, couples and families, kids with ice-creams, lots of noise.

I enjoyed people. They'd stop and look at my stuff, I'd give them a yarn, tell them what the symbols meant – the turtle for love, the platypus for wisdom, the goanna for journeying, all that good gear. "How much for this picture?" And I'd say: "For this original Indigenous painting, the waterhole, the goanna on his journey, Milky Way up there? Two hundred bucks." My pictures sold so easily, I had to think about raising my prices. "How much for this original Indigenous painting? The wise old platypus, the moorhen and her chicks, the Milky Way above? Three hundred and fifty bucks."

I had this knack for getting things right in my pictures. What I mean is that my canvases didn't look like some mug's attempt at Indigenous art; they *were* Indigenous art. You can be a blackfella and get it all arse-about when you try to paint. I was a blackfella who got it right. This was a time when white Australians were well into Indigenous art, a time when they wanted something from the original people of this continent hanging on their walls. Paul Keating had made his Redfern speech; Eddie Mabo had become a hero not only to black Australians but to white people as well – not to all white people, but enough to make a difference.

I'd just started at Turana when the judges of the High Court up there in Canberra got together in their big black robes and nattered away for weeks and finally said: "Australia wasn't empty when whitefellas came here in their sailing ships. Australia was full of Aborigines, damned right – full of blackfellas, Ajabathato Yorta Yortas." Which meant that Eddie Mabo's claim to title of the ancestral lands of his Meriam people could be upheld, by law. Now, when the judgement came down, people I knew, both black and white, were monster excited, but I was confused. I didn't know that the law said that blackfellas didn't exist in Australia when the white man came. It had to be explained to me by Aborigines with more education. It took me months to grasp that Indigenous people all over Australia could claim 'native title' to certain lands that were not held in ownership by anyone – crown lands, mostly. By the time that Paul Keating made his famous speech in Redfern Park in December 1992, I understood, mostways. The government was going to follow up on the High Court decision, clear the way for native title claims. Friends who understood more than me said: "You beauty!" Not only because they could claim their own land back, but because a rotten lie had been taken down. It was the Mabo decision and old Paul's speech that woke me up to the politics of my own people. When I spoke to other Aborigines, I was saying: "Mate, this is justice." That's what came to life in me. Justice. And it's been there ever since.

Soon the demand for my stuff was too much for me to handle. I drove to the north-west of the state in my rubbish Nissan to work something out with my uncles, aunties and cousins on Mum's side. They were all settled in Robinvale, no longer Swan Hill, Wathaurong people who knew their heritage and honoured it. I called on all of them, told them what I was up to. I said to Uncle Arthur, with his white beard halfway down his chest and his cowboy hat: "Uncle, you know how to make clapsticks, didges, boomerangs, yeah?" Uncle Arthur gave a shrug. "Uncle, you do some didges for me, paint 'em, some boomerangs, clapsticks, I take 'em back to the Sunday market in the big smoke, good money, pay you half of everything."

I told him I'd give him the paints. Uncle Arthur had a think for about twenty minutes, hardly said a word. Then: "Should be good, Stannie. Use me own colours, but."

Uncle Kevin Pearce showed up next, big Yorta Yorta man. Didn't know much about Uncle Kevin's past, but I saw that there must have been a past because when I sat with him under a big lilly pilly I noticed he was missing three fingers on his right hand. I said: "Bloody hell, Uncle, you've been in the wars, eh?" He held up his right hand and studied what was left of it. "Came off on the big circular saw I was using this one time, Stan. Shame." He still had his left hand, so I put my plan to him. Uncle Kev thought about it for about sixty seconds. "Yep! Clapsticks, boomerangs, yep."

Uncle Ralph Harradine sought me out when he heard about the deal I was offering, said he wanted in. I'd have to drive up and collect the art, but I could do that, long car trips never bothered me. Also, I was glad to give my uncles some income. Indigenous art is the only thing my people and my mum's people have ever had that white Australians wanted. It wasn't just the cash; it was the pride that came with working in your heritage. I was pretty sure that my uncles felt the same as me: nothing dishonourable in using your heritage to make things that white people wanted to put on show in their homes. That was okay. Wasn't as if you were giving away anything sacred. For me, everything sacred stayed the same.

In every picture I painted I put the Milky Way. That was my personal symbol. The stars of the Milky Way were above me when I slept with Dad in the paddocks, and that's how they got into my head, then into my pictures. But there was more. To paint a picture, you need a beginning, an image you can go to straight away. Once you have that beginning, it relaxes you, gives you confidence.

Anything might come your way after that. For me, the Milky Way let the spirit of my people into the picture I was making. It was as if I was saying to my ancestors: "Join me." It's a gentle feeling, to have the spirit of my people around me. I don't hear voices, nothing like that, but I feel comfort, encouragement, as if my ancestors want me to succeed, want me to make something strong and beautiful. I have to admit, though, that I want the picture to please the white people who come to look, too; I want my pictures to sell.

Getting up to Robinvale and the North West put me in touch with more of my family than I'd ever known, and man, I loved it. My people, my tribe. If I turned out to be related to every blackfella I ever met, so much the better. I *am* related to every Indigenous man and woman in Australia, yeah, but family is even closer.

And then one fine day back in Melbourne, out of nowhere, wham! – a brand-new daughter. I was down at my stall on the Esplanade giving my rave to the assembled punters – "Don't be shy, come and buy!" – when an Aboriginal woman stepped forward with a girl of maybe eight or nine beside her, gorgeous kid with big brown eyes. "Do you remember me, Stannie? I'm Sharon. Back in Shep, years ago?" I'm thinking, "Huh?" Because I did know a Sharon back in Shep in the days of the Warriors, but hell, every boy in Australia knew a Sharon at some stage. Standing there face to face with this Sharon, my Sharon, it all came trickling back – down by the river, hugging and kissing in the good old-fashioned way, and so on. We said cheerio, catch up soon, but we didn't catch up at all. Until now. "And this," said Sharon, nudging the girl forward, "is your daughter, Stannie. This is Tamara. Say hello to Daddy, Tam."

What do you think? Sharon had seen me on TV in one thing and another, came to hear that I sold gear on the Esplanade, thought she'd come down to the big city and drop by with my daughter, with this beautiful Tamara. Went for a cuppa at a café in Fitzroy Street, had a nice long chat, Tamara gazing at me with eyes full of soft light. Sharon said: "Tam wants to come down to the city and live with you. You think?" I'd have to speak to Sophia, that's what I said. So I did. Sophia said: "She has to live with us. She's your daughter. She's Kylie's sister, Stannie's sister. She has to come to Hoppers and live with us."

And she did. My family grew, and my heart grew.

There was only so much I could put on show in the space on the Esplanade, so I took myself up to Queen Victoria Market to suss out the prospects, and the prospects were good. Thousands came to the Queen Vic. I said to myself: "Stan, take the plunge." I negotiated a site with the market people, after they'd taken a squiz at my stuff. They wanted to be sure what I was offering to the public was genuine and that I had enough of it. I said: "Look at me, Stan the Legend, strong Wathaurong man, this is my art, this is Wathaurong art." I let them watch while I painted a canvas, and they were convinced. I did the spruiking and selling at the Queen Vic and left the Esplanade site in the care of my brother, Davy. But even a site in St Kilda and another at the Queen Vic weren't enough to get art into the hands of people who wanted it. I applied for a second site at QV, and a third. The didgeridoos and boomerangs and clapsticks I brought down from Robinvale made up half of all I had on offer at each site, but the paintings were all mine. That meant I had to produce up to ten canvases a week, probably a world painting record, Indigenous or not.

I was still off the booze, and I loved my new life. I was working a seven-day fortnight at Turana, but I was packed with energy. If you drink in the middle of the day, you're bound to get sleepy after an hour or two, need to flop down on a mattress. Stay on the booze for long enough, and you're going to get sleepy even if you're not drinking on a particular day. It's a terrific thing to feel strength flooding back into your body after years of floating around on the frothy stuff. My four years at Turana were divided into two years on the booze, and two years without it, and the second two years were a damned sight better than the first two years. Better concentration. It was the same with the painting. Once I was off the booze, I could hold that paintbrush for hours and hours, singing and whistling to myself. I was ready for anything.

I was with Bill, my mate from St John, one day down in Clarendon Street, South Melbourne, the both of us having a haircut. Next door to the barber shop was a travel agent. It was a bitch of a day, raining and cold, and as soon as we stepped out of the shop, Bill said: "The hell with this, buddy. You know what? We're going where the sun's shining."

"Yeah? Where?"

Bill led me into the travel agent's and said to the woman at the counter: "Need to get warm. Where do we go?" The woman's suggestion was Bali. "But you won't catch the last flight for the day," she said. "It leaves in two hours." Bill wouldn't hear of not catching the flight. "Time's wasting," he said, and we were out the door with our tickets, into Bill's BMW, no suitcases, nothing. By ten that night, we were in Bali. We shopped for shirts and shorts the next morning, soon lazing on our banana lounges on the beach. I could never have done that when I was on the booze – might've wanted to, but I would've been thinking of getting down to an early-opener, or parking somewhere with a twelve-pack. I've had a special feeling for Bali ever since that holiday with Bill.

# CHAPTER 15

# SHOWDOWN

The money was rolling in, hundreds and hundreds, then thousands and thousands. Sometimes I'd think back to my life as a kid and ask myself: "Stan my brother, are you dreaming?" Having a big comfy place to sprawl around in and driving a fancy piece of machinery – a Bentley by this time, big mother of a thing – was something I never got tired of.

For years and years, I'd been driving around in these clunkers and I was always waiting for something to go wrong, something to fall off, the carby to pack up, the head gasket to blow, and every day I was on the side of the road with the bonnet up. So when I bought my first new car, I was stoked; always started when I turned the ignition key, radio worked when I pressed the button, no need to pump the brake pedal to get the car to stop. It's one of the secret advantages of growing up poor. When you get some dough, man you enjoy it every second of the day.

Another thing I enjoyed was the hurly-burly of the crowds and the shouting and spruiking at the Queen Vic Market. Running a stall – actually, three stalls, then four, then five – is a job for an extrovert. Don't want to be too shy in the selling business. Around me were crazy people of every nationality: Greeks, Italians, Vietnamese, Croatians, Maltese, Russians, Africans of one sort and another, blacker than me, Arabs from wherever. And heaps of Jews. They enjoyed the spruiking and shouting as much as anyone. I know that being a Jew isn't a nationality, I know Jewish people come from everywhere, but they stood out because they loved the whole thing so much.

I'd get together with the Jews and natter away and tell them about how I was related to William Cooper from the long ago, a proud Indigenous man with a big heart who led a march of Aborigines to the German consulate in Melbourne in 1938 after the Nazis went berserk in Germany and smashed up all the Jewish shops, killed whole mobs of Jews. No white people marching on the German consulate, just William Cooper and his blackfellas. My mum was the one who told me about being related to William Cooper. Always made me proud. So I'd tell my Jewish mates about William and they loved me for having such a famous relative and made me an honorary Jew.

But I did have a bit of a dispute with one Jewish stallkeeper. This was Benny, an old bloke I hadn't met before, with a belly like a bass drum and big specs and one of those little Jewish hats. I'd been wandering around the market checking out the other stalls when I looked up at the top shelf of Benny's big shop, and hanging there was a boomerang, decorated with little shapes and figures about as Aboriginal as Santa Claus and his reindeers. I said: "Mate, what gives? Over in my places I'm selling genuine Aboriginal boomerangs and you've got this Mickey Mouse thing up there. Do me a favour." Benny introduced himself, shook my hand. He said: "So this is offensive to you? Okay, you buy it and I won't put up another one. I understand. You're sensitive." We had a chat, found we got along well. Friendly guy, Benny. I told him I was the only Indigenous guy in the world who was also an honorary Jew; told him about William Cooper, my big-hearted relative. I made it a habit to go around to Benny's side of the market each week for a rave, and one week he surprised me by saying that he'd sell his place to me if I wanted it.

Benny's shop was big, and in a brilliant position near the carpark, but he was selling toasters and electric jugs and heaters and all that gear, which was no use to me. "So what?" he said. "My licence is for selling anything. I could sell circus elephants if I wanted to. You buy me out, sell your Aboriginal stock, all good, my friend." He wanted $120,000 for the licence, and I had the dough, I'd saved it, so I stuck out my hand and said: "Benny, it's a done thing. Only now I have to find someone to man the place." Benny said: "Me, I'll do it, I'm an honorary Aborigine."

Six sites at the two markets. A licence to print money. All I had to do was clue Benny up about Indigenous culture, make sure he didn't go too far and try to pass himself off as a Wurundjeri, because he might have. Once the deal was done, I'd go around and listen to Benny spruiking my stuff. He told the punters he had the blessing of Stan the Man, the famous Indigenous elder. I said to him: "Benny, I'm not an elder, you know that, don't you?" He looked at me and shrugged. "Well, you should be," he said.

I was doing all this monster business in my stalls and shops, and that was terrific, but just as important was the involvement of my family. My rellies up in Robinvale, I now had them bringing down their stuff instead of me driving up all that way. I took whatever they brought down, paid them in cash, had them stay over at the

Hoppers Crossing house. We were like a new clan within our tribe, and even though I couldn't think of myself as an elder of this new clan, I was definitely the brains of the outfit. Money flowed back into the Robinvale Indigenous community and that gave me real pleasure. Since the coming of the whitefella, this was the first time that Aborigines in Robinvale or anywhere up there had been able to pay their way.

I was learning more about art, yeah, and also about human nature. If you're an Aborigine and you've got a few quid, people get puzzled. Not only white people; blackfellas too. They think: "Something's wrong here. Blackfella, big fat bank account – no, that's not right." If I was Lang Hancock sitting on a pile of banknotes you couldn't jump a Grand National winner over, people would say: "Brilliant, found a hill of iron ore and sold it on the market, bit by bit. Brilliant." But a black man with something to sell? Very suss.

Blackfellas, up until a little while ago, they've mostly thought of whitefellas as the ones with the wallets. Talking about money and big flash cars and huge houses with swimming pools? That's whitefellas. Things are changing, so I've noticed. Indigenous people around thirty, there's a big group of them who want in. They don't see anything crazy about a black man with money. They think: "Okay, I can see how the whole thing works, I can do that." Not just money, not just business, but getting into stuff like law and medicine and the arts and harvesting bush tucker, whatever. It's not closed to them, getting into uni, making it in the white world. But when my business took off, it was different.

I became known in the Melbourne Indigenous community as a brother with dough packed into biscuit tins and stuffed under mattresses. Sparked a certain amount of envy. Brothers were saying: "Hey, where's my biscuit tin full of fifties?" I had to defend myself damned near every day. "Where's your biscuit tin, buddy? It's up on your kitchen shelf but it's empty. Mine's up on my kitchen shelf and it's full because I'm selling pictures. You sell some pictures, fill up the bikkie tin."

I was pushing back against thousands of years of Indigenous culture, because for Aboriginal Australians, private property traditionally wasn't accepted in the way it is among whitefellas. Black Australians, we invented communism, property is theft and all that business. And as a matter of fact, it worked really, really well until Captain Arthur Phillip came along with his redcoats and English law and the idea of owning. If I own something, it's mine. I've got a receipt. Now, the traditional system was better: what's yours is mine, what's mine is yours. Works beautifully, unless you're paying a dozen people a fat wage to flog your stuff at the markets. But some of my brothers, they still wanted what I had in my bikkie tins, under my mattresses. And it happened that two of them came around to visit me one day with a proposition. I wasn't home, but Sophia was. She told me that the brothers wanted ten thousand bucks. "They're coming back, Stannie. These are bad guys. Baseball bats, house bricks."

I told Sophia and Stan Junior and Kylie and Tamara to hide out at a friend's place on the other side of Hoppers. I was there by myself when the chumps returned. One had an aluminium baseball bat; the other had a length of pipe.

"What is it, gentlemen? What can I do for you?"

And the bad guys: "Want ten grand, Stan, my friend. Only fair. You've got bikkie tins full of moolah, we've got nothing."

And me: "Suppose I say no? Suppose I say piss off?"

"Stan, my brother, we might have to put a few dents in your skull and break your arms."

It happened that I had in my possession an Anschutz .22 automatic, twelve shots. It'd been left in my keeping by an uncle of mine, and it was loaded. I told the brothers to hang fire for a minute.

"Just ducking into the kitchen for that bikkie tin."

I was back in ten seconds with the Anschutz.

"Now, you were saying?"

The two of them gaped at the rifle, then turned and ran out to their old Ford Escort. I should have kept chilled but instead I fired six shots at the car as it swerved away. How many bullets hit the vehicle I wasn't sure. More than one. What the hell was I thinking? It wouldn't have required a miracle shot to have killed one of the chumps. It could've easily ended up with a body behind the steering wheel with a bullet stuck in it. Then what? Murder, manslaughter, somewhere between five and fifteen years in the chokey, the brains of the business out of circulation. Well, the brains of the business was also capable of being a ning-nong, apparently.

Gunshots had been heard in Hoppers before, but not often, and not six in a row. Neighbours appeared with shocked expressions, saw me standing there like Chuck Connors in *The Rifleman*, and ducked back inside. Ten minutes later, the cops were on the doorstep. The rifle was leaning against the wall, and one of the cops took possession of it.

"Now, deary me, what's been going down here and what's your name?"

"Bad guys, officer. Trying to rob me. Had to defend myself. I'm Stan Dryden."

"Well, Mister Dryden, we've got laws against discharging firearms in a public place. But now, let me see, are you the guy who works with black kids out this way? Think I've seen your name in the local paper."

That was true. I'd been getting more and more involved in finding places for Indigenous kids to kip, getting some proper food into their systems, helping them find jobs. This all came from my memories of sleeping rough when I was a kid, and of my brother and sister competing with pigeons for crumbs and crusts back in Redfern.

"Yep, that's me, officer."

"And you sell boomerangs and all that sort of gear down in the Queen Vic Market?"

"Sure do."

So the two officers had a bit of a natter and came up with a solution.

"Mister Dryden, Stan, could be that this discharging of a firearm was what you'd call an accident. Might be that these bad guys rolled up, and you were holding this rifle out of fear of what was coming your way, and maybe you didn't know it was loaded. Is that right?"

"Umm, well ..."

"No, no – you didn't know it was loaded, did you?"

"Didn't know it was loaded, officer. No idea."

"Good. And then the bad guys come on hard, and first thing you know, the rifle goes off accidentally, bang, bang, bang, and you're shocked as much as anyone, and the bad guys hit the road. I think that's what happened."

"Exactly like that, officer."

"Good. Now let's see if we can catch these rogues."

They caught the rogues. But I didn't press charges. My dad was Frankie, after all, who'd seen a few chokeys from the inside. And me, I'd worked at Turana. Anybody who's been locked up doesn't want to see another person serving time, no matter how much the bastard might deserve it.

For Sophia, this business with the bad guys was another of those episodes in her life with Stan that made her wonder about me, maybe even made her ask herself if she'd have been better off with a more peace-loving hubby. She shook her head, told me not to expose the kids to this sort of mongrel nonsense. So, yeah, it worried her, but Soph was plenty worried about her life with me in any case, one thing and another, so the bad guys affair just got tacked on the end. I should've paid more attention to Soph's jitters at the time. Should've. But didn't.

# CHAPTER 16

# THE STAGE

A cting on television and in movies over the years gave me a mob of friends in the industry – producers, directors, sure, but mostly people like me who only ever found small roles. I still thought of myself as an actor before anything else, even if a whole year passed without a role. And I knew the people behind the scenes – the grips and focus pullers and carpenters and designers and make-up women, hairdressers, caterers, drivers, stuntmen, stuntwomen. The people in the industry form a network that supports actors, encourages us, gets us sharing our grief, tells us to forget about swallowing that bottle of sleeping pills. Someone hears of a production about to get off the ground and whispers in a buddy's ear: "Could work out good for you." (A funny thing, this was always in a quiet voice or a whisper, even if you were a day's journey from another human being – as if speaking too loudly would bring bad luck.) In 1998, I ran into a mate in the business who whispered in my ear about a play called *Stolen* being cast by Wes Enoch at the Malthouse Theatre down on Southbank, nearly all the parts for Aboriginal actors.

I went straight to Wesley down at the Malthouse, got my name on a list and chatted with Jane Harrison, who'd written the play.

It was about kids who were taken from their parents when they were littlies; five kids in the play, grown-ups at first but in some scenes, kids again. Both Jane and Wes had seen me in one role and another, the most recent in *Welcome to Woop Woop* – not a big part but okay because it gave me the chance to meet Barry Humphries, who played a madman, and also Susie Porter, Rod Taylor, Dee Smart and Johnathon Schaech. Stephan Elliott directed it, first movie after *Priscilla*, not the monster follow-up he was hoping for but it had its moments.

I'd met Wesley before, but not Jane. She was a Muruwari woman from up in New South, gorgeous I have to say, loved her straight off. She'd put her heart and soul into *Stolen*. She wanted it to become one of the true stories of the nation, something that would become as important to white Australians as Gallipoli or the Kokoda Track, and even more important to blackfellas. We had to grieve for the stolen kids, she said to me. We had to accept the sorrow of it. But we needed the whole nation to know what we were grieving about – that was Jane's point. She explained to me that she'd told the stories of those five kids – Ruby and Anne, Jimmy, Sandy and Shirley – in a way that would reach out to every kid who'd been stolen, and every mum and dad who'd seen a couple of white policemen bundling their son or daughter into the back of a van.

The role that might be mine – had to go through auditions – was that of Sandy, bloke of about twenty when we first see him, a true ratbag like myself, been on the run for years from the cops, who want to stuff him into an institution. Spends his life looking over his shoulder, no home to call his own, but the thing he doesn't know is that the cops stopped looking for him years earlier when these kidnappings were called off. He can't stop running, Sandy – that's his life. Even if he knew that he was safe, he'd do what he'd always done.

I was never stolen, but I knew what it was to be on the run, cops a few steps behind, Frankie calling out to me: "Keep up, buddy! Keep up!" The Sandy character, even though he keeps running, he's looking for something, for a place to call home, but he's so whacked out that he maybe wouldn't know home if he found it. I spoke to Jane about everything from my past, and made sure she understood that I'd never been without a mother and father – usually only one at a time – but that I knew exactly what was in the guts of Sandy.

Each of the five main characters had a different story. Jimmy had been stolen when he was a tiny kid, and his mum spends the rest of her life searching for him all over the bloody continent. She gets a hint that he's in one city or another and she's off. Jimmy spends years at a stretch in prison, never even knows that his mum is out there battling away. He thinks she's dead. When he does finally get the news of his mum's search, it's too late; she passes before the two of them can meet up. Jimmy tops himself, the poor bugger.

Ruby works pretty much as a slave in the homes of whitefellas after she's taken from her family. She's sexually abused over and over, and ends up crazy, sitting in a corner and muttering.

The Shirley character suffers a double catastrophe. She's taken from her family as a girl of twelve, then when she grows up and has her own kids, they're snatched away from her.

Anne is the only character who survives the experience of being abducted with her heart and her wits still holding up. She's given to a white family as a foster child, treated with kindness, educated, happy enough. Jane said she'd included the character of Anne so that the audience didn't think that they were watching a horror show. Not every kid snatched away became a walking disaster. But I could see that Jane still wanted the audience to understand that it was evil to take these kids, even if, like Anne, they didn't end up on the highway to hell. She wanted the audience to face that fact.

I was given lines to learn. Wesley knew that I was still struggling with reading but he expected that I'd be okay with a bit of help. The bit of help came from Sophia, as always when I had a script to cope with. We were once again in strife with each other over her boyfriends and my girlfriends, but I have to say that Soph could put all that rubbish aside when I truly needed her help. She sat on the sofa in the lounge room; I sat on a chair facing her. "This comes in the first act," Sophia said. "I'll just say the words normally, you say them in the character of Sandy. Okay?"

"Sure."

"'I'm sick of it, mate. Sick of running.'"

I was trying to get a set on Sandy, on the way he'd speak, and I tried out one reading then another, and another. And struggled to get the right expression. Sophia listened, watched, gave me her opinion.

"Don't do that thing with your eyebrows," she said.

"What thing?"

"That thing. Don't lift your right eyebrow."

"I wasn't."

"Yes, you were. And don't scratch your head. Sandy wouldn't scratch his head. Say the lines like you're tired, exhausted, like being exhausted is normal for you."

I changed the reading, worked it back and forward, remembered the lines until I could go through the whole scene without any corrections.

Something happened in the three hours of learning Sandy's lines. I went inside – that's the best way to explain it. I was inside the play and inside Sandy. This had never happened to me before, finding myself inside. Maybe that's not such a big surprise because most of my roles in the past had been pretty much surface stuff, especially the comic roles. But Jane's play was serious; you can't make any sort of comedy out of kids being taken from their families. After an hour, with Sophia's advice, I stopped looking for those comic moments I was used to. And the role of Sandy began to take shape around me, as if some real Sandy who'd once lived in the real world was watching on, nodding or shaking his head. The thing in my life it was most like was the mood that came over me when I was painting. When that happened, it wasn't to do with deep concentration, although, sure, I concentrated when I was painting. It was more like I was being offered someone else's concentration, drawing in the power of other forces, ancestral forces.

Learning Sandy's role, I told myself: "Stan, get it right." I didn't even have the role yet, but getting it right had become crazy important. Sophia could see it. She said: "You want this, don't you?" Hell, yes. All the other roles I'd tried out for, I wouldn't have collapsed in misery if I hadn't been offered them – a bit disappointed, not much more. This role let the politics of black Australia surge into my bloodstream. I was hot to trot for the justice of the cause once I'd listened to Jane and Wesley; I wanted people to know this story. Not just for the sake of black Australians. I could see that white Australians needed this just as much as I did.

I went back to the Malthouse the next day, faced up to Wesley and Jane, gave them all I had. No high fives, no backslaps, but yeah, I had the role. Next thing, big thing – learn to act on the stage, because it's not the same as acting in front of a camera. The gestures are bigger, the voice is bigger, you can't rely on the director to keep the focus on you – you have to draw the focus yourself. And another thing – you have to do it every day, not just three or four takes and then a wrap, but a new performance every day. This was real acting; this was Shakespeare stuff, doing it all on your feet, making the audience believe in you. The Sandy role made everything that had come before seem like kid stuff, sure, but without what came before, I couldn't have stood confidently on stage and made the audience believe in me. I needed that confidence. This was Jane's art, and if I'd let her down I would've felt sick.

I met the other actors as soon as I had the Sandy role: Tammy Anderson, who played Anne; Kylie Belling, who played Ruby; Tony Briggs, as Jimmy; and Pauline Whyman, who was Shirley. All of them were more experienced on the stage than I was. We liked each other. I think all of us had the feeling that we were in something special. We wanted to make it work. This story of the Stolen Generation, by the time I'd rehearsed for a week it was in my guts. I'd known about the stolen kids, of course I had, but knowing about it and having it in your guts, that's different; now it was something I was never going to forget. Archie Roach came down to the Malthouse before the play opened and had a chat as we sat around in a circle. Then he picked up his guitar and sang 'Took the Children Away'. Man, it turned me inside out. I stared at Archie's gentle face, heard his soft voice folding itself around the lyrics and it was as if I understood sorrow for the first time in my life. Frankie's passing, Charlotte's passing, that was grief and it was bloody awful. But this was sorrow, this was something that reached out wide and gathered in every Indigenous man and woman and kid in Australia.

Acting on stage, it's more from your heart and guts than movie acting. Especially in *Stolen*. Wes had to remind us that it wasn't our job to make every member of the audience collapse in a coma of grief. It wasn't our job to play for tears. He said: "This is a series of stories. All you have to do is tell your story. Don't even think about what's going on in the hearts of the people watching." That was Jane's message, too. It made an impression on me. The story was the thing. Now and again when I was on stage but not speaking lines, I'd glance at the audience. Man, the people out there were torn to bits. But I watched them dabbing at their eyes without feeling churned up myself. I thought: "The story, tell the story." I thought of my paintings, my sculptures. When I was at work on a canvas, I was in a zone, completely at peace, making something beautiful for the punters.

Acting on stage also gave me a chance to enjoy the others actors in a different way from shooting scenes on film. Watching Tony in the role of Jimmy, I could see at times how he'd changed a reading just a little from one performance to another. I wanted to say (but couldn't because I was in character): "Brother, that was magic."

We ran for five months at the Malthouse before Wes took the play out touring. We went from town to town in Victoria, then New South Wales, South Australia, one motel room after another, one theatre then another, the Royale, the Imperial, the Commonwealth, or maybe not a proper theatre, just a space indoors at the Wycheproof RSL or the Nhill progress hall. Wes wanted to cater to Indigenous audiences as much as possible so we took the play to places where blackfellas were thick on the ground. I saw Aborigines in the audience hugging themselves to stop the shaking. Jane's play, it went deep. Some of the Aborigines, they were at their first play ever. They didn't know that we were working from a script. They didn't know that Jane had poured her soul into the words of that script. They thought it was just our own words, coming up from our hearts, our own stories. We'd mingle with the audience after the show at times. "Brother, that wasn't just your story you were saying up there, you were saying my story too, believe it."

I have to admit that not everyone was a monster fan of the play, though. We went to Robinvale, where a number of my rellies still lived, and put on the show at the progress hall. My uncle Arthur was in the audience. I caught up with him after the show when he was enjoying a fag on the verandah, gave him a huge hug. "Uncle," I said, "what'd you think?" Uncle Arthur nodded his head as he puffed away on his gasper. "Yeah, good," he said, "but when are the movies coming on?" He thought he was off to see a double bill of *Fight Club* and *Sleepy Hollow*. Somebody must have conned him.

While I was touring with *Stolen* I was keeping an eye on the Queen Vic shops and stalls and the one I still ran at the Esplanade. It was more Sophia looking after the outlets than me, if I tell it honest. Lot of work for her. But I'd ring her on the mobile and listen to a report, ask her how the stock was holding up and if the people I had selling for me were turning up. I used to drum into the people looking after the shops that they had to be there at ten, and stay until five. Most were my rellies – cousins and nephews and nieces, even my own kids. I tried to go easy on them but they saw me as a hard-arse at times. They'd say: "You gotta chill a bit."

I did my chilling on the road with *Stolen*. Mooching from town to town I had time to natter in the bus, at the motel. I learnt the life stories of Tammy and Kylie, Pauline and Tony, and the stage staff. Sometimes a bit more than the life story. If my own story leaves out things I want to hide, it's not a book but an advertisement. Stan the Legend and two or three of the girls came to enjoy each other's company more than was strictly above suspicion, if I can put it like that. On the road in the way we were, it was like I was in a special space where right and wrong didn't count. Two lives, two different sets of rules. Back in the other space where right and wrong counted plenty, that was a bit awkward. I had to say to myself: "Stan, my friend, it's not as though you robbed a bank, just a little bit of fun, forgive yourself." It's a very important part of my make-up, the ability to forgive myself. I've had to rely on that knack a hundred times. Two lives, one at home, one on the road.

# CHAPTER 17

# SOPHIA

I'd wake up thinking: "You know what, Stan? Good on you." What with the money rolling in and me getting better and better at painting those canvases and that terrific season at the Malthouse, it was like the sun coming up and staying right there in the middle of that blue sky month after month. I saw nothing looming on the horizon that could get in the way of the happiness that was due to me; no warnings, no little twinges of doubt. But I should have, because the worst grief of my life was building up right there in the Hoppers Crossing house.

It was Sophia. For years and years – the booze years – she'd been all that had stood between me and the gutter. By nature, she was a very tender woman. She nursed me, comforted me, washed the pants I'd stained with urine, cleaned up my puke and told me: "You're going to get better, my love, you're going to give away the grog and get happy again." She was my wife, but she gave me heaps of mothering, even at times when she was seeing other blokes on the side. She was happier with the mothering than with anything else. She could show love in that mothering way when it was difficult to love me just in a man–woman way. I was a child to her, a problem child. Like a child, I'd run to her when I was suffering. "Need a drink, Soph, but I don't really want it." Or: "Soph, got these nightmares, awful stuff, make them go away." Yet when I gave up the booze and had Jackie Chris as my sponsor and guardian, Sophia's role of mother vanished. Not immediately, but bit by bit. I didn't go to her with my troubles and I had no nightmares to plague me. This is strange in a way, but as I became a better husband, the less often she could feel close to me. I came home with money that made us more comfortable than ever before and I was there for the kids, for Stannie and Kylie and Tamara, but Sophia had this sorrowful expression that she wouldn't talk about. I put it down to her remembering her life as a kid, when she was sexually abused in her own house. She'd told me about it years earlier. That abuse, it played some part in her mood, sure. But her blues were more to do with feeling that she couldn't get close to me in the way she once had. And Kylie was fourteen; Stan was twelve. Not as much of a role for a mother in their lives.

There was more that went into Sophia's sorrows. The girlfriends. I wasn't a Casanova, but yeah, sure, I got about. Not all addictions are to do with stuff you swallow or snort or inject. I was addicted to what I could kiss and undress. Every time I met a pretty girl, I was sixteen again; same lines, same charm. "Hi, darlin', how does it feel to be the most beautiful girl in Australia? Must feel great 'cos just looking at you is fab for me." Sophia knew about most of the girlfriends and it was agony for her. If I ducked out in the evening I always had an excuse prepared but Sophia knew where I was going and what I'd be doing. For me, the girlfriends were just a normal part of a healthy man's life. Sometimes, I didn't want anything from the girlfriends but happy sex, I admit that. Other times, I was in deep, cared like crazy about the woman. But whether in deep or just floating happily on the surface, Sophia was my wife, and that was a whole different scene. That was love. I had to duck and weave and sneak about to get time with the girlfriends, sure; that was part of the deal. But I loved Sophia forever, and I don't care if that sounds suss in any way. I loved her.

As I've said, Sophia kept herself busy too. Some of the boyfriends, they were just payback. Two or three, she was in deep, the same way as me. Tore me up whenever I found out. The famous double standard and all that rubbish, yeah, sure. But there's not a man on earth who can shrug and smile when the woman he loves is off with Tom or Harry.

Christmas 1999, six years after I gave up the booze, and we were at home for a big Christmas dinner with the kids (but not Tamara, who'd recently gone back to live with her mum) and Sophia's dad, Nick, and her stepmum, Persa, plus Soph's real mum, Bev, and her husband, Steve. The two couples got on really well, lots of joking and laughter, a good vibe in the house. And a big tree decorated with gold bells and red baubles with artificial snow; angels blowing trumpets, a golden star at the top. Underneath the tree, a pile of pressies for the kids. We had music playing on the CD player, all those Christmas tunes: 'O Come, All Ye Faithful'; 'Once in Royal David's City'; 'Good King Wenceslas'. Also a CD of Aussie carols: 'Six White Boomers' and 'Aussie Jingle Bells'. That good vibe going round didn't cheer up Soph, though. She was blue down to her boots when she should've been giggling – she'd always enjoyed Christmas. I got her to come into the bedroom away from the rellies and the kids and asked her again what the matter was. "I feel useless," she said. "Can't get myself going."

"What do you mean, 'useless'?"

"Don't know that I want to go on living, Stannie. Seems hopeless."

I could feel a claw gripping my guts.

"Don't say that, Soph. That's no good, saying you're useless."

"It's what I feel."

I gave her a kiss and she picked up a bit. "Don't worry about it," she said. I was thinking of doctors and medicine and getting people to talk to her, her friends, rellies. It was difficult for me to talk to people who'd lost all confidence because even at my worst in the booze years my belief in myself was never all that far away. Just a little thing, like a smile from a stranger when I was shuffling along the footpath, could give me a lift. I'd think: "Stan, you're curdling the milk. Cheer up." Or I could go to Sophia and put my head in her lap and enjoy having her stroke my hair. Even when Sophia talked about not wanting to live, I never accepted that she would ever do anything bad to herself, mostly because it was impossible for me to imagine being without her.

We went for a walk in the evening, Soph and I, around the footy ground at the local sports complex. We were walking Soph's dogs, a rottweiler and six chihuahuas, more dogs at our place than a boarding kennel. Soph adored them, the pooches, which was one of the reasons I was sure she'd be okay; she had problems with me, but she'd always want to care for those mutts. I had my arm around her shoulders, telling her I loved her, reminding her of all the good things in her life. "Stannie and Kylie, beautiful kids, both of them getting along to school regular, pretty much, except for Stannie, and Soph, they need you, believe me, a father's one thing but kids need their mum." And Soph said: "Do they? I don't know about that, Stan."

Christmas Day was on the Saturday that year. Sophia's mood was no better on Boxing Day or the next day, Monday. I kept a worried eye on her as I greeted the rellies and friends who dropped by for a Christmas drink, trying to take some of the effort out of her day when she was so low. She knew I was watching and every now and again she'd give me half a smile, but with the saddest look in her eyes. I think that everyone who called by could sense something was wrong. Nick and Persa, Bev and Steve, they picked up on it too. And the kids. They were used to their mother being down in the dumps over the past few years, but this time it was worse. I suppose, like me, though, they couldn't imagine Soph not being there for them, no matter how low in spirits she was.

On the Monday I left Sophia and the kids to themselves while I buzzed off to see Katrina, the woman I was spending time with; too much time, in fact. Gorgeous, she was, Katrina, if you can be gorgeous and poison at the one time. She'd been in my ear all week about making her feel special. I said: "Kat, it's Christmas time, gotta be nearby for the kids." Also, for Soph, in the state she was in, but I couldn't say anything like that. And Kat: "Couldn't care less. Need to see you, no excuses." I caught up with her in Coburg, bit of a kiss and a cuddle at the place she was living, a certain amount of the other. Then it was: "Stannie, Stannie, my darling, you never take me out to fancy restaurants, go on, take me somewhere flash." We jumped into the car heading for a place I knew in Brunswick Street, when Jesus suffering Christ, I caught sight of Sophia coming down Johnson Street towards us in her blue Toyota, probably out looking for me. She saw me at the same moment I saw her. I took off up Brunswick Street, Sophia just behind, and pulled up outside the cop shop in Dawson Street, the Major Collision Unit. I was thinking I'd be safe with the cops three metres away if Sophia was carrying an axe or a bazooka. Think again, Stan.

Sophia drove her car straight into the side of mine, pow, the passenger side, hoping to kill Katrina I think. It was only then I noticed Stan Junior in the car with Sophia. I said under my breath: "Stan, my friend, you'll have to kill yourself, only way out." We all climbed out of the cars, no injuries, but as I expected, a big shouting match, little Stan bawling his eyes out, Katrina dismissing everything Sophia was saying. "This is my husband. I want you to keep out of our lives. Do the decent thing and get lost." Katrina made a gesture with her hand as if she was waving a fly away. I kept myself between Sophia and Katrina because gentle as my wife was, I could well imagine her flooring Kat with a roundhouse right. The cops appeared out of the building, watched on for a few minutes then shuffled back inside. It was just a domestic to them. An Aboriginal domestic. Too complicated.

Sophia finally got back in the Toyota, but only after pleading with me to come home. I said I would, and Soph let Stan Junior come in my car with me, maybe as a guarantee that I really would head back to Hoppers after dropping Katrina back at her place. When Kat started caressing the back of my neck with her hand, Stannie grabbed her arm and flung it away from me.

It was difficult to know what to say on the drive home. "I'm sorry"? A bit lame, since I wasn't all that sorry. It was just problem-solving, more than genuine regret. I told Stan Junior not to worry about the whole shemozzle. "It's okay, matey. Bit of strife, nothing to worry about. You and me, kiddo, okay?"

Back at home, I kept up the happy talk, smiled my face off, kissed Stannie and Kylie about a thousand times each, gave Soph a hug every time she came within reach. By bedtime on that Monday night, I'd just about convinced myself that I'd patched everything up. It was all baloney, of course. Soph was still down in the dumps; the kids knew all my kisses and hugs and stuff like that was sus. But I wanted to believe I'd worked a bit of magic. Needed to.

Early on the Tuesday morning, before it was light, I heard Soph getting out of bed, and in my half-asleep state, I asked her what she was doing. "Nothing, go back to sleep," she said. Going to the toilet, I thought, and drifted off again. When I awoke a second time, hours had passed and I was late for an appointment. The appointment was with Jackie Chris. I dressed quickly, cleaned my teeth in the downstairs bathroom, took a bite out of a piece of toast. Sophia was nowhere around. I called out to tell her I was off, expecting she'd hear me, wherever she was. Steve and Bev and Persa and Nick, they'd all gone back to Shep.

Sophia didn't hear me. She was no longer alive. Later in the day Stan Junior found her in the upstairs bathroom. She had hanged herself by tying a length of rope around the rail that held the shower curtain above the bath, then collapsing at the knees until the rope strangled her. By the time I heard, Sophia had been taken to the morgue. Stan Junior told me later that he'd gone into the bathroom at about one in the afternoon to apply some Joop, a type of eau de cologne, and with his back to the shower stall, had felt something pressing against his shoulder. He turned around, drew the shower curtain and saw his mother hanging there, dead for hours. He said he'd run down the stairs to the lounge room where Kylie and a group of friends had gathered before heading off to a party. "I couldn't breathe," Stannie told me. "I stood there with my mouth opening and closing like a fish. I finally got out: 'Mum's hanging!' and Kylie said: 'What?' and I said again: 'Mum's hanging' and Kylie ran upstairs. Bawling her eyes out, Kylie, and I start screaming. We called the cops and the cops called the ambulance. I didn't know what to do. I'd started breathing again, but I didn't want to. I wanted everything to go away."

Kylie tried to call me but I had my mobile turned off, as I always did when I was with Jackie. So she called Aunty Tina, who lived a few minutes away in Hoppers. Tina dropped everything and came over with Marvin, her partner. Hugged the kids, decided to phone Bev and Steve in Shep, who said they were on their way. And still no answer from me on the mobile. The cops and ambos arrived. Stan Junior said that he was pleading with the cops. "Is she alive? Is she?" The cops said nothing for a little while, then one of then looked at Stannie and shook his head.

Then in walks Tina, who'd been trying one of my favourite places after another. "Stan, you better come on home."

"What the hell? Are you stalking me? I'm not going anywhere."

Steve appeared next. "Yeah, you need to get home, Stannie. Sophia's gone."

"Gone where? Bugger off!"

Jackie said, "Take it easy, brother."

"She's gone, Stan."

This time I got it. I stood up from the table, followed Steve outside, was told a bit more, climbed into my car. I was moving towards something I couldn't grasp for the moment, maybe the sort of thing I'd feel if I was standing before a firing squad and being asked if I wanted a blindfold.

I t felt like something I wasn't meant to survive. I told myself that the pain would soon kill me, that I wouldn't have to bear it for long. When I didn't die, I had to accept that the pain would go on forever. Most times when I've tried to look into the future, I've seen visions that are one thing and another, some of them likely to come true, some fantasies, some a mixture of both. Not this time. I saw the pain going on forever, and I was right. When Frankie died, and Charlotte, that was bad enough. But Sophia's passing was worse. And poor little Stannie – I wish I could've spared him that, finding his mum. It left him with nightmares. Kylie, too.

We took Sophia up to Shepparton to bury her on New Year's Eve. Her people all lived in Shep, including Nick and Persa, and Bev and Steve. We gave Soph a service at St Michael's Catholic Church, and also a traditional Aboriginal ceremony of farewell. At the church I'd been given a seat at the front with Stan and Kylie, but before the service began I sat myself on the floor, Sophia's coffin on a stand above me. I looked around at the altar and Jesus on the cross and the organ and all that polished wood and I couldn't feel that the church and religion had anything to do with what was going on in my heart. It was okay for some, but not for me, and not for Sophia, either. It didn't feel joined up with the world I lived in. At Indigenous ceremonies – and I'd been to a lot – everything that happens is about life, even though the reason anyone is there is because a friend or a relative has died.

There were hymns, speeches. I spoke my words when my turn came, not too many because my voice wouldn't let me. Later, I led the coffin out playing my didge. The churches, they try to keep the fact that the person being buried took his or her own life a secret. It doesn't go down well with any of the Christian religions. It's the same with Indigenous people, but for a different reason. For the churches, it's shameful; for Aborigines, it's just that it's too sorrowful to mention.

At the graveside, the Indigenous ceremony took over after the priest had said what he needed to say. We burnt gum leaves in the smoking ceremony; we called on the spirits who loved Sophia to gather close to her. Right next to Sophia, Charlotte was buried. We called on the spirits of Charlotte's people to stay close forever. Stan and Kylie kept themselves pressed up against me, Stan in particular. He hadn't let me out of his sight for the three days since his mother's passing. He held my hand with all his might. The grief I'd felt in the church was still there in my heart, but it was a different grief. In the church, I was trapped, as if I had to wait for the hymns and speeches to finish before I could play my didge and feel that contact with my wife again – that contact between the world Sophia had entered and the world I still lived in. By the grave, I could feel the current that joined us together, so the pain was at least good, clean pain. It was bearing me along on a journey of grief and mourning.

After the funeral, it was back to the city. What I wanted to do was contact an estate agent and sell the house. Couldn't live there any longer. I walked into the bathroom once we were home, looked at that shower curtain rail that Sophia had tied the rope to, then spent the next hour stomping up and down all over the house, wailing my guts out, smacking myself over the noggin with my hands. The kids were watching me, freaked out of their minds. I calmed down, called Stan and Kylie to me and hugged them half crazy. I told them I was getting rid of the house.

"You know why, don't you?"

"Yeah, Dad, we know why."

Earlier in the week, when Sophia was still with us, I'd arranged for us all to go to the New Year's Eve fireworks at Albert Park Lake. I kept to the plan. I'd let my sponsor Jackie Chris know about Sophia's passing, and he came along to the fireworks to keep an eye on me and brought a dozen people from the support group with him. It was all to do with solidarity. If any person in the support group was facing a crisis, everyone was. I was glad of the help and concern, sure, but my mood was pretty bleak. All the colours bursting overhead meant nothing to me, and I couldn't have smiled if I'd been guaranteed a million bucks just to try. Stan held my hand and I could feel in his grip the fear and panic that must have been there ever since he walked into the bathroom and found his mother. Jackie Chris came over to where I was standing on the bank of the lake with the kids and looked me hard in the eye. "You be strong," he growled.

I said, "Jackie, it's tough. The worst."

"You know what'll make it better?" he said. "Half a dozen VBs. Yeah, that'll bring Sophia back. Make you good and happy. You think?"

"Jackie, I'm not about to get back on the grog. Bloody hell."

"You know what will do it? Nothing. Nothing at all. It's you and me and your mates. It's in all our guts. Sophia is gone, but you're not. You're bound to live the good, strong life you've made for yourself."

"I know, Jackie. Don't worry."

This was all pure Jackie. Did I think he was about to go soft just because a bloke's missus has hanged herself? Pain is a bastard of an enemy. You think, "Nobody on earth can put up with this." You'd feel justified if you hid yourself away and popped the caps on a few stubbies. That's what Jackie was worried about, and why he said what he did.

Aboriginal mourning ceremonies go on for weeks. Family members and friends come to the funeral from all over. If there's a brother in Western Australia and he needs to get to Redfern for the ceremony, he flies in on time, gets the money from somewhere. Out in the settlements where the rituals are still as strong as ever, funeral feasts are prepared three times a day for a fortnight, sometimes even longer. There are always a couple of aunties who take control of the mourning and make sure that everything that's supposed to happen takes place. The people at the mourning ceremony sing in language and the men paint their bodies and the women paint their faces. Sophia wasn't Aboriginal, didn't have a tribe or aunties, and she wasn't given a full Indigenous send-off. But my mourning came from what I'd had inside me since my birth. My mourning was Aboriginal. A couple of days into the new year and the new millennium I picked up my didge and a big boomerang and told Stan and Kylie that I was heading out to be alone for a bit. They understood, but little Stannie, he followed me out to the car and grabbed my hand. "Dad, don't do what Mum did, will you?" I told him, no way. No way. "I have to take some time to be alone, Stannie. You know? It's important. But I'm coming back, matey. Don't worry."

I drove down the highway towards Geelong, then turned off for the You Yangs national park. All around the You Yangs was Charlotte's country, Wathaurong, coming down through my great-great-great-grandfather John Charles, who stood up to the white settlers in the 1880s and was given grief for being a 'troublemaker'. He would only speak his own language, Dja Dja Wurrung; refused to utter a word of English. He hanged himself. Before I knew about Granddad John Charles or Charlotte's country, I was down below the You Yangs off the Bacchus Marsh–Geelong Road, shooting a scene for a miniseries, *Snowy River: The McGregor Saga*, just standing around in my character's 1880s clobber (Joe Possum I was, an Aboriginal tracker) waiting for the director to tell me what to do. I had my back to the hills, thinking about all sorts of stuff, can't recall what, probably girls or grog or what a meat pie would taste like just at that moment. And something came over me. I felt that I was being watched. I turned to see who it was, but there was no one. No, not no one. The hills. They were staring at me steadily. I thought: "Bloody hell."

I ran into my Aunty Caroline the next day at a welcome to country ceremony she was performing for the film crew. She was a Wathaurong elder who knew my mum and also damned near everything about Indigenous history in Victoria. I wandered over to her and told her what I'd felt the day before – the hills boring holes into me with their gaze. Aunty Caroline said: "Yeah, that's your people, Charlotte's people. The You Yangs, they're your ancestors, my young friend. They're your mum's mob." She told me about Granddad John Charles. "They took Granddad John out of the Coranderrk mission up north of Melbourne and gave him to the white people on a property at Anakie. He didn't like it, slavery. They called it 'trouble making'. When those hills talk, you make sure you listen, Stannie. Charlotte's in those hills, and John Charles himself. You listen." She told me to look at the clobber I was wearing for my role – an old shirt and dungarees from the days of Great-granddad John. "You're probably wearing what he wore. Do you know that?"

At the You Yangs main entrance the gate was shut. I took my didge and the boomerang and walked up the track deep in the park with the scrub closing in on both sides. It was well into the afternoon and the sun was sliding down the sky in the west. Man, my state of mind! All over the place like a madwoman's washing, frightened in the way of a little kid, but curious about the place I'd come to, also angry that Sophia had left me behind, strong one minute, about to blubber the next. I could hear a couple of koalas over in the honey box gums on one side of the track but I couldn't see them. They make a sound like a tractor motor with a dodgy ignition, koalas do, not really spooky but in my state, spooky enough. The grey kangas in the bare patches of scrub took off when I came close. Maybe they took my didge for a spear because they crashed away through the tea tree and black wattle with a noise like a threshing machine. I called out to them: "Coming back one day with a .22, chuck one of you buggers on a campfire."

I reached a place where waterholes had formed in outcrops of smooth granite. I knew how those waterholes got there; Aunty Caroline had told me. They'd been made over thousands of years by blackfellas like myself coming for a drink and scraping their kalus (like a drinking cup made from wood) over the bottom of the ponds. The holes would have started off small, then become bigger and bigger. They were perfectly round, and each one was a bit more than my height across. In the first colours of sunset, they shone bright silver with flecks of crimson. I took the boomerang and heaved it into the sky with all my strength. It made the sound it was supposed to make if you throw a boomerang the right way, a deep whirring noise that frightens the prey towards you. And with the boomerang in the air, out of nowhere appeared the silhouette of a bird, a big bird, a wedge-tailed eagle. It stopped in the sky, hovering, and the whirring of the boomerang faded. The eagle was Bunjil, who can make and unmake and who, in his mood of making, created half of all we know. While he floated in the sky, my heart went from fearful to joyful.

Now I knew I'd come to a sacred place. My skin told me. And I knew what I needed to do. I stripped off all my clothes and stood naked beside one of the waterholes and bowed my head and cried. I'd cried for Sophia before, cried hard, but this was different, this was a torrent, salty water gushing out like all I had inside me was tears for my wife. While the tears were gushing, I danced. I don't know how I knew the sort of dancing I was doing. It came to me from the place. I danced and cried all around the edge of the waterhole, a slow dance because the dreaming that was guiding me was slow dreaming; all Aboriginal dreaming is slow, like a wombat in the bush when there's nothing to scare him, one slow step and another. All the time I was dancing, Sophia's spirit was watching. I was dancing her into the dreaming. She was white, and she needed to be drawn into the dreaming. I thought: "She wants this. She wants to be with the Wathaurong. They're welcoming her." Every step I took was the right step.

At just the right time, I stopped dancing. I picked up my didge and stood tall and raised it to my mouth. I saw that the stars were coming out; soon the Milky Way would be up there. I made music that lifted Sophia into the stars, made a home for her. I could've stayed there playing by the waterhole for hours, but I had to think of Stan and Kylie. If I was gone for too long after dark, they'd get frantic.

Walking back along that track in the moonlight, I knew I'd been through something and come out the other side. That feeling of entering a place, learning stuff, leaving the place. But I could come back whenever I wanted to. That place beside the waterhole, it had been waiting for me to arrive. If anyone else in the world had come to that place that night, nothing would have happened. It was waiting for me, and I was ready.

# CHAPTER 18

# RECONCILIATION

T he two lives I'd led when I was on tour with *Stolen* – the road life, easy and breezy, and my life back in Melbourne, much more complicated – became one after Sophia's passing. Just the one life, full of pain, but pain that I was meeting head on after my trip to the You Yangs. If I was hoping for something else – forgetting, maybe – I was hoping for something that was never going to be. I had the strength to bear the pain, and that was as much as I could ever expect. And I had Tamara helping me out. She'd moved back in with her big heart to be on hand for Kylie and Stan Junior.

Wes and Jane took *Stolen* to Sydney in April 2000. The cast was the same, but with Robert Patten sharing the role of Sandy when I had to get back to Melbourne for the kids and for my business. We opened in the Belvoir Theatre in Darlinghurst, and it was only when I walked in and gazed down at the stage from the top of the centre aisle that I realised I'd been there before, when I was a kid of thirteen living in Redfern with Frankie. It was the old Nimrod Theatre, where I'd had that terrific, floaty feeling up on the stage. Standing there at the top of the aisle, a monster smile spread over my face.

Wes said: "What's up, mate?"

I said: "Been here before. In this theatre. When I was a kid."

"Yeah? Good for you."

Not all good, of course. There's a scene in *Stolen* that did my head in every performance. The Jimmy character – Tony Briggs – hangs himself. Couldn't hack it anymore. I was on stage for the scene but I always made certain I was looking away. That was how I coped. All the cast knew what I was doing and felt for me. If I'd turned my head and glimpsed Jimmy hanging by that rope, I would've been buggered. I not only turned my head away, I sent my mind into the stars, into the Milky Way. I chanted silently to myself: "Out in space, brother. Hold on. Way out in space. Hold on." Then one night something went sideways. I looked over my shoulder much earlier than I should have, and there was Jimmy hanging by his neck with his tongue sticking out. Nothing in *Stolen* is fantasy. If the Ruby character is muttering away half insane, it's because there truly were Aboriginal women like Ruby who went off their heads with despair and sorrow. If Shirley's eyes filled up with tears every day, that's because so many women like Shirley had to weep to get by. And if the Jimmy character hanged himself, he was taking the way out of a thousand other Jimmys. I saw Sophia. Tears rushed into my eyes and streamed down my face. I'd been sitting when I caught sight of Jimmy hanging but I stood and walked to the back of the stage and ground my face into the wall. I wandered up and down aimlessly, torn between abandoning my character altogether and getting the hell off stage, or holding on for the sake of the play. The other cast members could see what was going on and tried to cover for me, as if this was all part of the drama. And it worked. The audience thought what I was doing was in character. After the curtain, backstage, Tony and Tammy and Kylie and Pauline took turns to hold and comfort me. Wes said: "Brother, you going to be okay?"

Most of the time – that is, when I wasn't stupid enough to look at Jimmy hanging from a rope – I was okay. More than okay – I was even happy, all because of that ecstatic feeling I'd enjoyed as a kid on that same stage. Whenever one of these floaty experiences comes my way, I never think: "Nice coincidence." No, I think it was all meant to be. When I was on the Nimrod stage at twelve, the thirty-four-year-old Stan was there, too. I've got uncles and aunties on Charlotte's side who'd agree with me, take it for granted. But after I let my character break down, I understood that Sophia was on the stage with me. Everything that had happened in my life between the ages of twelve and thirty-four was there with me.

Wes and Jane had plans to take *Stolen* overseas – New York, Japan, London. I signed up for Japan, enjoyed a huge buzz in the Ginza district – like a carnival with all that neon, more people on the footpaths than I'd ever had to dodge. The whole story told in *Stolen* was a bit of a trial for the Japanese, who had no idea of the background. I could see on the faces in the audience the slow dawning of what was going down. "What, they took the children of these people from the arms of their mothers? Can this be true?" The shock of it – that's what I saw on the Japanese faces. In Australia, the audiences were prepared; people knew. For the Japanese, the full horror came to them as they watched, and their reactions brought home to me all over again the crime it was to part kids from their families.

By the time the New York gig came round, 9/11 had played out on television screens all over the world, that jetliner flying between the skyscrapers, looking normal enough, before burying itself in one of the twin towers, and then the next jetliner and the next tower. Like everyone else, I watched over and over as those jets ploughed into the buildings. I thought: "Jesus Christ! No way I'm flying to New

York when I've got Stan Junior and Kylie to care for, no way." Both
kids saw the Twin Towers come down on the telly and were dead set
against me going. I pulled out of the New York season, and London.
Both seasons went well for the cast, for Wes and for Jane, I'm happy
to say. And even though nothing happened, I have the feeling that
I did the right thing.

I had another opportunity to do the right thing in May 2000,
five months after Sophia's passing. If somebody I love passes, it
takes me a long time to part with them, and I was in the middle of that process when the Walk for Reconciliation got underway.
Up in Sydney, 250,000 people joined the walk and shuffled over the
Harbour Bridge; took them ages. Down in Melbourne, we walked
down Swanston Street, over Princes Bridge and along St Kilda
Road to the Domain, where all those with something to say got
their chance.

I'd been invited to head the walk with the leaders of the Jewish
community, including a mob of rabbis. They wanted an Indigenous
person up there with them for a number of reasons, number one
being that this was a day that was all about Aborigines and Torres
Strait Islanders. But the Jewish community also wanted to honour William Cooper and his buddies who marched to the German
Consulate in 1938 to protest the treatment of German Jews. There
I was, surrounded by Jews in traditional clobber, shawls and big hats,
a few with long curly locks of hair trailing down, also beards galore;
the Jews are a little bit insane about costume and haircuts. Mind you,
me and my brothers and sisters, we were decked out in a traditional
way ourselves, body paint, clay in our hair. I was playing my didge as

we walked along; not all that easy to do, holding up a didge and playing it as you walk. Anyway, best of mates, Jews and blackfellas, we've both been battered from pillar to post just for being who we are. I was thinking: "This is one of the best things ever, one of the best." Because what we were doing was making the country again, giving it a story people could believe in. We'd had a story that was part lies, part fairytale, but now the people I was walking with were saying: "Something better for all of us. Something true, this time." I didn't think of 'reconciliation' as just being sorry, just asking for forgiveness. I wanted it to be about creating something, like what I was doing when I painted. I wanted to paint this huge new canvas for the whole of Australia. Everyone who had an itch to join in – sure, pick up a brush, make your mark. Even those who thought that blackfellas were a waste of space, make your mark. All part of the big picture. But by the looks of that gathering shuffling down to the Domain, we'd end up with the picture I wanted. Damned right.

A big, important reason for me getting my arse into Indigenous politics was fatherhood. I needed my kids to be free. Not only Stannie Junior and Kylie, but also Aleira, my daughter with Katrina. As I've indicated, ours was not the happiest of relationships, but I adored Aleira from the moment she was born in 2001, hell yes; she was way beyond gorgeous. Aleira was with me a few years later when Queen Elizabeth was in Australia for something or other, hopping from city to city and telling us all how much she loved Aussies and admired our spunk and our cricket team and our gum trees. She was down there in Carlton Gardens making a speech, about a thousand well-dressed people ready to applaud, including lots of kids from various communities in national costumes. A bit of a protest had been organised by the blackfellas of Melbourne because we wanted an admission from

Her Majesty that the British had ripped us off a couple of hundred years earlier. We had our signs and our songs, made a racket; we were pretty well-behaved, but. I was looking over to where all the people were assembled and I couldn't see a single Indigenous person, certainly not a kid. Apart from Aleira, I had my nephew Josh with me, same age as Aleira, the three of us outside the fence they'd put up to keep people like us out. I was huffing and puffing, maybe making a few rude comments, and over wanders the commissioner of police in charge of security for the whole shebang. "Now, now, my friend, what's all this bellowing about? Do you want to offend Her Royal Majesty? Surely not."

I made my complaint: "Came all the way here from Buckingham Palace to see Australian kiddies, but just take a gander. Not a single Indigenous kid in sight. Crying shame, Mister Plod, sir."

And the commissioner: "Now, now, what I'll do is take these two kiddies of yours and introduce them to Her Royal Majesty, all sweet." He did just that, lifted Aleira and Josh over the fence, held their hands and trotted them along to Queen Elizabeth. Her Royal Majesty shook my daughter's hand, shook Josh's hand, patted them on the top of their noggins. Aleira and Josh took their place among the A for Afghans all the way to Z for Zimbabweans. As it turned out, Good Queen Bess has something to say to the crowd in support of blackfellas. "A land with such wealth should find a way to improve the condition of its Indigenous people," she said. "Crying bloody shame." It surprised me to hear her say that, and pleased me. I've had warm feeling for ever since. Does she know about the stolen kids? I think she might. And I think she'd sympathise. She's got kids herself. Mostly ratbags, but still, they're hers.

As important as Indigenous politics is, this white v. black thing, there are times when I'm sick to death of it, sick of the struggle, sick of the ignorance that fuels racism. Sometimes I just want to be a good old natural human person getting on with my life, happy to be judged by what I do and don't do. Sometimes I get tired of being an Aborigine before anything else in the eyes of white Australians. I do. Every Aborigine in Australia gets tired of it at times. They want to say – same as me – "Listen, mate, listen, missus, here I am, just cop it sweet." Most days of the year, sure, I want to be Black Me, I want to stand there in my pride, watched over by my ancestors. But I never get a rest, never get a holiday from politics.

I was up in Alice one time, 1997 it would have been, filming *Welcome to Woop Woop* with Rod Taylor and Barry Humphries and Stephan Elliott, who was directing. I went with a buddy, a white guy, Trevor, to a restaurant; we were enjoying the nosh when a brother wandered in looking for a glass of water. The bartender gave him the water, the brother gulped it down, said his thank you, and off he went in his singlet and shorts and thongs. Once he was out the door, a white couple at the next table started in bad-mouthing him, carrying their chatter along to the point where they were making massive statements about the short-comings of blackfellas. I'm sitting there, about as obvious a blackfella as the Commonwealth of Australia can provide, and these two idiots are happy to slag off my brothers and sisters. I leant over and caught their attention; young couple, maybe married, maybe just boyfriend and girlfriend. I said: "Take a look at my face. What do you think? New Orleans? Memphis? Or maybe here. What do you think?"

The girl left it to the guy. "Here?" he said.

"Damned right! Here! Give that man a cigar! So how do you think I feel when I hear you talking all this bollocks about blackfellas? Hey?"

"Sorry. I didn't realise."

"You didn't realise what?"

"That you're an Abo."

"An Aborigine, is that what you mean?"

"Yeah, an Aborigine."

"Okay, now let me ask you a question. Do you know why tourists come to Alice? Tourists like you, why you came all the way from Sydney or Melbourne? Which is it?"

"Sydney."

"From Sydney. You came to see Indigenous culture. That's why tourists come to Alice. To see Indigenous culture. They don't come to see the architecture. There isn't any architecture. And they don't come to see other whitefellas. They can do that in Sydney. They come to see something unique in the world. So try to appreciate it, Syd. I'm telling you this instead of giving you a whack across the chops."

The couple ate the rest of their meal in silence. I might have ruined their night out, but I mean, what the hell? Back in the privacy of their hotel room, if they wanted to carry on with that sort of anti-blackfella nonsense, okay. But not when I'm two metres away.

# CHAPTER 19

# STARS AND STRIPES

O ut of the blue in 2002 came an invitation to show my paintings in an art exhibition in New York City. It was the idea
of a bloke who collared me at the Queen Vic Market in one
of my shops. He introduced himself as Tony, an executive
with Nike, short, balding bloke, maybe thirty-five, cheerful
guy. I made him a cuppa and listened to this plan he'd dreamt up. He
wanted to get into art, Tony, not as an artist but as a spruiker. He told
me that a monster exhibition was opening in New York in a month or
so, artists from everywhere in the world, a couple of thousand of them,
like the Olympic Games of painting. Seemed that some lovely person
had told Tony Nike to bring along some Indigenous art, probably said:
"Stan the Legend, see if he's up for it." Damned right I was. Tony
said he'd buy fifteen paintings from me for a big bag of money then
send me and the pics to the exhibition at the Jacob Javits Convention
Center on 11th Avenue, where I'd flog the pics to punters. "Airfare,
accommodation, all taken care of, my friend." I thought: "Thank you,
God!" Because I wanted to see New York, home of the Warriors, after
missing it when Wes and Jane took *Stolen* to America. Make a tidy
sum, meet girls, take myself out on a boat and have my pic snapped

under the Statue of Liberty, buy hotdogs on the street – all good. Also maybe go to the Metropolitan Museum of Art, the Guggenheim. And Central Park, bloody oath, I'd heard about that, enormous chunk of the outdoors right there in the middle of Manhattan.

I sold twelve of my pics right off the wall at Jacob Javits. Piece of cake. People would ask me what was going on in the paintings and I'd give them a rave and they'd say: "My black brother of Australia, please accept this big bag of money in exchange for your beautiful painting."

When I wasn't selling pics I wandered the streets of New York, didge in hand, soaking up the vibes. Took myself up to Harlem, a big item on my New York to-do list. I came up from the subway into the light of day on Malcolm X Boulevard. Man, the amazement I felt when I looked up and down the street and saw black faces in every direction, hardly a single white face, black brothers and sisters grooving along the sidewalks, filling the cafés, selling every sort of whatever from shops and booths and kiosks. It struck me after five minutes of shuffling along on MXB and Adam Clayton Powell Jr Boulevard that I'd never before been in any place where the majority of people were black. I was used to being a black man in an ocean of white people. And it made me more relaxed than I could ever remember being. This was Black City, and it had a place for Stan Dryden Yarramunua of Australia.

I stopped a brother on Adam Clayton Powell and asked where I could find the Apollo. He said: "Good place to find, my man. You take yourself down to West 125th in between this here boulevard and Frederick Douglass and you'll see that big sign." The guy wanted to know where I came from, since he could see and hear that I wasn't American. I told him Australia. "Oh, man, Australia? How great is that! Australia?"

I mooched my way down to the Apollo and stood smiling up at the sign, enjoying the currents of joy and genius. I thought of so many legends who'd performed there, people I worshipped: Ray Charles absolutely, also Aretha, Ella, Otis, the Supremes, James Brown most definitely, Mahalia, going all the way back to Duke and Dizzy.

On my way up Malcolm X Boulevard a guy stepped out of a restaurant, Sylvia's, a soul food place, and asked me with a smile what I was carrying. "That's for, like, music, yeah?" I told him it sure was, a didgeridoo of my people the Wathaurong, Australian Aborigines. He wanted me to come into Sylvia's and play something for the brothers and sisters, for a free feed of his renowned soul food. Didn't need to be asked twice. Stood there with black faces all around me bringing up deep soul stuff from my didge; shouts and whistles and applause when I was done. Also Sylvia's corn bread, famous all over Harlem.

Harlem, the Statue of Liberty, Central Park, girls, hotdogs, they were all double-fab, but I also wanted to do something else in New York, something for all those men, women and children who'd been murdered on 9/11. It had spooked me at the time, same as most people. It was a massacre, and my people knew about massacres and the horrible sorrow that follows.

I headed down to what was being called Ground Zero, didge in a long bag specially designed for it. I was on foot, all the way from my hotel just opposite Madison Square Garden along Broadway in the direction of Lower Manhattan. As I was passing through Times Square, a big black cop stopped me in my tracks and asked me what I had in the bag. I said: "That's my didge in there, brother – my didgeridoo."

"Yeah? Best show me."

Unzipped the bag, reached in for the didge. My black brother of Manhattan, all he could see was something that looked like a shotgun barrel. "Whoa!" he said. "You take that out nice and easy." He needed educating. "Mate, it's a musical instrument. A didgeridoo. I'm from Australia – an Aborigine from Australia. Taking this down to Ground Zero to play it for the people who died. A tribute, brother."

By this time we'd gathered a crowd. I could hear my audience saying things like: "Says he's an Aborigine from Australia, says this is like for music." The cop looked at it with suspicion, then he told me to play it. I was only too happy to oblige him, lifted the didge, started into a dirge I was going to play down at Ground Zero. The crowd around me were like: "Oh wow!" And the cop nodded, impressed. "You go on your way, Mister Aborigine."

Down at Ground Zero, huge hole, rubble, and a vibe of true sorrow. I got myself as close as I could to the big wire fence, took out the didge and played sad and low. Tourists gathered around, and they somehow knew that this was a tribute, this was my dirge for all those people who went to work one morning and never did another living thing. The vibe came back at me even while my dirge was filling the air. I was thinking of my ancestor William Cooper back in 1938. He would have felt that vibe of sorrow coming all the way from Germany, where the Jews were caught in their nightmare. I think they never go away, those currents of sorrow; they stay in the air of the earth forever. My people were murdered at Waterloo Creek, Myall Creek, up in New South Wales on the Nepean River, all over Tasmania in the Black War. Their sorrow is still in the air, same as the Jews' sorrow at a thousand places in Europe and all over the world, same as so many other people down through history. All that can be done is what I did by sending out the music of my didge to show my sympathy.

Back in Australia I was still going through the stages of mourning Sophia. My ceremony up in the You Yangs hadn't taken away the pain, but it did bring Sophia into the care of my people. After that, the pain was like a current that connected two worlds. It would always be there, but it was like something that had to be. It was right, in a way.

Then along came a little guy from Minnesota in the United States, and he brought Sophia with him.

I'd been back at work at the Queen Vic Market for almost three years when Prince came to town in 2003 on his world tour. I'd loved what he did with music from the first time I heard him back in my Shep days. He was a genius, sure, but musical geniuses come and go; Prince had something in his soul that lifted me up, and the same thing touched Sophia. Her favourite song was '1999', but she was crazy into 'Purple Rain', too, those lines about never meaning to cause pain, just laughing in the purple rain. I planned to see him at Rod Laver Arena, wishing that Sophia was there to sit beside me at the concert and jive about in her seat and call out: "Legend!" I was mucking about in my big shop up near the carpark and picturing the joyful look Soph would've had on her face when these two black girls stopped to check out my stuff, lovely girls with big smiles.

When people stop for a look, I talk to them, always. For one thing, I'm a talkative bloke; for another thing, customers will buy something off someone they like, but never off someone surly. It was a lesson I tried to teach my brother, Davy. He painted, too, fabulous stuff, and we had his canvases up in one of my shops. But he'd sit there like he had a huge pain in his guts when people looked at his stuff. They'd ask him: "What can you tell me about this one, Mister Dryden?" And Davy would grunt: "Just what you can see. Goanna, wagtail." Then he'd stare at his feet. I said: "Davy, people aren't buying a picture. They're buying their way into the whole Indigenous thing. You gotta help them along." And Davy: "Too bad."

So I'm nattering away to these American girls, Rhianna and Kyusha – they gave me their names as soon as I showed them my smile; very warm people, Americans, mostly. And they told me their whole life stories before I could get a word in edgeways: where they were born – Minneapolis, Minnesota – their travels, and what they did for a living. Make-up artists. For Prince. With him on tour. I gave a monster shout and clapped my hands. Prince! "You're only telling me you're with Prince! A guy I love like a brother? Okay, I want to marry both of you. Now." Then there was space for me to tell the girls my life story. They loved it that I was an Aborigine, loved everything I told them about the life of an Aborigine. I laughed like a drain listening to them struggle with words like 'didgeridoo' and 'goanna' and 'kooka-burra'. I told the girls I wanted to give Prince a didge, one painted in Yorta Yorta designs. Rhianna said: "You coming to the hotel. Hell, yes. You coming to the hotel, you give that doogery to Prince himself." And she gave me the name of the hotel, the Park Hyatt, up the east end of town, near St Pat's Cathedral and the parliament.

That's where I went at close of business with my didge for Prince. It's a swish place, the Hyatt, fountains and statues, polished wood, everything gleaming, including the guests in their designer clobber. Me, I was wearing what I wore in the market, Acca Dacca T-shirt

(*Back in Black*), jeans; I might have changed out of my thongs and into lace-ups. Attracted a few down-the-nose looks. I didn't care. How many of these swanky dudes could go and see Prince with a didge as a gift? I told the guy on reception, all kitted out in his blazer: "Stan Dryden for Prince. Just give him a call. Expecting me." Blazer Boy offered me a smile you could have packed fish in, dialled the room. "Sir, I have a Mister Stan Dryden here who says you're expecting him." A pause, then Blazer Boy, monster amazed, handed me the phone.

"Mister Dryden, I'll send someone down for you."

Prince himself. That voice. Me: "Thanks, brother."

Rhianna and Kyusha stepped out of the elevator, kisses and hugs right in front of Blazer Boy, who was still blown away. A crowd was up in the suite, enough for a party but there wasn't a party, only people sipping away at drinks with fruit and umbrellas sticking out of their glasses – and I had to say no when I was offered the same sort of thing. The music playing wasn't Prince; it was hip hop from ten years back, Salt-N-Pepa, 'Shoop'. Good to see so many happy people, a few with Ray-Bans on indoors looking too sexy for their shirts. Over by the sound system stood Prince, and man – nobody there got close to him for chill. I just stared at him – so beautiful, so relaxed, all in black. He noticed me and strolled over. "My girl Rhianna told me about you, Mister Dryden. 'An Aborigine, a black brother,' she said. I know about your people. Forty thousand years in this country. An honour to meet you, Mister Dryden."

His voice was soft, almost a whisper, but you could hear every word clearly without leaning in close. I said: "Stan," and shook his hand. I wanted the experience of calling him by his name, and I knew I could because he'd gone back to 'Prince' after ten years of going about as a madhouse symbol. "An honour for me, too, Prince."

"You have something for me. A didgeridoo, most like?"

He pronounced the word exactly right. He held the didge, turned it this way and that and asked me to play it for him. I gave him a couple of riffs. He took it from me, studied it close up, put it to his lips, and boy – he got a deep gorgeous sound out of it straight off. I knew he played damned near everything – keyboards, sax, bass and acoustic guitar were just the instruments I knew about – but a man can play everything in a huge orchestra and still be knocked arse sideways by the didge. Because you don't play a didge like anything else in the world. The breathing is a bastard, just for starters. So you could say I was impressed. Also, I was glad that the first conversation I had with this man was about something from my culture. I took real pride in playing the didge. This was an instrument that my people had been mastering for fifteen hundred, two thousand years, and the sound I got out of my didge, it was ancient, full of the music of the earth.

I stayed for an hour and was introduced to everyone, most of them with the same colour skin as me. "Yo, Ab-or-ig-in-e! Man, so glad to meet you." I heard that over and over. Before I left, Rhianna asked me to come down later to a club in the city, Bennetts Lane, where Prince would be jamming with local music folk. "You can get there?" said Rhianna. "We need to send a limo for you?"

I said: "I'll be there, won't need a limo."

Bennetts Lane was crowded with people I'd seen before here and there; people who knew music inside out, some of them session musicians with big reps in the business but not monster famous with the public. When I walked in I spent a minute or so just smiling, enjoying the vibe. Prince was at the bar sipping at something. Kate

Ceberano was singing a bluesy number at the mic. I stood against the wall keeping out of the way, but Prince saw me and walked over. He didn't say a word, just stood beside me. I'd heard from Rhianna that he didn't like people to stare at him so I satisfied myself with a quick sideways glance. I'm a talkative bloke, as I say, but I was picking up something from the zone Prince was in and I knew I had to be quiet, just listen. Nothing to drink, no dope, but I was floating. Tears built up in my eyes and ran down my cheeks. I felt someone beside me and even before I looked, I knew it was Sophia.

I don't know where it came from, but ever since I'd first met Soph on that date up in Shep and fallen in love, I'd had this crazy thing in my head that told me where she was at any time. Even when there was no reason to expect that she was near, I'd get that feeling and glance around and there she was; usually a big smile, sometimes tears. I'd felt her near a number of times since she passed, but not like this. I turned my head and Soph was standing there in a summer dress I knew well, and she was smiling her face off. Prince stood on the other side of me as still as if he'd been a wax model. But then he looked at me, only for a few seconds, not a word from him, just that gaze. He could feel Sophia's presence too, but maybe not who she was. I don't know what I'd call this power of Prince's, but he was the one who made it happen, who stood there channelling my wife to me in Bennetts Lane. I think if I'd taken my feelings apart, I would have found awe and wonder and gratitude. I thought later, when I'd left the party and gone home after receiving a type of blessing from Prince, that I wanted these things to keep happening to me; I wanted whatever power I have to see a little bit beyond the world around me to stay with me. And Sophia standing there, her message to me was: "I know you love me, darling. I know that."

I ended up dating Rhianna before she headed off on the next leg of the Prince tour. Gorgeous woman, I have to say, and we got on fabulous. She contacted me from back in the United States, wanted to come and see me, which she did. She said: "Stan my darling, Stan you handsome Ab-or-ig-in-e, come back with me to America, I'll make you crazy happy." I had to turn the offer down. I needed to consider Stan and Kylie. I also had to consider that I might end up trapped in the freezing wastes of the northern USA. Rhianna said: "You breaking my heart, Stan my darling man." I said: "I'll email you."

# CHAPTER 20

# COLLINS STREET

I was walking along the footpath in a classy suburb of Melbourne – High Street, Prahran, might've been – when I noticed an art gallery with a sign on the door that read: 'Open to the Public'. Good-o, I was the public, so in I shuffled. The whole place was painted white and the walls were hung with canvases, maybe twenty of them by the one artist, pretty depressing, figures bleeding and screaming. The message I was getting was that the artist needed serious medical attention. A skinny woman was sitting at a white desk wearing an expression that said: "Drop dead." I told her I was just having a gander, gave her a smile to cheer her up, and her lips moved about one hundredth of a centimetre. A list of prices told me that the poor devil of an artist had a very fancy idea of his worth. I thought: "Open a gallery, give it some class, and sell Indigenous art from all over for about four times what I'm asking now." When a big idea comes to life in my mind, it's all I can think about. I had to have that gallery. I thanked Morticia, who gave me an extra one hundredth of a centimetre, and headed straight for the office of an estate agent in the city. "What have you got on the books, brother, that's good for a gallery?" What he had was a place in Collins Street, the New York end, big glass windows, fancy shops just down the way a bit. I was told that I'd be required to attend an interview with the proprietors of the space. Seems they were not about to say: "Yeah, happy days, move in," to just anyone. Had to be a certain amount of snoot about you.

I rolled along to the interview a couple of days later. A lady related in looks to the chick in the slaughterhouse gallery asked me to take a seat. "A few minutes," she said. Magazines had been provided to keep people patient while they waited. I flicked through one then another, and came across an article – this was fate, or Fate – about the Indigenous people who'd enjoyed the site where Melbourne was now, the Wurundjeri. A few black-and-white pics of the Wurundjeri looking worried, as they should have been. I saw an opening, and when I sat in front of the three-man panel half an hour later, I had the magazine with me.

"Mister Dryden, you're proposing an art gallery. I assume we are talking about Indigenous art?"

"We are, brother. High-quality Indigenous art."

"And you've had some success in selling your art, Mister Dryden?"

"Damn right, brother. Six outlets at the Queen Vic, another on the Esplanade in St Kilda, crowds of customers."

"And now, as I understand it, you're planning to go upmarket?"

"Something a bit classier, I thought. New York end of Collins, big gorgeous gallery, the best Indigenous art in Australia."

The three Mister Suits were holding off, just a bit. Not completely comfortable. They asked me if I thought a display of Indigenous culture would 'harmonise' with the building, the snooty big business offices. They told me that the building was in the most prestigious commercial area of the entire CBD; home to accountants, an investment bank. The main mister doing the talking, he said that the clients of the building might not feel that Indigenous art "enhanced" (I remember that word especially because I had to ask him what it meant – "improved", he said) the status of the address. I could see what was going on. I expected it. They were worried that I'd slap up a hundred canvases, then invite in a dozen black brothers to a barbeque of goanna and wombat haunch with a nine-gallon laid on. But they didn't want to say that, because they weren't racists, they were gentlemen.

I stepped over to the desk and laid down the magazine open at the Wurundjeri article. I said: "You know who these people are? These people in the pictures? They're men of the Wurundjeri tribe, my people. That was the tribe that lived here in the way back. Proud people. Lots of the names of places around Melbourne, they come from the language of the Wurundjeri. One time, blackfellas were walking about right here, in Collins Street. My gallery, it picks up the history of the Wurundjeri. I'm talking about something beautiful, not a hole in the wall, something gorgeous that reaches right back to the Wurundjeri. These blackfellas in the pic, they're my rellies, my people." (Not entirely true, since my people were the Wathaurong, but I had to improvise.)

The panel was impressed. Mister Suit A glanced at Mister Suit B and Mister Suit C. A nodding of heads. Then more questions, this time about money. What sort of turnover did I anticipate? I said: "About a million. A hundred thousand a month." And now these boys were properly impressed.

"A million dollars' worth of Indigenous art?"

The misters couldn't help themselves. Money was the thing they understood best. And I must admit, I played it that way, whacking them over the noggin with a big figure at exactly the right time. I was in business, and I had to let these boys know that I understood business.

I told them that I'd be asking for the first three months rent free. This would give me time to set up and attract customers. As I happened to know, it was pretty much expected that a new client in an expensive building would want a no-outlay period. If I hadn't asked, the misters would have wondered about my savvy.

"We will give it serious thought, Mister Dryden. You'll have an answer in a week."

"One day would be better."

"One day? Very well, one day."

"Or we could make a deal right here on the spot."

"Well, well, my goodness gracious, ha ha, could you allow us five minutes?"

"Gents, you're going to say yes. Just do it."

"Ha ha, you're very shrewd, Mister Dryden. Very well, we'll have a lease drawn up, ha ha!"

So it came about that Stan Dryden, now known by his ancestral name of Stan Yarramunua, settled into his new shed in Collins Street, and man – it was a knockout! Three of my canvases were up there on the walls, one of Davy's, also two by Eileen Stevens from up in the Central Desert, one of the best painters in Australia. And a Tommy Watson, a complete ratbag of an artist but a genius, a Pitjantjatjara man from west of Irrunytju. Kuntjil Cooper, who painted up in the Western Desert – a couple of her pictures. Also Minnie Pwerle and her sister Emily Pwerle, and Barbara Weir, Minnie's daughter, all of them in the Central Desert.

What I was counting on was the tourist trade up there at the New York end of Collins, where you've got ritzy hotels like the InterContinental Melbourne in the Rialto. I made sure we were ready to ship canvases back to where the customers came from: Taiwan,

Hong Kong, China, the United States, Germany. I also kept a big stock of the carry-it-with-you gear – boomerangs; small carved statues of turtles, bush turkeys, waterbirds; bullroarers; clapsticks. Tourists wanted souvenirs that were truly Australian, and that left me with the whole market. An original work by an original Australian – way better than a Ken Done T-shirt or a Jenny Kee jumper. And I was on hand to tell the Taiwanese or the Yanks the whole story of a particular picture, all about the artist, about Indigenous culture itself.

The tourists took it on board in a different way from white Australians. A mister and missus from Taiwan, they just saw the art, saw its power, didn't know much at all about the politics. I didn't give Mister and Missus Manhattan the whole story of Indigenous Australia; they weren't in the gallery to hear about massacres and stolen kids, and it would have been useless to load them up with that nightmare. I just let them see the beauty that had survived. But now and again, a Yank maybe or a German would ask me about the past. They had a bit of knowledge to go by. Might say: "Mister Yarramunua, I understand that many black Australians lost their traditional lands when Europeans came to Australia." I'd give them the story, sure, but the fact was that I felt uncomfortable. I couldn't talk sorry business looking out on Collins Street through shiny plate glass. I needed to be sitting on a log in my own country down at the You Yangs, a fire burning, moon in the sky, the Milky Way blazing above me. And a strange thing: it wasn't really the business of people from New York or Berlin. I didn't want to make the story of my people just one more tale of the rotten stuff that happens for tourists to carry back home. It's my business, it's blackfella business, and it's the business of white Australians, too. But the Yanks? What are they going to tell people? "Yes, I met a blackfella by the name of Stan Yarramunua who told me about the terrible things that his people were put through in Australia"? It's too personal. When I talk about all that, I need the Milky Way and the fire.

The gallery wasn't a supermarket with half a dozen checkouts and the sound of cash registers opening and closing. Maybe only ten people would come in all day. I had a lot of time to sit at my desk, watch pedestrians passing, think. It was Frankie who came into my mind most often. Man, I wished he could've lived long enough to see the gallery, see me smiling away at the customers. He would've been impressed by what the gallery was making in dollars and cents. In his whole life, I don't think he ever held more than a hundred bucks at a time in his hand. And yeah, he would have noticed that part of the craft of selling was the butter I spread on the bread: the charm – but he would've approved of that.

Another big thing for me was just sitting there among the paintings and soaking in the vibe. I was showing some of the best artists in the world in that gallery. It was like I was a guy with a gallery in Paris more than a hundred years back with a dozen Matisses and Cezannes and Gauguins and Van Goghs on the walls. I'd looked in art books at all those guys. I knew what was special about Matisse and Picasso, and the same special stuff was right there in Indigenous art.

Some of the paintings, I'd bought from dealers and from relatives of the artists who'd been given them as gifts; some came straight from the artists. I handed over money to Tommy Watson himself for three pics, at his shack in the desert. I didn't know him or anything about him. I was driving out in the desert looking for people who could paint. Tommy was sitting there in the red sand, staring at the horizon. I got out of my car – this was about 2001 – and wandered over. I said: "Good day for it, brother." Tommy just stared at me as if to say: "Who the fuck are you?" I wasn't offended, introduced myself, and just on spec, asked with mime if he knew anyone around who painted in the traditional way. Tommy had a terrific beard, a Pitjantjatjara beard, big and bushy, almost completely grey. He rubbed his hand in those whiskers for a bit then took me into his shack and showed me six paintings that made me want to shout out with joy – I'm talking about colour and design like nobody had ever seen in paintings by an Indigenous artist. Tommy's shack was a monster mess but those paintings resting against the wall shone like the sun and the stars. A kid of about twelve was sitting on a chair eating an orange – a grandson, so I learnt.

Tommy gestured at the paintings with his hand and said something is his people's lingo; he didn't speak English. The boy with the orange translated without being asked. "He says, 'What do you reckon?'"

"Sell me the three of them, brother. I've got the cash in my pocket." Tommy named his price, chickenfeed, total rubbish. Tommy, he never had any bloody idea about money. No idea. I heard a story about him a few years later, how he was given five hundred bucks in bank notes for a picture, put it in his pocket and when he was caught short for toilet paper the next day, wiped his arse with fifties. I gave him three hundred for each pic. He took the money and dropped it on the table with the unwashed plates and apple cores and burger wrappers. The only thing I could get out of him about the paintings – I wanted some info to put in the provenance certificates – was that he painted to share the culture of his Pitjantjatjara people. "They don't know all this business," he said through Orange Boy. "Whitefellas, lots of blackfellas. They don't know." Anybody who ever wants to understand what it means to be an artist pure and simple needs to look at Tommy's life and work.

Barbara Weir gave me as much as Tommy. One of her pics, *My Mother's Country*, had something about it that I'd never seen before, traditional but changed, like she'd seen patterns in her mother's country that were more delicate than anyone else could see. She painted with a very fine brush and I got the feeling that every single brush stroke, and there were tens of thousands of them, was made on the perfect place on the canvas. She'd been to Indonesia on a grant, Barbara, she and a whole mob of Aboriginal women, to study batik. I'd spent time in Bali, short holidays of a week at a time, and I'd seen artists at work with wax and fabric. I could tell that batik had made an impression on Barbara in the way she got her colours to merge. She was from the red soil of the Utopia region up in the Territory, north-east of Alice and south of Tennant Creek, and was stolen from her family as a little kid. She returned to Utopia when she was twenty, stayed with her aunty, Emily Kame Kngwarreye, a terrific artist herself, who put a brush into Barbara's hand and said: "Go for your life."

There was nothing about her experience of being stolen in Barbara's work, nor in the work of any female Aboriginal artist. That sort of grief is faced in other places, in sorry ceremonies; it can't be shown in the way that a woman's country can be. Maybe in *My Mother's Country* there's just a hint of it in the tracks that pass the big, dark, central shape without touching it. I don't know. I wasn't about to ring Barbara and say: "So, Barb, what do you think? That picture got some stolen grief in it?"

There was more grief for Barbara when she finally found her mother, Minnie Pwerle, again at Utopia in 1975. By the time of meeting up with Barbara, Minnie had already farewelled her stolen daughter in ceremony. She couldn't bring Barbara out of the spirit world.

Minnie's paintings, inspired by the Awelye body painting of Aboriginal women, made me crazy happy every time I looked at them. Nobody had ever put anything like this on canvas before. She hadn't just imitated the body-painting designs; she used them as a springboard to create her own vision of a black woman's dreaming power. There's nothing in her brushwork like the slow and careful painting of Barbara; it's all done in a hurry. Awelye is meant to draw the spirit of people and things to the woman and release the woman's dreaming, and Minnie's paintings on canvas do the same thing. Strange to say, it was Barbara who encouraged her mother to take up painting – Barbara already had a big rep before Minnie ever picked up a brush. So in the end, there was a reunion of mother and daughter through art.

Eileen Yaritja Stevens from the Western Desert only painted for four years, but man – she filled up those four years with fabulous stuff. I saw her pictures and thought: "The best thing on earth to be is an Australian Aborigine with a dozen canvases waiting for you and a hundred tubes of colour." These were works of genius pouring out of my brothers and sisters and into galleries in Paris and London and into my own gallery in Collins Street. Eileen, her first job when she was a kid at Ernabella Presbyterian Mission, a long ways north-east of Adelaide, was milking goats. She moved to the Nyapari community in the same region as Ernabella after she married, and lived there pretty much for the rest of her life. Eileen's life was a bush life, full of the traditions of her Pitjantjatjara people. I think because she had never painted until she was an old woman, she was free to use her colours and brushes in any way she pleased. She didn't have to think:

"Got to paint in the same way as everybody else." In her community, among her people, there was no tradition of painting on canvas. Eileen invented painting for herself. She was maybe eighty-five when she picked up a brush for the first time.

I came into art in the middle of a big change in Indigenous painting. Artists like Barb had brought new designs, new colours, new brush techniques into Aboriginal painting. Later, when Tommy Watson came along, he released visions of the dreaming that had never been seen before, colours so strong that people at first thought he'd gone mad with his brushes and painted the massacre of a kangaroo over and over. But then they saw that what he was doing with colour and design was so powerful that it amounted to a whole new way of showing the soul of the land. My own painting was pretty much traditional. When I was alone with my dreaming, I saw the goanna showing the path of a journey, I saw the turtle carrying love on top of his shell, and I saw the stars of the Milky Way twinkling with the wisdom of the ancestors.

Another thing that made me happy: watching customers in fancy clobber with rooms upstairs in the Hyatt studying the paintings of brothers and sisters who'd put the paint on these canvases out in the Western Desert, the Central Desert, most times sitting on the floor with the colours on handmade palettes, dozens of tubes squeezed out of shape. And I'm thinking: "Tommy, Barbara, Minnie – one day people will study these pictures like they study Cezanne. And one day people will say it was Stan Yarramunua who went up to the desert and gave a big howdy to Tommy and brought these pictures back to sell in Collins Street." The customers, they didn't always know what they were looking at. I could see little cogs and wheels spinning round in their brainboxes, and I could hear the voices that played while the wheels were turning: "Hmm, I think I like this one. But is it good? I'm not sure. Maybe it's just colour splashed about in any old way. But that Jackson Pollock, that's what he did, and look at what a Pollock is priced at these days. This guy, Tommy Watson, maybe his pictures will do the same thing. God, I don't know!"

At the right time, exactly the right time, I'd mooch up to this guy in his Hugo Boss and ask him if he needed some guidance. That's the word I used: 'guidance'. Because that's exactly what he was hoping for. And the guy would say: "Hmm, guidance, yes, I think I do. Can you tell me a little about this picture, this Tommy Watson? What's going on here? What does it mean?" I'd tell him about the dreaming and how the dreaming was different for different people, very different for women and for men. And I'd say that this was the same for non-Indigenous artists, different for Cezanne and for Van Gogh but that Cezanne and Van Gogh both had their dreaming, which was different again from the dreaming of Aborigines. Then I'd tell the guy, Mister Hugo Boss, that nobody could paint anything true and strong without dreaming. Then Mister Hugo Boss would buy the Tommy Watson. I'd arrange for delivery, shake hands, and make a cuppa, strong and black.

The customers I appreciated most were those who knew what they enjoyed. Some customers wanted a chunk of Indigenous art because it was becoming fashionable, well and good, but this was art, not something chic to wear, and I was happiest when I got the idea that the client was into a painting in a personal way. I had a lady from Singapore who strolled in to look at what was on offer. I asked her if she needed a bit of info. She said: "Walk around with me."

This was a classy gal, so I had to put on my classy Stan routine, which meant shutting up unless a question was asked. She studied each picture lovingly. When she came to a Tommy Watson, she smiled. "I'll take this one," she said. It was a terrific piece of work, I have to say. "The price?" she asked. I told her ten thousand. She nodded and reached into her bag for her chequebook. All pleasure: a customer who was likely to look at that picture on the wall of her apartment in Orchard Road ten times a day; a decent payday for Tommy and for me; the enjoyment of sending Tommy out into the world.

And a difference experience – still good – with a couple who popped in on the Grand Prix long weekend in 2011. Super stylish, this couple. I heard them chattering to each other in front of a canvas and it sounded like Italian – same as the Italian ladies used to talk back in my delivery driver days. The guy – really handsome bloke – called me over and asked me about the paintings. Lots of questions, mostly to do with painting techniques. I couldn't tell whether they'd actually buy, but in the event, the woman said: "This one, this one, this one, this one and this one." Bloody hell! I said: "You realise that would come to one hundred and eighty thousand?" The woman – well, the wife; you can always tell if a man and woman are husband and wife – said: "Yes, I know." I reduced the total to a hundred and fifty thousand in the spirit of goodwill, said I'd accept a cheque. And the name on the cheque was Alessandro Benetton. I suppose I should have kept myself all aloof and sophisticated, but instead I said: "Benetton! Jesus Christ! Heard about you, mate, damned right!" Alessandro and his missus, Deborah, were in Melbourne for the Grand Prix, where the Benetton team was racing. We had a little rave about Ferrari and Mercedes and Jordan and so on, made arrangements for shipping, shook hands happily. Somebody or other must have recommended my gallery to Mister and Missus Benetton. I mean, they wouldn't have just been tooling along and caught sight of Art Yarramunua and jumped in to spend a fortune on impulse. That tickled me, knowing that someone told old Alessandro: "Yeah, call in on Stan Yarramunua up there in Collins, got a fabulous range, fix you up no worries."

And not long after Alessandro and Deborah practically drowned me in dough, along came a woman who was desperate to do the same thing. She was in her fifties, attractive in a mature way, nicely decked out in a fashion that showed me she wouldn't be asking to put anything on lay-by. I spoke to her about the pictures, and like the Benettons, she was keen on a Tommy Watson with a monster price tag. But she wanted to talk about other things, too. She was unhappy, I could see that. In the way of women, some of them, she wanted some love and support even if it was from a stranger. She told me that her hubby had died, and sure, I was sympathetic, of course I was, but when she told that he'd committed suicide a few months back, man, I couldn't stop the tears; had to share a bit about Sophia, couldn't help it. She was a private sort of person even though she'd handed over all this personal stuff to me, so I'll protect her identity by calling her 'Jane'. Now the pic she was attracted to, the Tommy Watson, the reason she loved it was that it seemed chock-a-block full of life, absolutely true about every pic Tommy painted. She wanted it on the wall so she could sit in front of it whenever she had the struggling blues. I took it to her place in Camberwell, the most fabulous place, art everywhere, ornaments; difficult to think of her being miserable with all this beautiful stuff surrounding her, but there you go.

I hung the Tommy Watson and boy, did it shine. But Jane, she was still down in the dumps, trying to smile but finding it hard. I knew what that was like. That pain inside, and outside everything is grey and lifeless. The only way to escape is with booze or drugs. No booze or drugs for Jane. All she had was her courage and her heart. I spotted a hi-fi with a turntable and a huge collection of albums – not CDs, proper vinyl albums. I flipped through them and picked out Engelbert Humperdinck, scanned the tracks and found 'The Last Waltz'. "Come on, Jane, we're gonna dance." And we did, waltzed around the lounge room like Fred and Ginger, the smile on Jane's face getting bigger and bigger. When the music stopped she plonked herself down on her swish sofa and caught her breath. "Oh Stan, that's the first few minutes of happiness I've known since Bruce died." It wasn't just grief she was suffering from, but loneliness. It's murder when you need someone close, and it's you by yourself.

Jane bought heaps of pics, and she could afford it since Bruce had left her a fortune. I was invited to her place in Camberwell for dinner again and again, and I was well into it, loved Jane's company. These close bonds can develop easily in the gallery business. It's not like selling someone a new kitchen. It's emotional. People buy art with their heart and soul, many of them. And yeah, I'm making money for myself and the artist, but I sell with my heart and soul, too. I wanted that Tommy Watson to hang there in Jane's shack. And a couple of my own pics, big expensive ones, twenty and thirty thousand. It made me happy.

CHAPTER 21

# GOOD INTENTIONS

I heard somewhere, maybe on the telly, that everything important there is to know about a man can be discovered without
ever speaking to him. All that's needed is to look at the women
he's known – not ask them questions, just study their character.
Suits me. I don't mind being judged by the women I've known
because I've known some wonderful bloody women. Sophia, of course,
and Debbie, and Lisa. I knew each of them for years and was married to
two of them. Maybe also a number it wouldn't do me any good to speak
about in any detail. I admit that. Lisa and Debbie, though – anyone
who studied their character would end up thinking that I must be a
champion sort of bloke to have hooked up with them.

I met Lisa up at the Queen Vic Market in 2003. She was running a shop there, terrific place, menswear, new and second-hand.
I saw her sashaying along on the way to her shop one morning and
I thought: "If I can't smuggle my way into that woman's affections,
I'll have to kill myself." I wandered into her shop, introduced myself,
learnt her name, asked her out. She said: "Ha ha, this is a bit sudden,
ha ha, no." I persisted, as any man who caught sight of her definitely
would. I strolled over to her shop two days later and repeated my

request: "You and me, babe, dinner, a movie, what do you say?" She said: "Well, Stan, your offer is very sweet, I'm sure, but, ha ha, no." I was thinking: "What's wrong with me? I've showered, powdered my body with Old Spice, sprayed on a bit of deodorant, clean shirt and daks. I'm presentable. Why's she so negative?" I went back to her shop a half-dozen times over the next ten days, always with the same request, always got the same reply: "No." I took flowers. "What beautiful flowers, Stan, my darling man, I'm touched. But no." Until finally she said: "Yes." What in God's name goes on in the heads of some women? It's like there's a legal number of times they have to say no before they can relax and say yes. Like, it might be a test. If you keep coming back, you pass the test. All I know is, every time I went to ask Lisa out, I bought a shirt, what the hell. Some of those shirts I haven't even worn yet.

We went to and fro, Lisa and Stan, found we could get on happily. And so: "Maybe the two of us under one roof, Lisa darlin'?" And Lisa: "Suits me, Stan, you handsome devil." We married, set up our lives together in the Hoppers Crossing house – not the house I'd lived in with Soph, that one I'd sold; this was the second Hopper's house I'd bought. But then we happened to take a short holiday up in Cairns, lovely and warm in July while in Melbourne polar bears were stalking people along the streets. One night out walking we came on the night market, big show it was, hundreds of stalls, tourists in a relaxed mood opening their wallets and throwing big notes all over the place. I said: "Lisa, we've got to get ourselves some of this."

I went the next day to talk to the manager of the night market, a redneck walloper as it turned out, who looked at me as if I'd crawled out of a cellar. "I need a stall or two, my friend," I said, and he asked me what I intended to sell. "Indigenous art, fabulous stuff, what do you say?" What he said was that the market already had a few Indigenous art stalls, didn't need another one. "Yes, but Mister Redneck, sir, my stalls will be Aboriginal owned and operated, the genuine thing, ridgy-didge, kosher." He didn't care, he said, didn't want any more Abo art. I told him I'd buy a couple of stalls if he wouldn't lease them to me, asked him how much. And he gave a laugh. "Two hundred and twenty thousand each," he said, as if this was likely to flatten me with shock and awe. I said: "I'll take two." I gave him a twenty thousand deposit on each, balance in six months, brought up a load of pics and sculptures from Melbourne, made more money than an ice-cream shop in the Sahara. Then I took a leaf out of Captain Arthur Phillip's book on colonisation and invaded Port Douglas just up the road, sold Aboriginal art to the billionaires.

Lisa was pregnant by this time, beginning to develop that gorgeous mum shape. We were what's known as a contented couple. We drove all over the coast roads and inland around Cairns, just being happy. One day out in Smithfield I noticed this terrific place built like a treehouse, with posts rising from it like boughs. In my reckless way, I drove up to the house, roused the owner and, after a bit of folderol, offered him a big bag of money for it, which he eventually accepted. I don't know exactly what sort of plans I had for the house. I just liked it. Whenever I have a rush of blood to the head in that way, I always go with it and it works out beautifully nine times out of ten. Okay, eight times out of ten. Seven. Whatever.

One possibility was that Lisa and I would move into the treehouse ourselves. But at six months into her about-to-be-a-mum state, Lisa said that she had to go back to Victoria for the sake of having her own mum and her whole family around her as the birth approached. Lisa's heritage was Italian and it's a big thing with Italians to be in the bosom of the family when the time comes to push. I thought: "Better go along with this, Stan. Can't stand in the way of culture." I sold the treehouse for a monster profit, finished up at the night market, tootled back to Melbourne. Lisa and I moved in with her mum and dad, big house in Park Orchards. Lisa's aunty lived next door; her uncle lived on the other side. The whole Italian clan would gather for meals a number of times each week and were always very welcoming to me. "Stan, good to see you, have a seat here at the table. You're looking good, Stan, so handsome." Lisa's dad was from Sicily, her mum from Calabria. The roots of their heritage went down deep. "Stan, we are the true Italians. Sicily, Calabria, the soul of Italy. When we accept you, it's forever."

Living in the Park Orchards house with Lisa's mum and dad was like having a team of servants caring for me. Lisa laid out pyjamas for me on the bed at night. (Pyjamas? I'd never worn pyjamas in my life; I didn't even *know* anyone who wore pyjamas.) Lisa's mum put the toothpaste and my toothbrush on a ledge in the bathroom, ready to use. My shirts were always freshly ironed. First thing in the morning as soon as I wandered into the kitchen a glass of OJ was stuck in my paw. "Did you sleep well, Stan? That's nice to hear. What can we do to make you comfortable today? Any special requests for lunch? Would you like us to fly in some oysters from Sydney?" I'd never in my life had such a fuss made of me. It drove me crazy. The whole Italian mob of them lived and breathed family harmony. I felt like I was being remade as a pasta freak from Calabria. This feeling for family was nothing like what exists among Aborigines. Sure, we reach out north, south, east and west to our rellies, but it's a very relaxed thing. We never try to live in each other's laps. An uncle might wander off somewhere or other for a year, then turn up one fine day and resume the conversation he'd been having just before he disappeared. Relaxed, as I say. So it drove me crazy, this tight family unit thing, this Calabrian/Sicilian hugging and kissing.

Lisa gave birth to our daughter, Alkira, in June 2004, gorgeous little bundle of joy. But the family madness only got worse. A bambino comes into Lisa's family, it's a month-long celebration, gifts from everyone, songs, laughter and yet more kissing. It's like the birth of Jesus all over again. I shouldn't be complaining; it's life, isn't it? Joy, tears of happiness, koochie-koo. But it wasn't my culture. No room to be an Aborigine. And at this time, my boy, Stan Junior – living out in yet another Hoppers house I'd bought with Kylie, who now had a baby of her own – he was in a monster struggle with ice. Kylie would call me half hysterical saying that Stan was off his head, aggressive, abusive, impossible to have in the house. I couldn't bring Stan Junior into my life with Lisa, into the Festival of Italy. Ice addiction was way beyond anything Lisa's family could cope with. I spent more and more time out in Hoppers with Stan Junior and Kylie. Not good for the marriage, of course, but if I had to choose between the Festival of Italy and my boy, I was bound to choose my son.

And I chose other things, too. Even when I was with Lisa and the baby at Park Orchards, I'd be out late at night. What was I doing? The traditional thing. Finding comfort in the arms of other women. It was a nightmare for Lisa. She'd look at me out of deep pools of sadness. Ruining a marriage in her family was like a bad, bad sin. One of the worst sins. So when Lisa looked at me in that way, it wasn't just for herself that she was sad; it was for me, as if I was destroying my soul. The whole Italian mob of them were disappointed in me. It was like: "We welcomed you into our family and look what you've done, it's heartbreaking."

I arrived home very late one night and found Papa waiting up for me with smoke coming out of his ears. "Where have you been? My daughter, she cries her eyes out for you. I am Sicilian. Do you know what that means? Do you want to make an enemy of a Sicilian?"

I stood there in the lounge room, looking straight back at Papa with cold, hard anger. "Do you know what I am?" I said. "I'm an Aborigine. I'm a blackfella. So don't tell me about Sicilians."

And that was the end. Yet again I'd stuffed up. None of the break-up was down to Lisa. It was all my handiwork. If I kept going at the rate I was clocking, I'd have fifty kids with fifty mums all over the continent. When I moved out of Park Orchards and into a place in Northcote, close enough to Stan Junior and Kylie, I promised myself to keep out of strife for the next ten years. "You hear me, Stan, my friend? Ten years of good behaviour. Meanwhile, you look after all your kids, Kylie, Stan Junior, Tamara, Aleira, Alkira, smother them in love. Are you hearing me? Good."

Hmm, good intentions. It was 2007 when Debbie came into my life at a bar in Manly, the Boatshed, where I was chatting with my mate Bill Byrne. Neither of us were drinking, of course, just sampling the nosh – oysters, prawns. She was by herself, Deb, and so I naturally thought: "A crying shame." I sauntered up to her at the bar and made my intentions known. "Stan Yarramunua from Melbourne. Pleased to meet you. Well, I would be, wouldn't I?" Deb was willing, so we launched into a natter, and at a certain point – just out of sheer inspiration – I asked her if she was an artist. "Now," she said, "how did you know that?" Wide-eyed, amazed. And me: "I'm an artist myself, and I can always tell if someone's got a gift." Could I? I'm not sure.

Maybe. Anyway, it got us chatting happily, and Deb revealed that she wasn't a professional artist; it was just something she was into when she had the time. She was an engineer. Damned right, an engineer, worked for PricewaterhouseCoopers. I maybe knew an engineer or two, but Deb was the first female engineer I'd ever met. The more she spoke about her work, the more I appreciated what a strong, independent woman she was.

We dated up in Sydney, had some lovely experiences. Then I returned to Melbourne and it seemed all over, short but sweet. I shuffled on with my life, thought about Debbie each day; there was something about her I couldn't shake off. I often enough needed to shake off affairs. At a certain point, I'd have to say to a girl: "Listen, sweetheart, I have to give you the low-down on Stan. Five kids, four different mothers, what you might call restless, also what you might call promiscuous, try my best but have been known to cause a bit of grief and pain. So what do you say?" And the girl might well say – could you blame her? – "Sounds a bit risky, Stanley, my darling man, better go my own way." After all the sweet experiences, all the mucking around, all the laughs and tender words, I'd have to shake that girl off. Debbie, no. I had this feeling deep down that we had further to go, so when I had a call from her six months later, I said: "You and me, babe. Get yourself down here."

I was in an Ilbijerri Aboriginal and Torres Strait Islander Theatre production at that time, *The Dirty Mile*, by Gary Foley and John Harding, a genuinely original piece of work that told the history of Indigenous Fitzroy. We performed it on Gertrude Street, the legendary byway of Fitzroy known forever as 'Dirty Gertie', once home to crime boss Squizzy Taylor, not to mention a hundred others hoods – a story we told right out there in the open, walking up and down Gertie. Kylie Belling was the director and she encouraged us to ad lib when we thought we could, make use of the moment. Man, this was real acting, this was my soul and my heart and whatever wits I had left to me all striving to make my role work. Some members of the cast were in period costume from the 1900s; some were in not much more than rags. It was a play I was proud of, and I asked Deb to come and see me when she got down to Melbourne. She did. She loved what we were doing, and she loved my canvases when she saw them. I was thinking, "This is going well, Mister Yarramunua." In a few days, we went from people who'd once had an affair to a definite, double-fab item.

Something else huge happened in my life around this time: I went to Federation Square to hear Kevin Rudd make his apology speech to the Stolen Generations. That apology, it was a long time coming. And it wasn't only for the stolen kids and their parents, but to all Aborigines and our brothers and sisters on the Torres Strait Islands. I wanted to hear that apology as the words were spoken. Hundreds of us there in Fed Square, some painted up as if for ceremony, a fair few didges about. Some people had brought their pooches with them for the occasion; they wanted everyone they loved, even their pets, to hear what was coming. I was embracing buddies every minute. "Great day, Stannie, great day."

I found a possie close to the screen. Stan Junior and Kylie were at their various homes, watching on telly. They didn't want to put up with the crowd and the crush. The big screen was showing the scene inside parliament in Canberra, Kevin 07 in his suit and tie just letting the motor idle for a few minutes. Down in the crowd at Fed Square, we were all calling out: "Come on, Kev! Get your arse into gear, buddy!" I had a brother next to me stuffing Smith's chips into his cakehole; he offered the packet to me but I was too choked up to think of swallowing chips. Then I got a call on my mobile from Kylie and Stan Junior: "When does it start, Dad? When's he gonna speak? What's the hold-up, Dad?" And then: "Oh wow!" because the camera was showing all the brothers and sisters out on the lawn, watching on a screen, some of them already in tears, never thought they would see this day. The camera switched back inside. The Speaker in his humungous armchair said: "The Prime Minister," and Kevin 07 stood and nodded, and began reading from his speech (I have a printed copy of what he said):

"Mister Speaker, I move that today we honour the Indigenous peoples of this land, the oldest continuing cultures in human history. We reflect on their past mistreatment. We reflect in particular on the mistreatment of those who were stolen generations – this blemished chapter in our nation's history."

While he was speaking, I felt something I'd never felt before, a feeling that blackfellas had become *important* – that's the word I have to use, important. We'd always been important to ourselves and to each other, but now we'd become important to the nation, and that's very different from being ignored or forgotten. That's real. We'd somehow come in from the cold, and actually been seen and heard. And the people in that crowd who'd been stolen as kids when they were not important, I think they understood that they were now in the story of this country, and that what they'd suffered was known about. Not the same as having a broken heart mended, but it was something real.

I hadn't been stolen but, hell, I knew exactly what those stolen kids had been battling. Exactly. A hundred or more performances as Sandy in Jane Harrison's play had given me insight, sure, but so had my mum, Charlotte. She'd grown up on a mission station and used to tell me about hightailing it into the mulga when the Aboriginal Welfare officers turned up, hiding away for the whole day and night. Leah Purcell has a song, 'Run, Daisy, Run', that tells the same story about her people.

Kev said: "We apologise for the laws and policies of successive parliaments and governments that have inflicted profound grief, suffering and loss on these our fellow Australians ... For the pain, suffering and hurt of these stolen generations, their descendants and for their families left behind, we say sorry."

That's why Jane wrote her play – Indigenous people having their story told, and white Australians seeing the hurt, the grief. Times on the stage, playing Sandy when the audience was mostly white, like at the Malthouse and the Belvoir, I'd gaze out over the audience and see men and women shaking their heads in sorrow, and I'd think: "This will never happen again." What I meant was that in Australia, the government can never again decide that it's in the best interests of Indigenous families to have their kids chased down and kidnapped by white cops following orders. Everyone knows it would be an atrocity. But within the lifetimes of some of those people in the audience, it wasn't an atrocity. It was government policy. That's why those whitefellas were shaking their heads. I think they were saying: "How did we let this happen? How?"

Once again, the camera showed the people outside, the elders up the front, a number of people sitting in chairs. Man, the tears! Especially the elders: they could remember lots of Daisys being told to run, lots of Charlottes heading into the mulga. Nobody was howling; it was all quiet weeping. Those words of Kev's: "We are sorry." I think they were sincere, and I think the brothers and sisters accepted them that way. I did.

The apology by Kevin 07, Sorry Day, the Mabo ruling – they had all had seeped into the minds of Mister and Missus Public and by 2008, 2009 all sorts of organisations wanted to show their respect for Indigenous Australians. One way and another I was becoming known not just to people who wanted some Indigenous art for their walls, but to community groups and corporations, which was how I was able to help Deb get a job in Melbourne that did some credit to her education and intelligence and experience. Deb was the first woman I'd known with a proper education, and that was something else I was well into, knowing that the woman I loved was smarter than me.

I was asked by the management folk at NAB to conduct an Indigenous ceremony of welcome for a new building of theirs up in Lonsdale Street. After the ceremony, I wandered up to a guy in a five-thousand-dollar suit and told him I had a talented friend who had come down from PwC in Sydney and needed a Melbourne job. Mister Five Grand said: "Mister Yarramunua, my new best Indigenous friend and brother, not a problem, I will meet this Debbie and good things will follow, absolutely." I thought: "This is disco, this is so fab. Here I am, zero education and I've got the NAB Five Grand Man listening to me like I'm one of his expert people."

That's the great thing about being born Indigenous and growing up in a shack in Swan Hill. I never get tired of those little victories, looking at myself and thinking: "Black me, black Stan, you had something to prove and, my brother, you proved it."

# CHAPTER 22

# LOVE AND LOSS

**D**eb and I had moved in together, and I had the feeling that this was something special, more than special; that feeling that sits in your heart and your gut that makes you glad about being a living, loving human person. The kids got along with Deb; my friends liked her, admired her. I woke up beside her in the morning and it felt right. We made love, and it felt like this was one of the great things happening in the world, anywhere.

But dear God. There's always something. Little tests I need to pass, and don't pass. Jane in Camberwell, she was still heavily into the art of Stan Yarramunua – well, into my art and the art of a half-dozen other Indigenous artists. She was at the gallery again and again. And I loved seeing her, loved the sweet things she said about me, loved her feeling for art. "Stannie, my beautiful friend, my lovely black Stannie, I want that picture, yes the one with the seventy-thousand-dollar price tag. And Stannie, my beautiful man, I want you to come for dinner tomorrow night, and dance me around the living room, and tell me stories. Okay?"

And me: "Sure, honey!"

Two weeks later: "Stan, my darling, dearest Stan, I want that big picture there, ninety thousand, wrap it up. And on Friday night, can you take me to the opera? *La Traviata*. You'll love it, and I'll love having you there beside me in your handsome Henry Bucks suit, holding my hand."

And me: "Sure, honey!"

What could I tell Deb? "Sweetheart, I've got an AA meeting on Friday night. Might go until late."

Here's the thing about women – something I've discovered. When I'm telling porkies, they know. They have no right to know, no clues, no love notes left in the coat pocket, no overheard telephone calls. But they know. It drives me crazy. I think: "What the hell? How could she possibly guess? That's voodoo." Deb began to go about with a frown.

"Something on your mind, darlin'?"

And Deb: "Well, yes, as a matter of fact. A lot of late-night AA meetings. That's what's on my mind."

And Stan: "What can I tell you, babe? It's an obligation."

I tried a new tactic. "Babe, Jane wants me to go over for dinner tonight. Just me. That's cool?" This new tactic was called 'the truth'. Hadn't attempted it in the past so far as women were concerned, but for the sake of my soul, I thought I should give it a shake.

After my experience of telling the truth, I have to say that I wouldn't recommend it with wives and girlfriends. Mind you, the truth I was telling was just a part of the truth. A big chunk, sure, but not the whole truth and nothing but the truth, so help me God. This radar that women have, it homes in on the part of the truth being offered and a big red light starts flashing. Deb knew damned well that my 'truth' was 90 per cent dinky-di and 10 per cent suss. And it made that frown of hers permanent.

Jane had an appetite for Indigenous art, but she also had an appetite just as big for male company of a particular sort, of my sort. There was a connection between the purchase of art from my gallery and the trips to the opera and the theatre. Well, of course there was. But all unspoken. If I'd said: "Let's keep our relationship strictly a business thing, Jane," I was pretty sure that would've been the end.

Deb, with that frown on her forehead, told me she knew something fishy was going on between me and Jane. And me? "No, no, Deb, it's all innocent, just business." She said I must think that she was a fool. And me: "No, no, Deb, I think you're the most intelligent person I've ever known." But there came a point when I knew that one more porky would be one more too many. Deb and me, our relationship was just barely hanging on. I had to think: "Do you want to keep Deb, or do you want to keep selling pictures to Jane?" The rent on the Collins Street gallery was murder. Without Jane, I'd be toast. Jane came into the gallery, took a look at a big canvas with a price tag over a hundred thousand, and said: "Wrap it up. Oh, and Stan, my love, I want you to take me to a concert at Hamer Hall on Saturday night. Beethoven." I stood there with my hands in my pockets, thinking: "This it it, Stan, my friend. Which way you going to go?"

Now, I don't want to be comparing myself with the great men of history, but there's a story in the Bible about Jesus going out into the mulga for a bit of me-time; he's up on a hill and he can see all these cities with their lanterns blinking. Satan creeps up the hill and stands beside Jesus and whispers in his ear: "What do you think? Want to be king of the world, rule over all these cities? King Jesus the First? Follow me." Jesus says no. "I'm good," he says. "I'll just get about with my sandals and my swag, empty purse, all sweet." And me? "Wrap it up. Oh, and Stan, my love, I want you to take me to a concert at

Hamer Hall on Saturday night." What did I say? "Right you are, Jane, my dearest. Right you are." And a couple of weeks later, Deb was gone. Too much pride to put up with my yarns any longer. Moved back to Sydney. Bloody catastrophe, because I loved that woman with all my heart.

After a break-up – a big break-up – I always feel that I want to stay breezy and free. I think most people, men and women, have the same feeling. Keep it light and loose. At least for a while. Say, a hundred years. If you meet someone, take her to a bar for a sherbet, maybe step into a disco for a bit of a skylark, show her the moves, later in the evening shimmy on into the boudoir for a certain amount of kissing and hugging, then: "Lovely time. See yuh!" With Stan Junior in the state he was in, light and loose was all I could commit to with girlfriends.

My heart was with Stan Junior. The ice was doing him over in a monster way. I'd ask him: "What's up, buddy?" And Stan Junior, looking at me out of eyes with all the light a long way back, like he was in a cave that went for miles and was holding up a match I could barely see, he'd say: "Nothin'. All good." When I heard that, I thought of me in the booze years. My mate Bill would say: "How's your journey, brother?" And me: "Yeah, all fab, mate." The hardest thing for me to locate in those years was an honest answer.

Ice, though, it was a tougher gig than booze. Takes years for your brain to frizzle with booze; with ice, about ten minutes. I hated the sound of the stuff – worse than smack or coke, far worse than dope. Think about it: heroin, coke, dope, you can pretty much find them all in nature – poppies, the coca plant, good old Mary Jane. Mightn't do you much good but at least you can say they come out of the living world of plants. But ice – that's the lab. Smack? Get your arse on methadone. Coke? Addicts have success with dopamine and serotonin. Marijuana – what can you say? Go for your life. Ice? Nothing. It's just you versus the crystals.

I got Stan Junior into rehab for the first time in 2010, but going into rehab is always a 'for the first time' deal. You might need three, four, five, ten trips to rehab. It's the 21st century, after all. There's a whole smorgasbord of drugs out there and a number of kids are going to give them a go. Stan was always one of the more likely kids to stump up his dough for a little baggie of crystals. I wasn't in a position to ask him why he wanted to go down that trail of escape. He'd had to survive finding his mum hanging in the bathroom, for one thing. And for another – genes. My genes. I followed on from Frankie; Stan Junior followed on from me. What I could do was take a vow that I'd never abandon him, and boy, I needed a vow like that because time and again I got to thinking: "Bloody hell! Enough!" Getting him into Odyssey House did some good, but the cure didn't take for very long.

And while I was waiting to see if it was meant to be, I occupied my time with capitalism, using money to make money, then using what I made to make more. My ambition was to build up a pile of dough it'd take a sherpa from Nepal a month to climb. No, that's going too far, but at the same time, I had a knack for making moolah, mostly out of property. There's a nice twist right there because when whitefellas came to this country the first thing they did was take away blackfellas' property, all in one go, terra nullius: "Sorry, mate, you don't exist but your land does, see yuh!" I don't know when it was but one fine day I realised that houses mostly went up in value, not down. If I could get the dough together for one house, I'd be able to jump on that gravy train. Bought the house at Hoppers Crossing, sold it for a big fat profit. Then another house in Hoppers, then another and another. Each time, a big fat profit. I thought: "Stan, my friend, this whitefella system for getting rich is totally disco, and it's legal, what the hell!"

I had good instincts for the racket. I was sitting outside a café in Barkly Street, Elwood one morning when I caught sight of a big 'For Sale' sign down the road a little ways. Wandered over, took a squiz. It was a big place, what's known as a California bungalow, pillars at the front holding up a verandah roof, solid brick. An agent was hanging about inside in a snazzy suit with pamphlets for the punters. He took a gander at me, thought to himself: "Aborigine; won't be getting an offer from him." I'm always getting that look from whitefellas, I'm used to it. The mindset behind that look helps me at times because it means the dude is underestimating me, and if I'm being underestimated, it gives me an advantage. Inside on a sofa sat two old blokes a bit on the shabby side who turned out to be the owners. It wasn't only the owners who looked shabby; the whole place was full of rubbish, newspapers and magazines tossed about, cardboard cartons stacked against the walls, cobwebs, dead flies on the window ledges, same in every room. Up on the wall behind the sofa a whole row of pictures of players from the Geelong footy team had been stuck up with pins. I had a natter to the old guys about Geelong, about footy in general, and after five minutes they were doing something I wouldn't have thought possible at first sight of them: smiling. I could see past all the rubbish lying about; I could see that the house would come up fabulous with a bit of love.

The agent sidled up to me and whispered: "I don't think you realise that the house is not for lease, it's for sale." I said: "Good,

I'm buying." My offer was lower than the asking price, but the old Geelong supporters, they wanted me to have it and we came to an arrangement, as they say. I gave the place a decent sort of birthday and six months later sold it for a fortune, damned right. What I was doing with houses was exactly what hundreds of thousands of other people were doing in the capital cities of Australia – getting into the property market at a magic time for it, interest rates going down as values were going up. But as I say, people don't expect a blackfella to be part of it, and not just because they think we wouldn't have the capital – no, they think that it's against blackfella culture, that we'd have to be throwing out something sacred in order to own a house in Elwood or Brighton. I've seen worried looks on the faces of whitefellas I've known, like: "Stan has sold out to the establishment, he should be up in the desert whittling boomerangs and roasting wallabies." Boomerangs, wallabies, both good. But while I'm sitting by the campfire, I want to be thinking of the right time to put that two-storey terrace in Rathdowne Street in the city on the market. This idea that a blackfella shouldn't make money in the way that whitefellas do is just racism of another sort.

Even people with hearts full of goodwill for Aborigines can muck up in amusing ways. I met a gorgeous woman at a party a few years back – I'll call her Margot – and while we're chatting I happen to mention that I'm a painter. "Oh, really?" she said. "That's handy, because I need my fence painted. Do you think I could hire you?"

I said, "Not that sort of painter, darlin'. I paint pictures. Art."

Not a racist bone in her body, but if I'd been a white bloke, she would have considered the possibility that I was talking about canvases. Who cares? We dated, got along in a madhouse way, but I was always a worry to the people in her circle, all from Wesley and Melbourne Grammar and MLC, made buckets of dough. I moved in with her, with Margot, swanky place in a toffy suburb, got to know the neighbours. For most of them I was the first Indigenous person they'd ever seen up close. "Well, Mister Yarramunua, so you're an Aboriginal, how delightful, my goodness." (Nervous smile.) "So you've, ah, settled in here, have you?"

And me: "Yeah, brother, settled in proper. Got another fifteen family members on their way down from the desert, might have to set up a camp out here on the nature strip. Don't mind, do you?"

And the neighbour, neat as a department-store dummy in his Country Road slacks and beige cardie: "Well, no, not at all, ha ha, fifteen did you say?"

Margot and I took different roads eventually, but it wasn't anything to do with race. She got tired of my excuses. "Sorry, darlin', it's one o'clock in the morning, sure, I was abducted by aliens up in Toorak Road."

Jackie, my guru, my friend, the man who'd kicked down the door to my soul twenty years past and chucked out the furniture, became ill at the age of seventy. It was dementia. Awful thing to watch as it took over his brain, which had been a bloody good brain. I found myself talking to him in the nursing home more and more in the way you talk to little kids: "Want a glass of orange juice, do you? Whaddya think, nice glass of juice, hey? Do you need a wee first? Want Stannie to take you to the loo? Yeah?" Once I realised

I was doing it, I stopped. Mostly kept quiet, eyes full of tears. That's the thing about life – you live long enough to wish you were dead. I mean, look at Jackie, all that wit and wisdom turned into jelly, wobbling about on a dish. Every time I visited him, I said, "Jackie, I love yuh," when I left. And by Jesus, it was the truth. So that's something stronger than demetia – love, because I could see in his eyes that he knew I loved him. If nothing else, he knew that.

His funeral was held up at St Ignatius on Richmond Hill. The church was full of people Jackie had saved from the scrap heap, like myself. He'd been a social worker by occupation, Jackie, but to say he'd been a social worker was like saying Elvis had been a singer. Elvis was the King, and Jackie, he was a king, too: something about him that would have made him a ruler in a different age, a natural authority. A few people spoke at his funeral, and for once all the over-the-top things that are said at the end of someone's life were not exaggerations. He was one of those blokes you listen to. You can't help yourself; he speaks, you listen. I played the didge for Jackie as the coffin left the church, my personal tribute to this fine human being who reached out and rescued me. Something I can contribute to all the information about grief and sorrow and its impact on human beings: it's possible to play the didge with tears running down your cheeks; it's possible to play the didge with a broken heart.

Meanwhile I was becoming concerned about my mate Bill. He'd once carried a bit of weight but over the past couple of months he'd lost heaps. It couldn't have been worry over his setbacks. Bill didn't have a worry gland. He always thought: "Stormy weather doesn't hang on forever, my friend. The sun's too big to hide for long." I said to him: "Mate, you need to let the quack check you out, give you some pills.

You're fading away." Time was when I relied on Bill for guidance, when I listened to his message of sunny days ahead. Now he was relying on me. "You think?" he said. I got him into the Alfred Hospital for a complete once-over, tested every damned part of him from his toes to his brainbox. He was in a bed on the third floor when I called in to be with him on the day the doc brought him the results. Bill, he was anxious in a way I'd hardly ever seen him, rubbing the back of one hand with the other, nothing remotely like a smile to offer.

The doc sat himself on the foot of Bill's bed and asked him how he was feeling. "Been better," said Bill, "have to confess." The doc nodded. Then he went into an explanation of the test results, this and that and the other and then a bit more of this, technical stuff that neither Bill nor I could follow, like sitting in a science class – well, not that I've ever sat in a science class, but I could imagine it. What I did understand, and I'm sure Bill did, too, was the graveyard look on the doc's face. Finally he paused. Then he said: "Bill, you have stage four cancer of the liver. Stage four is about as serious as it gets. You've got two weeks left."

I was standing but I sat down when I heard 'two weeks'. I was bewildered. Both Bill and I looked at the doc, thinking he couldn't be serious. What, two weeks? Fourteen sleeps, then nothing? The doc was serious all right. "Two weeks, Bill," he said again. Tears came gushing out of my eyes. I don't mean a little trickle; I mean big, fat, round tears. Same with Bill – tears that turned into sobbing. The doc was silent. I went and sat on the bed beside Bill and picked up his hand. I didn't know what the hell I could say. This was like being in a courtroom with the judge handing down the death penalty. What I did say was that I'd be there for him, for Bill, my friend of twenty-five years, this man I loved like a brother.

The doc said: "I'm sorry. We'll do everything we can to manage the cancer, but the outcome will be the same. I'm terribly sorry."

As soon as the doc left the room, Bill threw back the blankets. "Gotta help me get out of here, Stannie. Don't want to spend the last of my life in a bloody hospital. Got these gorgeous nurses everywhere and I can't do a thing."

I took him home to his family. I came back to him every day. One of his friends had been reading about miracle cures for cancer on the internet, and had discovered some bloke in Mexico who saved people who had one foot in the grave, nothing that ordinary medicine could do for them. Bill listened with a big smile. Then he stood up and lifted his arms above his head. "Hasta la vista! Mexico, here we come!" Yeah, yeah. Miracle cures. What can you say? Bill never went to Mexico. He died exactly two weeks after his diagnosis. Bloody hell. I loved that man, and he loved me.

But here's a bit extra. Not long ago I was in Bali for a holiday and I was down on the beach on a banana lounge soaking up the sun, just as I had with Bill years back. Same beach, might have even been the same banana lounge. A little ways off, entertainment was being offered by the hotel people, a talent show: a marquee, a stage, a mic. The emcee asked the people who'd gathered around if any of them would like to sing a song, and a kid of about eighteen with a groovy look about him stepped up and took the mic. I was watching and listening in a drowsy way when this kid started into 'My Way', the huge Frank Sinatra hit, and he was almost outdoing the master, just fabulous. I sat bolt upright on the banana lounge. The Sinatra version of 'My Way' had been Bill's favourite, number one, he was always flinging out a verse or two like it was his personal anthem. Just like at the Prince party when I felt the presence of Sophia, I now knew that Bill was beside me. I don't mean that I thought of him because of the song – I mean he was there, my mate, that beloved man.

Why does this happen to me, this sense of the presence of a loved person who's passed? I can't put it down to the grog; none in my system. But it is important that I'm Aboriginal. That much I know. All the blackfellas I know experience the same thing as me, and not one of them thinks it's the least bit strange. My old man used to say: "Stannie, no person who's passed wants to harm you. If you feel someone near, it's because they love you." So it's something I'm glad about, having spirits close to me. Zombies, vampires – they feed on your blood. The spirits of the people you were close to – they come to you and feed on your love.

# CHAPTER 23

# MAN WITH A PLAN

I was still mourning Bill when I got it into my head to move a gallery I'd recently set up in Acland Street, St Kilda, to Church Street in Brighton. The Acland Street gallery took the spot of my Collins Street place; the rent there had become more than any sane person would pay. The idea of moving to Brighton was to pull in the Brighton crowd. Brighton was old money. People there had been used to shopping at Henry Bucks and David Jones for generations. They used their money to make money, not just by investing on the stock market or running factories and merchant banks, but in everything. If they bought something, they wanted its price to go up, and that included art.

In Acland Street, people wandered into the gallery, took a gander at the canvases and sculptures and said: "That one – I'll take that one; wrap it up and I'll put it in the boot of my car." I loved the St Kilda folk, and should've stayed where I was. But I began having dreams full of dollar signs raining down from the sky. It was a mongrel punt. The St Kilda people were ready to buy on impulse, even for a canvas worth eight thousand bucks. In Brighton, the customers came in for a look, asked a few questions, went away and came back a week later, then came back again a month after that. They had to think about it, and ask more questions, and do some research. It didn't suit me, the Brighton way of doing things. Caution didn't suit me. And it wasn't long after I opened the Brighton gallery that I realised that Brighton itself didn't suit me.

I live in Brighton in a big, fancy house with a swimming pool and gardens and four shiny bathrooms, enough bedrooms to board half the population of Melbourne, glass panels at the back of the place opening onto trees and shrubs. The house whispers to people passing: "What do you think? Stinking rich." Yeah, stinking rich. Three-metre-high walls to keep the bad guys out, to keep out people like the Stannie Dryden I used to be. I bought the house thinking of the Stannie Dryden I used to be. I imagined him at age twenty driving down the leafy street, maybe delivering something from Snuggle-Rite or tooling along in his old bomb of a Toyota. And looking out the window at the mansion I was to buy twenty years later. "Bloody hell!" says the twenty-year-old Stannie. "Imagine living there? I'd think I was God Almighty in his heavenly palace." My story is one of those famous rags to riches yarns, and I'd spent years saying to myself: "Wow, Stannie, my man, look at you. Are you a huge, raging success or what?" But it's possible to get tired of that yarn. It's possible to think: "Well, yeah, huge success, so what?" For a time I thought of myself as an example to other Indigenous people, like I was saying: "Aborigines, we can be millionaires. Aborigines, we can buy big fancy mansions in Brighton. We need to believe in ourselves, my brothers." It's possible to get sick of that, too. Because up and down my leafy street, the owners of mansions have put up the sort of three-metre walls that surround my place. Brick walls. One day I was feeling puzzled by this blue-down-to-my-boots mood that had come over me, until it struck me that this wasn't the first time I'd been surrounded by walls. Years back, I'd worked in the Turana youth detention centre, and that was walls, walls and more walls. So what progress had I made? Still living with brick walls.

Now, I've heard any number of Indigenous people – my brothers and sisters in race and heritage – asking me how come I deserved all this comfort. "Where's my swimming pool? Where's my pop-up toaster that takes six slices of bread at once? Where's my seventh and eighth bedroom? And if it comes to that, where's my Merc? Where's my Ferrari?" I always say: "Mate, I worked for it." And they say: "I've worked all my life. I haven't got a pop-up toaster that takes six slices of bread at once. Where's the justice?" And me: "Stop whingeing, you're doing my head in." The whingeing drives me crazy. But look at me, I'm about to have a whinge of my own. I've got a first-world problem. The house in leafy Campbell Street, the gorgeous gallery in Church Street, the Merc and the Ferrari in the driveway – none of it's making me happy. I'm thinking: "There must be more to life than this." Dear God, listen to me!

My thoughts keep drifting back to hitching on the highway with Frankie when I was ten, had nothing, happy as a lark. "Hey, Dad, can we have tinned sardines tonight? Aw, go on, Dad, yeah, tinned sardines. Please!" And Dad saying: "Nah, can't afford it tonight. Have to wait until I can find a wallet somewhere." Then the next day the old man applies his craft and finds a wallet in the pocket of some punter and brings four cans of sardines back to whatever dump we're living in. "Here you go, don't say I don't love yuh, hey?" I know that people all over the world who've made themselves super comfy often have the same sort of complaint: "Must be more to life than this." It's boring in its way, but the fact that it's boring doesn't make it less real.

I can't get rid of it by saying: "Cheer up. You can have tinned sardines seven days a week if you like. Wake up to yourself."

I go to Bali six times a year. I'm happier there. I stroll about in Denpasar or down near the beach at Kuta, up in the hills at Ubud, all over the island. Some places people sit out the front of their shops chiselling away at a block of wood that will become a Hindu statue for sale to tourists. I always stop and watch. The guy with the chisel, the sculptor, he's doing the same job as me: turning the words of legends into art. The difference is that he's been toiling away since he was a kid, and he'll still be at it when he's seventy. He's never going to drive through Ubud in a flash new Merc. Most of the Balinese, they live for a year on what I spend in a week. Cheerful, smiling themselves silly. I might pass some cove who's eating his rice from an earthenware bowl and he calls me in: "Please. Sit. Eat." I'm envious of the poor, and that's a sad, sad thing to confess. I should be ashamed. But Jesus, the simplicity of the lives of these Balinese. That's what I envy.

I know what I have to do. Even when I grizzle about wanting there to be more to life than this, I know what's wrong. That drive that got me here, I've used it up. I wanted to show everyone that a blackfella could roar along the Nepean Highway in his own Merc and shout his mates dinner at Philippe in the city. But buying my mates dinner is not the same as giving something back. That's what I want to do – give something back. I don't mean to say I've been ignoring others. I've been doing what I can for years now – reaching out in AA meetings with my personal testimony, sponsoring one booze hound after another, helping them become ex-drunks. Also getting my arse along to court to testify for young blackfellas in strife with the law, accepting the responsibility for keeping them clean while they're on bail, on parole or doing community service. Hundreds of brothers, some not much more than kids, some in their twenties or thirties. I stand up there in front of the beak or the judge and pretty much plead for these ning-nongs to be given a second chance. It's what's called a 'bittersweet' experience to run through my resume in court. "Yes, Your Worship, I'm an artist who is paid tens of thousands for my pics and sculptures, big flash house down in White Town, i.e. Brighton, fancy gallery in Church Street, buckets of dough." It impresses the big guy up on the bench, much more so than if I were a whitefella with a fat bank account. The big guy thinks: "Well, what do you know. Here's a blackfella with a monster bank account. He's an example to his people." Bittersweet, as I say, because each time I impress the big guy, I think: "Why does he (or she) think it's such a novelty for a blackfella to have a few quid in his wallet?"

I want to do more. And I think I can. A year ago, I had plans for a property I own up in Shep, wanted to build accommodation on the land for young Indigenous kids. Couldn't get it past the council, but. Now I've got an option on some land out the back of Burleigh Heads on the Gold Coast. Same sort of plan as I had for Shep: build three houses, one for me, the two others for black kids, give the kids some training and a lot of encouragement, get them into employment they can stick with. In a way, my plan is based on old-fashioned values: you get what you want by working for it.

When I'm giving testimonials in court, I tell the judge or the magistrate that I'll make sure whoever-it-is gets to school, or gets to work or doesn't become a no-show on community service. I'm not just coating the bread with thick butter for the big guy; I mean it. If I'm speaking up for a kid, that kid better damned well listen to what I'm saying. I'm with Noel Pearson – welfare is toxic, and the more of it you get, the deeper the poison sinks in. I want welfare for a mum who's looking after her kids by herself, sure; and I want welfare for anyone who's had his leg off at the thigh and has to hop about on crutches. But Jesus, welfare's not going to make a life for a kid who's shrinking his brain with diesel fumes. Whatever way I can, I want to get that kid's face out of a plastic bag, want him to find in his gizzard the determination that gets him along to work each day. At the same time, I want him to honour his culture, because our culture isn't diesel sniffing, glue sniffing, and it isn't booze. And okay, it isn't sitting at a workbench for eight hours a day drilling little holes in the tops of toothbrushes either. But the kid can spend six months drilling little holes, then move on to something a bit more satisfying, maybe college. That's what I mean about my old-fashioned values. Roll up your sleeves and work, then use your imagination to go further. Am I oversimplifying? I might be. I probably am. But deep down, it's not oversimplifying all that much to say to kids that rolling up their sleeves is going to be much better for them than sitting on their arses. Also, living and breathing their culture.

And I've been into black communities all over to make my point about our culture and the better life you can have off the gear. I'm like one of those travelling preachers who sets up a tent in one place and another and fills it with bad boys, lost boys who need saving. These kids listen to me because they know I've been a bad boy myself. It's called credibility. It's like when I was at AA meetings down at the church in Victoria Parade. I listened to Bill and to Jackie Chris because they'd been through all sorts of shit and had come out of it with a better life to lead.

Another plan, what I'd call Shep Plan B: I've got some land up outside Shep that might become an arts and crafts community. What

I visualise is a big house and a number of workshops. I'll set up one of the workshops for weaving, one for carpentry, one for painting, and so on. I'll open the place to kids who want to get out of drugs and booze, give themselves a purpose. Not just Indigenous kids – kids from all over, black, white and rainbow. I see raising money from corporations, because I want the Shep spread to be self-funding, nothing from the government; that'd give us much more freedom. If you take government money, you have to appoint a committee before you open a window: "A motion has been put forward regarding the opening of the window on the north side of the living room, all those in favour? Against?" I'm working on a submission I can present to various boards, give them a bit of a rave: "Ladies and gentlemen, here's your chance to do a whole lot of good, just throw a big bag of money on the table, make it the folding sort, we'll use it to change lives, damned right, lift kids out of the gutter, give them a dream to chase down." Corporations usually come through. Big banks, finance people, manufacturers – yeah, they want to do some good if they believe in the project. I'd put my brother Davy in charge of the community and come down once a month from the back of Burleigh to show my face, smile my smile.

As important as anything in these plans for the future is my own art. Big changes going on in Indigenous art over the past few decades, new designs, different ways of using colour. In the old times, designs would remain the same for thousands of years, and always use the same colours. But Indigenous artists now have heaps of new colours from tubes to work with, and canvases that are completely flat and take the paint easily. And something else. The world around Indigenous artists has changed. The whitefella world is bound to get into our art. I don't mean images of cars and aeroplanes and fifty-storey buildings; I mean the spirits of the whitefellas' world. Because believe me, whitefellas have spirits following them, too, some of them pretty bloody spooky, but some of them full of good-will. The life that blackfellas live in the white world isn't all about racism and exploitation. Some good stuff, too. We don't feel like we want to paint the Eureka Tower, but the mojo that goes into the building of the tower, sure, we can see something in that. Same with my Ferrari. There's real beauty in that car, and it comes out of a sort of white dreaming. Indigenous art is all about a spiritual way of con-necting with the world, the universe, with other people – mostly with our ancestral spirits, yeah, but we're listening to the whitefella spirits, and they change what we put on canvas. Just a bit. I want my painting to show some of what I've seen and felt in my life among whitefellas. I want it to be subtle – I love that word, now that I know what it means. Subtle. But strong at the same time.

So, lots to feel confident about. As much as anything, the turn-around in Stan Junior's life. After one stint and another and another in rehab, the cure finally took. A friend gave him a copy of the Qur'an while he was at Odyssey House the last time, and he read it cover to cover, again and again. It reached into his heart, into his guts, that message of mercy and commitment. He read me passages that made me understand exactly what this ancient book must mean to fol-lowers of Islam. Stan adopted Islam with all his heart, and it's the foundation of his days, the prayers, the duties and customs. I'm not about to join him in his faith, but I respect him in his commitment, top to bottom. It gives him the best chance he's had for years to build a big life – he and his little daughters, Charlotte and Chantay. Look at me: Granddad Stan. Dear God. Granddad four times over, because there's also Kylie's daughter, Sophia, and her son, Anthony.

Nobody gets the chance to change lives, switch to a new story. I wouldn't, even if it were possible. I want my story to be the one I've lived, the one I own. I'm an Australian Aborigine, a Wathaurong man, and that's an identity I had to grow into. I'm an artist who draws on the life of blackfellas in this big red and yellow and black country. My heritage is the richest on earth. I've known joy and grief, and I'm bound to know more of both. I earnt my name of Yarramunua after years of struggle, and I'll keep that name for the rest of my days. Any strife that lands in my lap, no matter what it is, will have to be a bloody awful brew before it can overcome the pride I take in myself and my people, and in my name, given to me as a gift by Mate Mate that day at Galiamble. Yarramunua, son of Frankie Dryden and Charlotte. Stan Yarramunua.

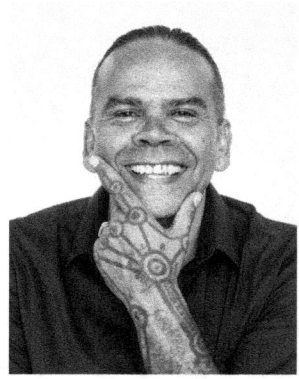

**STAN YARRAMUNUA** started painting more than twenty-five years ago, and began selling paintings, didgeridoos and clapsticks at markets and galleries. He built strong relationships with Aboriginal desert artists, representing their work in Melbourne.

In 2008, Yarramunua was proud to open one of the first privately owned and managed Aboriginal galleries in the world, at 500 Collins Street, in the heart of Melbourne's CBD. He later moved the gallery to hip and busy St Kilda, where today it is located at 112 Acland Street.

Yarramunua has graced the stage of the MCG as a speaker and a performer, and completed several commissioned works for private companies and charities. He continues to paint and to represent artists from across Australia in the Art Yarramunua Gallery: www.artyarramunua.com.au